The Practical Leader

A Guide to Creating Highly-Engaged and High-Performing
Organizations that Achieve Extraordinary Results

Through the Integration of
Self-Leadership, Business-Leadership &
People-Leadership

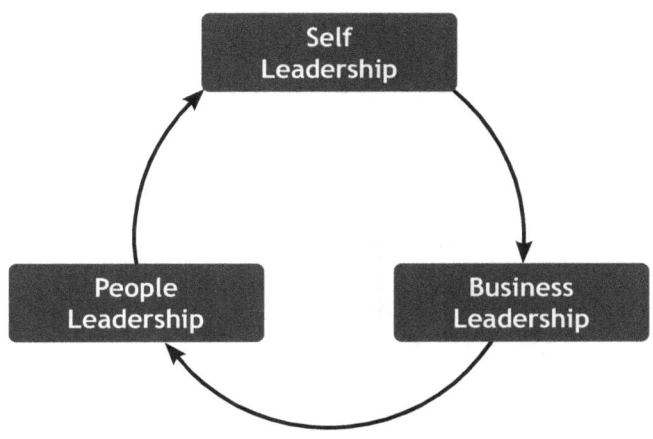

By Kevin Reynolds
with Brent Conkle

Integrated Leadership

No part of this book may be reproduced, or stored in a retrieval system, or transmitted in any form or by any means, electronic, mechanical, photocopying, recording, or otherwise, without express written permission of the publisher.*

Copyright © 2021 Kevin A. Reynolds
All Rights Reserved
ISBN: 9798740548012

*Feel free to photocopy the various templates and worksheets for your personal use.

A Practical Guide to Effective Leadership

This book is for you if...

- You're relatively new to a leadership role, and want some ideas on how to go about creating a Highly-Engaged and High-Performing Organization.
- You're looking for a quick "Leadership 101" guide
- You don't have access to leadership development programs (not every company has one), and so you need a resource to get you started in the right direction.
- You've read some leadership books, attended courses, watched a series of videos on-line, downloaded a multitude of Apps - but you need some practical suggestions on how to implement those ideas.
- You want to be a better leader, wherever you are in the organization.

This book is also for you if...

- You know you should do some succession planning and people development but you're not sure how.
- You need to brainstorm with your team to create innovative business ideas, but need some guidance on how to do that.
- You need to generate a vision - but are unsure how to do that.
- Your team is under-performing, and you want some ideas to change that.

Are you a Leadership Coach?
The Practical Leader can be used for "Structured Coaching" - supporting you on a 1:1 basis with your clients.

THE HIGHLY-ENGAGED & HIGH-PERFORMING ORGANIZATION — 9
- Fundamental Leadership Outcome — 10
- Assess Leadership in Your Organization — 13
- What Employees Want, What the Business Wants — 15
- The High-Performing Organization — 19
- Quick Case Study — 23
- The Leadership Matrix — 25
- Leadership Self-Assessment — 27

SELF-LEADERSHIP — 29
Highly-Engaged in the Role — 32
- Your Leadership Challenge — 33
A High Level of Self-Awareness — 35
- Your Personal Focus — 37
- Strengths and Challenges — 39
- Adjusting Your Focus for Someone Else — 42
- How You Prioritize — 45
- How Productive Are You? — 47
Be a Values Role-Model — 48
- Your Personal Values — 49
Clear Sense of Purpose — 50
- Your Life Role/ Purpose — 51
Clear Philosophy of Leadership — 52
- Create Your Leadership Philosophy — 53
Self-Leadership Action Plan — 54
- Build Your Self-Leadership Action Plan — 55

BUSINESS-LEADERSHIP — 57
Ensure Everyone Understands the Vision — 60
- Creating Your Vision — 62
- Creating The Team Vision — 63
- Connecting the Team to the Vision — 65
Connect to the Organization's Strategy — 66
- Link to Organizational Objectives — 67
- Make it SMART — 69
- Align Job Descriptions to Mission/Goals — 71
- Example Job Description — 73
Build a Strong Organization — 74
- The 7R Model — 75
- Key Role/ Key Person Analysis — 77
- Right Person for the Role? — 81
- Assess Organizational Capabilities — 87
- Bridge Capability Gaps — 89
- Using the 9-Box for Succession Planning — 91
- Right Organization — 93
- Right Cost — 97

Create a Sense of Urgency 98
- Do the Right Thing at the Right Time for the Right Reasons 99

Hold Regular Performance Conversations 100
- For More Difficult Situations 101
- Assertive Communication Technique 102

Business-Leadership Action Plan 104
- Build Your Business-Leadership Action Plan 105

PEOPLE-LEADERSHIP 107

Create a High Trust Environment 110
- Building Trust 111

Encourage & Empower 112
- Delegation Self-Assessment 113
- Three Levels of Delegation 114
- Where Can You Delegate More? 115

Discuss Career Development 116
- One-on-One Development Conversations 117

Coaching & Feedback 118
- Giving Both Positive & Corrective Feedback 119
- The GROW Model of Coaching 121

Build High-Performing Teams 124
- High-Performing Team Assessment 125
- The Tuckman Model 131
- Actions to Build a High-Performing Team 133
- Celebrate Success, Learn From failure 135

People-Leadership Action Plan 136
- Build Your People-Leadership Action Plan 137

Integrated Leadership - Quick Summary 138

Measuring Leadership Outcomes 140
- Combine HR and Business Measures 141
- Link to Business Priorities/ Employee Engagement 143
- Changes in Overtime, Retention, 360 Surveys 145

Additional Resources 147

Improving Your Personal Productivity 148
- Do the Right Thing at the Right Time, with the Right Result 148

Activities for Building High-Performing Teams 162
- Team Alignment, Vision 163
- Who we are, What we do 165
- Improving Team Communications, Solving Problems 167

Making Transparent Decisions 170
- 4 Fundamental Decision Making Methods 170
- Criteria Matrix/ Dot Voting for Group Decisions 171

Risk Analysis 172
- The Risk Analysis Matrix 173

Developing Innovative Business Ideas	174
• Business Trend Analysis	175
• Brainstorm Categories	177
Developing the Strategy	179
• Present - Where Are are Now	181
• Future - Where We Want to Be	183
• Strategy - How We Will Get There	187
Delivering Objectives & Performance Reviews	190
• A Process for Deploying SMART Objectives	190
• Delivering the Performance Review	197
Leading Change Initiatives	200
• 7 Steps to Creating the Change Story	203
Employee Engagement Full Question Set	**209**
Working With HR on Leadership Interventions	**213**
Example Organizational Analysis Report	217
• Leadership Interviews - Inputs	223
The Robo-Doc Case Study	225
Presentation from Head of Robo-Doc	229
HR Data Analysis	235
• Organization Overview	237
• Engagement Survey	239
• Leadership Effectiveness	241
• Key People, Key Positions	243
• Headcount Cost, Capabilities	245
Analysis & Solution Development	247
• Brainstorming Issues & Solutions, Adding Structure	249
• Impact Analysis	251
Presenting the HR Response	253

Becoming a More Effective Leader through Integrated Leadership

It doesn't matter whether you are the "big boss" of a department, or a team leader on a small project. All of us, at every level in an organization, need to know how to become a more effective leader. A leader of ourselves and the people around us.

Leadership is not about position, power, job title… or being a "hero." It's about credibility, relationships and what you do.

The good thing is, leadership can be learned. In fact, this book is based on our leadership training classes - which we have distilled down into a self-study format.

If you're looking for in-depth analysis and deep guidance on leadership, then there are many resources available to you. *The Practical Leader* is designed as a fast, self-study, quick reference guide to becoming a more effective leader, through the concept of "Integrated Leadership."

The Integrated Leader

- Provides a positive, innovative atmosphere.
- Creates highly-engaged teams.
- Delivers excellent results.
- High concern for actions/results.
- High concern for people.
- Role-models company and personal values.
- Can effectively lead teams and organizations in any location around the world.

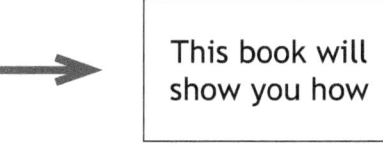

This book will show you how

About The Practical Leader

- *The Practical Leader* is essentially a 3-day leadership workshop in a 'self-study' format.
- The idea is to give you a useful, quick guide to being a more effective leader.
- We suggest that you work through Self-Leadership, Business-Leadership and People-Leadership, and develop action-plans for each area.
- Resources such as "Developing the Strategy" are not meant to be an in-depth analysis of how to go about creating the group strategy, but instead are designed to give you a method you can use now, particularly if you don't have a business degree.
- That said, feel free to use *The Practical Leader* in any way you choose. We hope it proves useful!

THE HIGHLY-ENGAGED & HIGH-PERFORMING ORGANIZATION

Your Basic Goal as a Leader is to
Ensure your People Succeed

Inspired by Jay Galbraith's Star Model

> The Fundamental Leadership Outcome

A Highly-Engaged and High-Performing Organization that Achieves Extraordinary Results

Let's look at some quick definitions

The Highly-Engaged Organization
- "Engaged" employees are aligned to the organization's mission and vision, and personally want the organization to succeed.
- If the overall "Engagement" level in the organization is high, then the organization is more likely to achieve, and exceed, its goals.

The High-Performing Organization
- Delivers excellent results that exceed expectations.
- Has a clear "Line of Sight," where individual & team mission & objectives are clearly linked to the organizational mission and objectives.

What Does it Mean for Your Organization?

In Your Organization
- What does "Highly-Engaged" mean?
- What does "High-Performing" mean?
- What are "Extraordinary Results"?

Use this space for Reflection/ Analysis/ Notes or Brainstorming

The Highly-Engaged & High-Performing Organization

Try this Organizational Assessment

		Engagement & Performance	
Performance - Business Leadership	1.	I understand the vision of my company.	
	2.	I feel connected to organizational strategies.	
	3.	I understand what is expected of me.	
	4.	I am given the necessary authority for getting my job done.	
	5.	I have confidence in my Business Group's senior management to lead us to achieve our goals and objectives.	
	6.	I feel the organization where I work is strong.	
	7.	I feel there is a strong sense of urgency.	
	8.	I feel encouraged to take risks.	
	9.	I feel encouraged to come up with new and better ways of doing things.	
		Avg. Business-Leadership Score -->	
Engagement - People Leadership	10.	In my Work Group, diversity among members is respected.	
	11.	In my Work Group, bottom-up approaches are respected.	
	12.	I am able to speak candidly with the leader of my Work Group about my problems & concerns.	
	13.	I receive ongoing feedback that helps me improve my performance.	
	14.	I am satisfied with the feedback I receive.	
	15.	If I fulfil what is expected of me, my success will be recognized.	
	16.	My Business Group leader assumes management responsibility for the results of her/ his subordinates' work.	
	17.	I feel my ideas are listened to/heard.	
		Avg. People-Leadership Score -->	

1= Strongly Disagree, 2= Disagree, 3= Neutral, 4= Agree, 5= Strongly Agree

Assess Leadership in Your Organization

Plot Your Results on the Integrated Leadership Matrix*

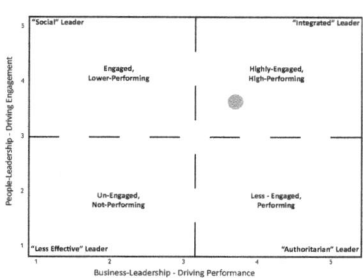

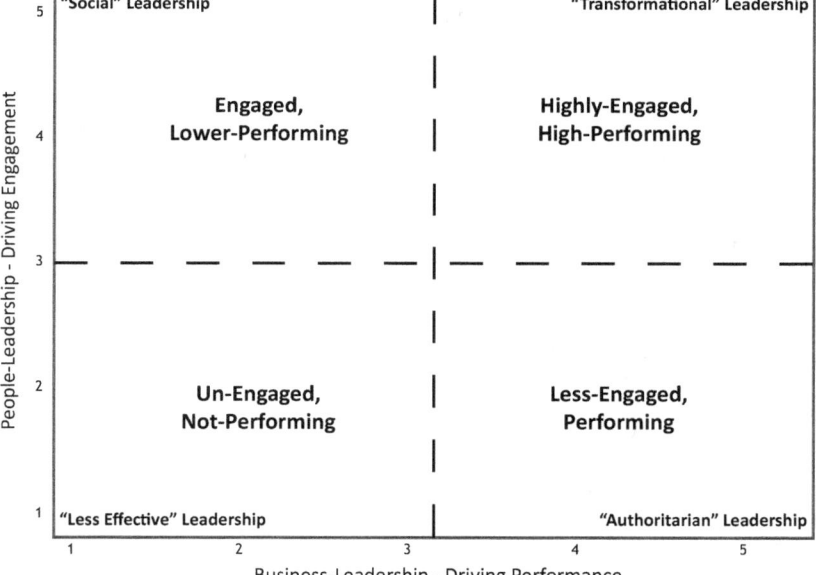

What do the results tell you about leadership in your organization?

*See page 25

13

The Highly-Engaged & High-Performing Organization

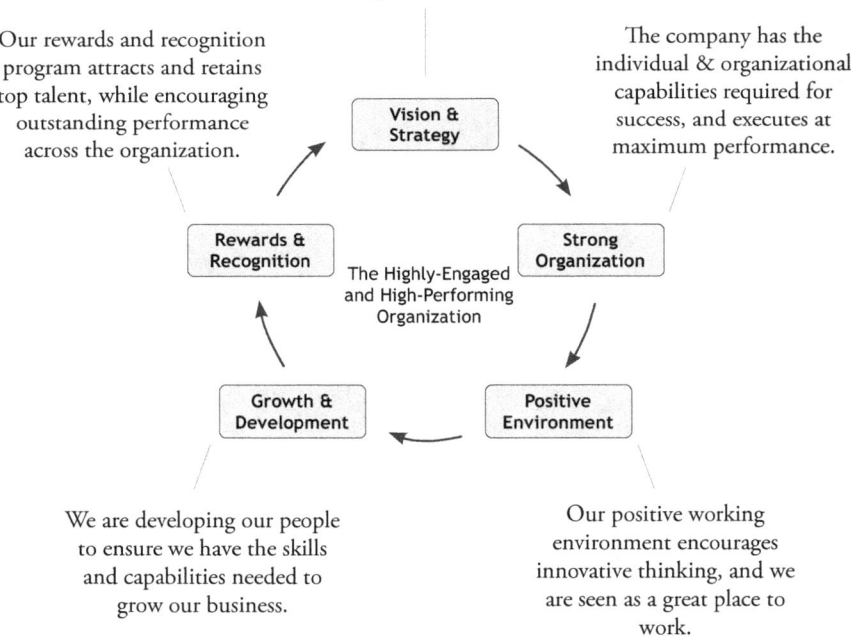

"Engaged" employees are aligned to the organization's mission & vision, and personally want the organization to succeed

What Employees Want, What the Business Wants

	What Employees Want	**What The Business Wants**
Vision and Strategy	• Clarity of purpose and direction. • Feeling connected to the strategy. • Clear understanding of what is expected. • Confidence in Leadership.	• The whole organization is aligned to the vision. • Everyone is working together to implement and achieve the business strategy and objectives.
Strong Organization	• High-Performing teams. • Company making changes to succeed. • Elimination of non-critical tasks. • Confidence in decision processes. • Pride in company.	• The company has the individual and organizational capabilities required for success. • Our organization is efficient and effective, with lean processes and elimination of waste. • Our top talent are in the most critical roles. • The organization continues to execute effectively, at maximum performance.
Positive Environment	• Making a personal contribution. • Use of skills and abilities. • Encouragement to be innovative, take risks. • Desire to stay in the organization. • Trust/Open communication. • Support for work/life balance. • Good office environment.	• We are seen as a great place to work that attracts and retains top talent. • The positive working environment encourages innovation and out-of-the-box thinking.
Growth & Development	• Improving skills & knowledge. • Training & Development opportunities. • Clear and relevant feedback.	• We are developing our people to ensure we have the skills and capabilities needed to grow our business.
Rewards & Recognition	• Appreciation for contributions made. • Ideas and opinions are listened to. • Success is recognized and rewarded.	• Our rewards and recognition program attracts and retains top talent, while encouraging outstanding performance across the organization. • Ideas gathered throughout the organization are recognized & rewarded.

The Highly-Engaged & High-Performing Organization

Example Employee Engagement Survey Result

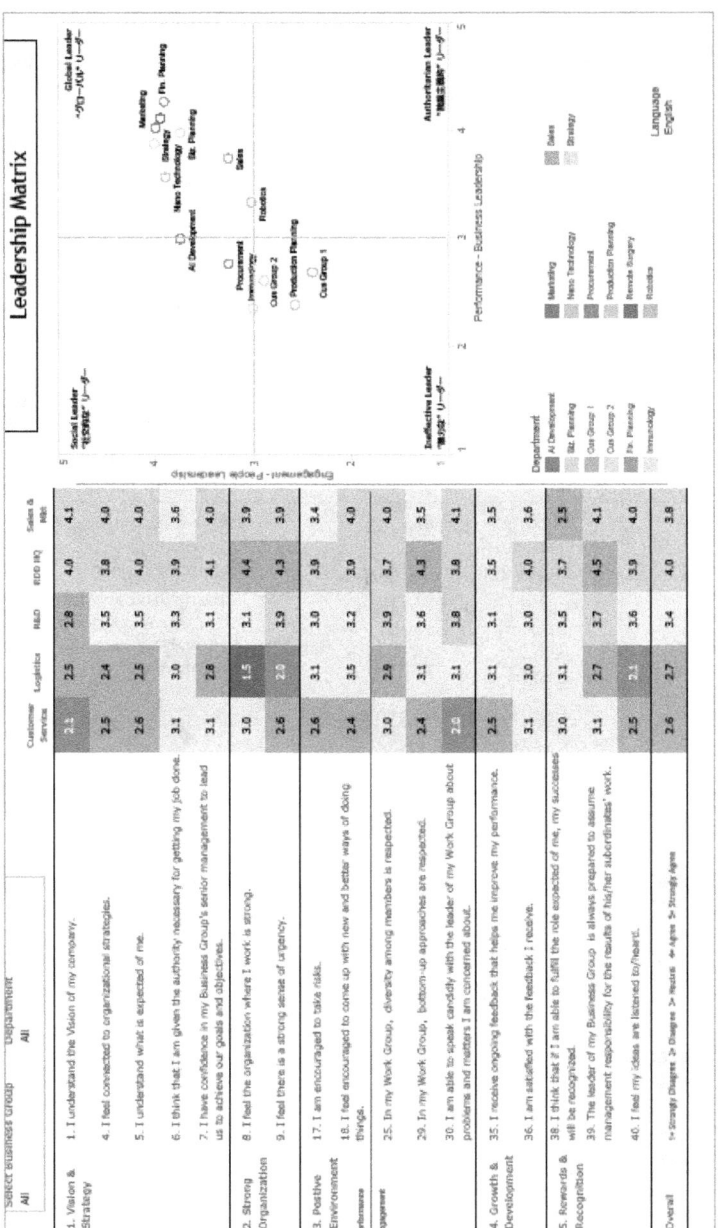

Note: The original graphics throughout this book are in full colour - some clarity might be lost when printing in monochrome

Example Employee Engagement Survey

	Assess Your Own Team/Organization
	Do this subjectively, if you do not have actual data to use
Vision and Strategy	
Strong Organization	
Positive Environment	
Growth & Development	
Rewards & Recognition	

Is the organization where you want it to be?

The High-Performing Organization

"High-Performing" is not only about business results - it includes people and organizational results, too.

Line of Sight
Link Team Mission & Objectives to the Organizational Mission and Objectives.

For example:

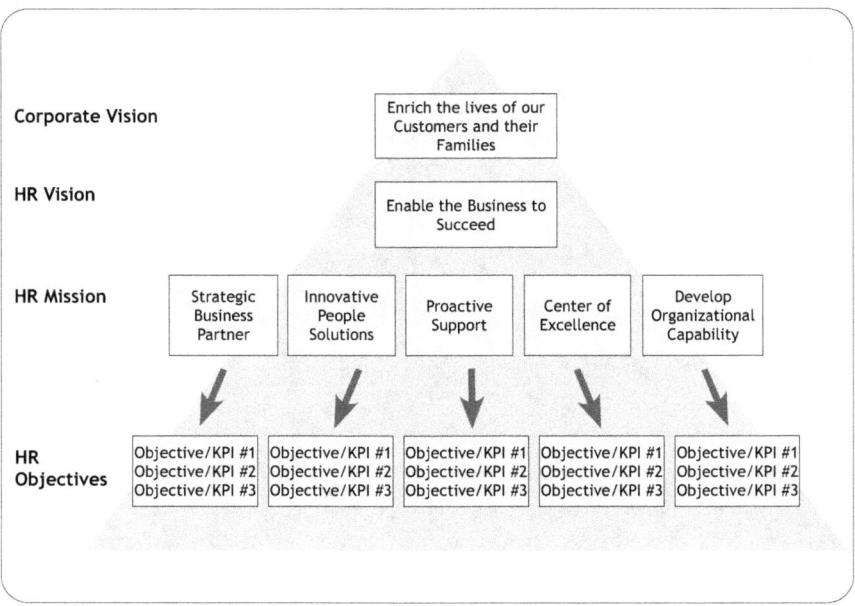

The High-Performing Organization

More examples:

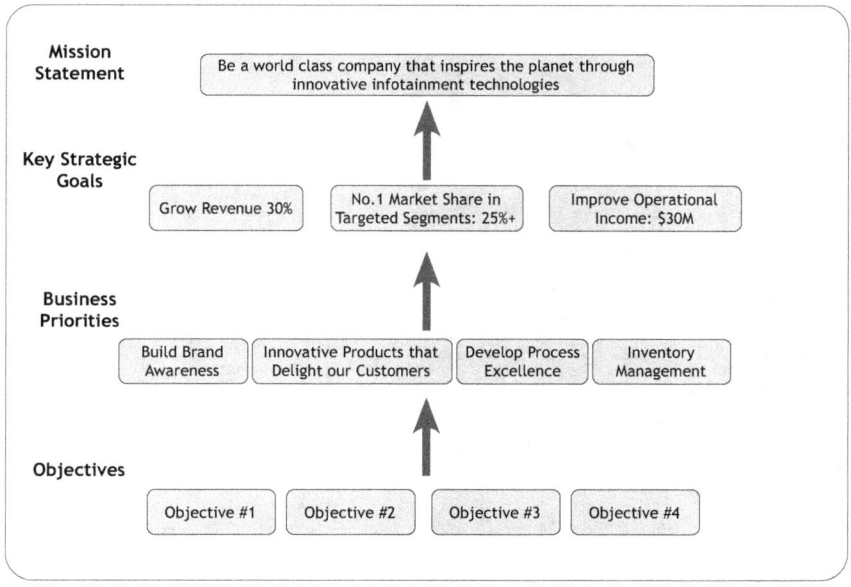

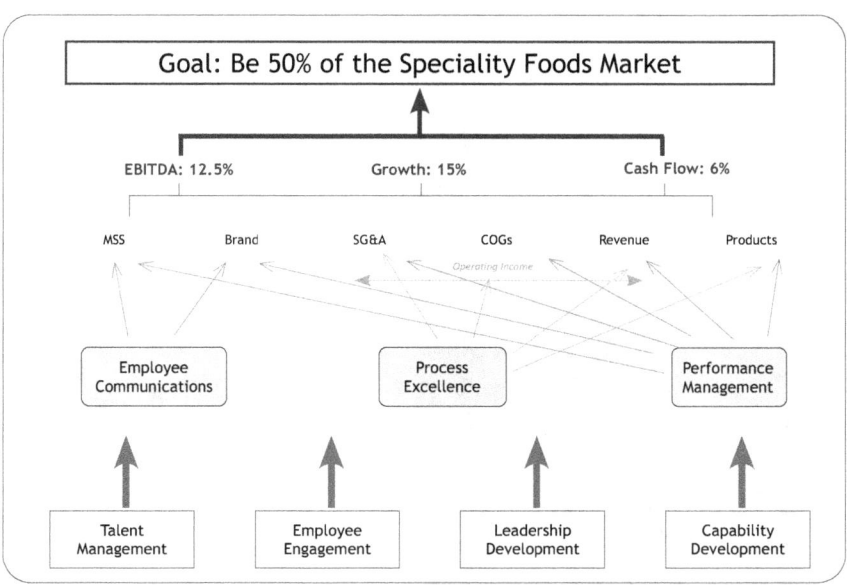

The Highly-Engaged & High-Performing Organization

Line of Sight
Link Individual Objectives to BU & Company Goals

Company Goal	BU Goal	Manager's Objectives: (KPI)	Weight
Grow Revenue Across all product lines	Revenue Growth in all markets	30% increase in USD revenue across assigned markets by end of year	35%
Achieve no.1 Market Share	Become the recognized Market Leader	Achieve 25% Percent market segment share in assigned Domestic & International markets, by end Q3	15%
Improve Operational Income	Improvement in Operational Income	Achieve 20 Million USD operational income by end of year	10%
New Product Introductions that delight our customers	New Products that Inspire and Perform	Launch 10 innovative New "A" class Products, by end year, with: a) Customer response = 75% "delighted", b) Sales Traction & Profitability 100% of goal	10%
Build a highly engaged and innovative organization that achieves extraordinary results	Making our Organization the best that it can be	10% improvement in Employee Engagement Survey Result	10%
Build a highly engaged and innovative organization that achieves extraordinary results	People development: Create succession plan for organization, including key player development	Succession plan in place. Key players identified with development plans, by end Q2.	10%
Build a highly engaged and innovative organization that achieves extraordinary results	Personal Development: Leadership Competency	70% score in Leadership Assessment Tool result from Direct staff and other Stakeholders, by July 31st	10%

Is Your Organization High-Performing?

In addition to business performance, consider these HR-related measures:
- Retention - how many people are leaving the organization?
- Productivity - how much overtime is being done? (or other measures)
- Sick leave - how many sick days, or other days? (not holidays)

	Considerations	Cost / Value Impact to Your Organization
Business Performance	• What is the current level of performance to team / organizational /company objectives? • Is this improving, decreasing?	
Retention	• How many people are leaving the organization per year? • What is the total cost of replacing them? Including recruiting agencies, training, etc. • Is this number increasing, decreasing?	
Productivity	• How much overtime is being done? • What other productivity measures do you use? (e.g., no. of contracts created by by legal team, etc.) • Is this number increasing, decreasing?	
Sick Leave	• How many sick days, or other days? (not holidays). • Is this number increasing, decreasing?	

The Highly-Engaged & High-Performing Organization

A Quick Case Study

On the opposite page you can see the outcomes of an intervention that myself and my colleagues conducted at a global Japanese manufacturing near Tokyo, where we are based.

The initial request from the department manager was to help fix some "problems" in the team, mainly concerning the poor-quality relationships between the Japanese local staff and the foreigners who were managing that organization. Initially he saw this as a leadership issue, but we soon realized that there was more to it than just "doing some leadership training." In fact, the program moved from a few planned leadership classes into a full-on two-year program that dealt with a variety of concerns.

The key points to note about this program were:
- At first, the low Engagement Survey score was the driver - the department manager's manager essentially said "Get those scores higher!"
- That said, there were no additional performance measures being used - such as turnover, cost to replace, overtime, sick leave or even individual performance scores. The only goal, at first, was a "better" engagement survey score - in other words, "stop being last in the whole company and so make us look bad."
- You can see the range of interventions in the table - they were extensive, and included 1:1 coaching for leaders and individual followers, too. The key thing is that the final outcome was *measurable*:
  – ~39M JPY (~390K USD) annual cost reduction
  – Improved engagement - the original goal
  – Improved individual performance, with reduced turnover, overtime, sick leave.
  – Other 'subjective' outcomes included "work is flowing through the department more quickly" (not actually measured!)
  – Note: this was a support function, so there were no measures such as "increased sales," and at that time there was no internal customer satisfaction survey.

What's the message here?
Leaders are responsible for the entire output of their departments, and should look for ways to create high-performing organizations - at all levels.

One goal of this book is to help you to obtain similar results in your own organization.

Quick Case Study

Issue / Situation	Year One Solution	Year Two Solution	Program Outcome

Organization
• 27 FTEs with imbalance of foreign mgmt. & leaders
  – 9 Japanese assistant mgr. & mgrs. vs 6 Non-Japanese sr. mgrs. & director.
 	
Engagement & Performance
• Lowest Engagement scores in org:
  – 56%
• Lowest performance score average in org.
  – 8 below, 17 meet, 2 exceed expectations
 	
Staff & Cost Impact
• Turnover ratio: 4 FTE left dept.
  – 14.8%
  – 22.5M yen 'cost to replace'
• High overtime
  – 42M yen annually
• High amount of sick leave
  – 21 days individual average annually
	Assessments
	• 360 Global Leadership survey :
	  – Assistant mgrs. up to director
	
	Workshops
	• 3 day leadership workshop x 2
	• 1 day performance management workshop x 2
	• 2 days inter-cultural training workshop
	• 2 days presentation skills training x 4
	• 1 day change management workshop x 2
	
	Coaching
	• 9 months coaching - core topics:
	  – leadership, performance, W/L balance, career development, others
	
	Note: Workshops & coaching were for Individual Contributor up to director
		Assessments
		• 360 Global Leadership survey :
		  – Assistant mgrs. up to director
		
		Workshops / Projects
		• Change management project
		  – Bottom up approach
		• 4 half day change management workshops
		• 2hr. twice a month Change Management team mtg.
		• Change initiative categories:
		  – Employee value proposition, performance management, authority, resources, training, collaboration & work structures
		• 1.5hr. monthly performance management meeting
		
		Coaching
		• 9 months coaching - core topics:
		  – leadership, performance, W/L balance, career development, others
			Organization
			• Department Growth: Increased headcount from 27 to 32 FTEs
			  – 1 local staff promoted to assistant mgr.
			  – 2 local staff promoted to mgr.
			
			Engagement & Performance
			• Engagement score increased
			  – From 56% to 83%
			• Improved performance scores
			  – 20 'Meet Expectations'
			  – 12 'Exceed Expectations'
			  – (vs. 8 below, 17 meet, 2 exceed expectations at start)
			
			Staff & Cost Impact
			• Turnover ratio; 1 FTE left dept.
			  – From 14.8% to 3.1%
			  – 'Cost to replace' reduced from 22.5m yen to 4.8m yen
			• Overtime reduction
			  – From 42m yen to 21m yen annually
			• Sick leave reduction
			  – 21 days to 11 days average annually

~39M JPY (~360K USD) annual cost reduction at program end

The Highly-Engaged & High-Performing Organization

> High levels of Self-Leadership, Business-Leadership & People-Leadership will enable you to create Highly-Engaged and High-Performing Teams & Organizations that Achieve Extraordinary Results

Self-Leadership
- Knowing your own leadership style
- Where you focus
- What are you good at
- How you react under pressure
- How you interact with others
- How you impact others
- How to adjust your behaviour according to the situation

Business-Leadership
- Vision & Mission
- Defining Strategy & setting Goals
- Planning, organizing operations
- Focus on Results
- Measure success through Key Performance Indicators

People-Leadership
- Motivating, coaching, supporting
- Creating Understanding
- Working as a team
- Developing the organization
- Encouraging others to succeed

Refer to the Leadership Matrix on the following page.

The Leadership Matrix

Provides a quick reference for where you are now, and where you want to be as a leader

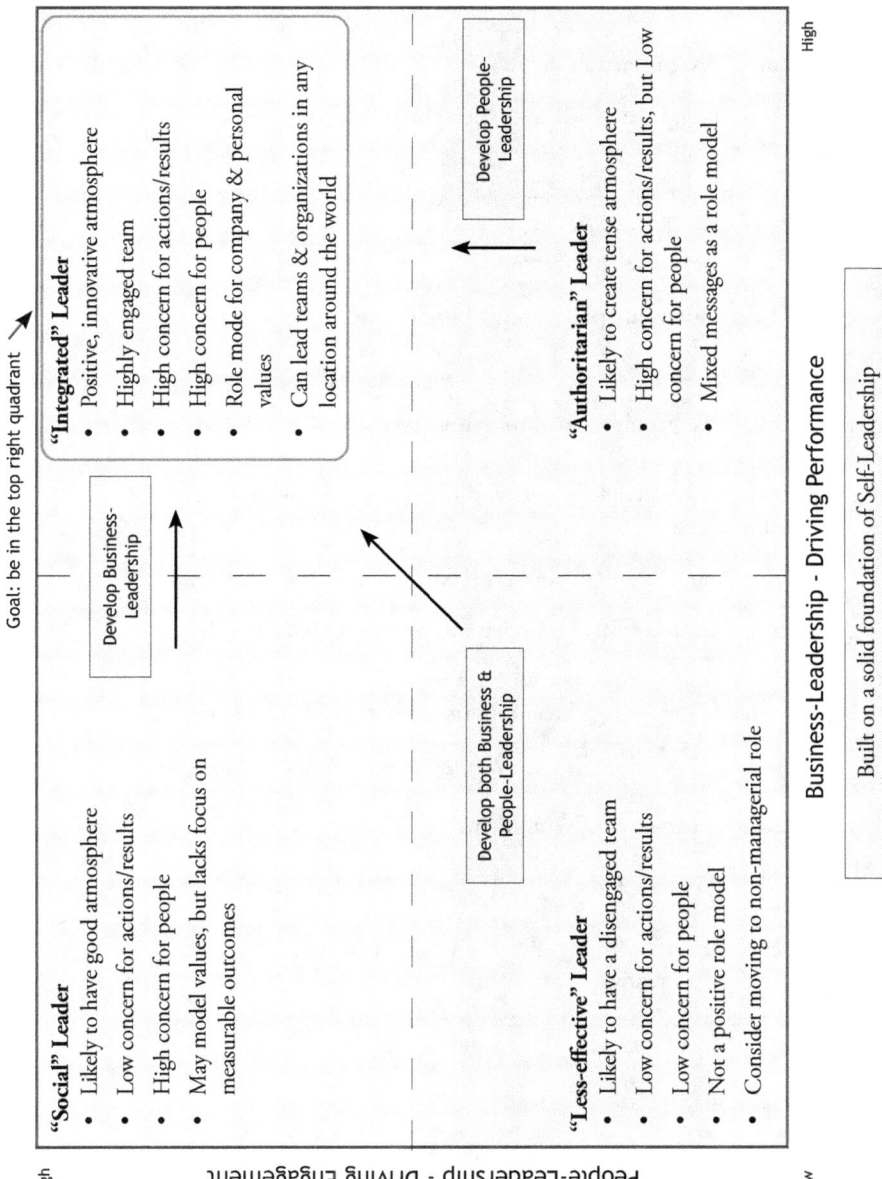

The Highly-Engaged & High-Performing Organization

Try this Leadership Self-Assessment

	Leadership Self-Assessment	
1	I am highly engaged in my role.	
2	I have a high level of self-awareness (behaviours, strengths, weaknesses, etc.).	
3	I am a Role-Model for company and team values.	
4	I have a clear sense of purpose.	
5	I'm clear about my philosophy of leadership.	
	Avg. Self-Leadership Score -->	
6	I make sure people in my group understand the organization's vision.	
7	I ensure other people understand how their work is connected to the strategy.	
8	I have built a strong organization to implement the strategy.	
9	I ensure people in my group have a sense of urgency to achieve the objectives.	
10	I regularly talk to my direct reports about their performance.	
	Avg. Business-Leadership Score -->	
11	I create a high-trust environment.	
12	I encourage and empower other people to deal with issues and develop solutions.	
13	I schedule time with my direct reports to discuss their career development plans.	
14	I actively coach people to develop their skills and grow in their job.	
15	I create high-performing teams.	
	Avg. People-Leadership Score -->	

1= Strongly Disagree, 2= Disagree, 3= Neutral, 4= Agree, 5= Strongly Agree

Leadership Self-Assessment

Plot Your Results on the Integrated Leadership Matrix

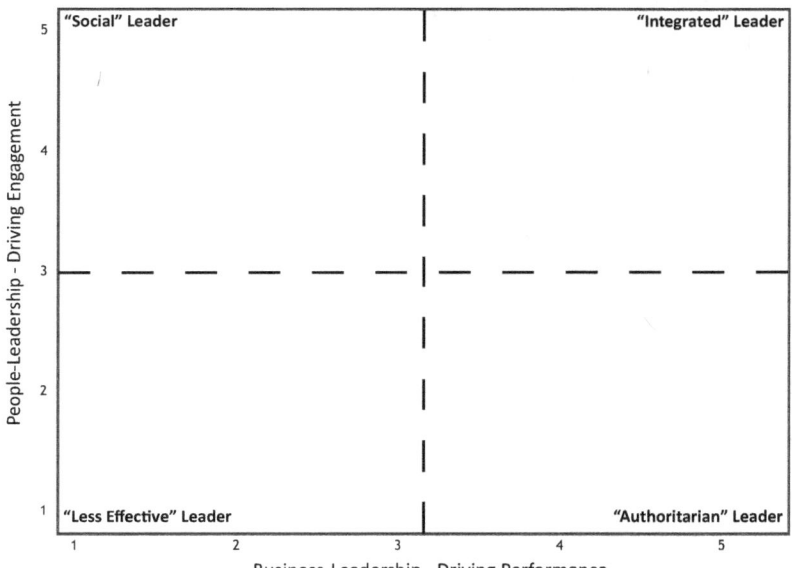

Hint: use a "bar" in the Self-Leadership box

What insights/surprises did you find?
- What would you like to change/develop?
- What do these results suggest about the effect you are having on people around you?

Why is there no "Self-Leadership" on the Matrix itself?
- Think of Business/ People leadership as how your leadership manifests to the people around you, but which rests on the foundation of your Self-Leadership.
- See over if you prefer Radar-Maps

The Highly-Engaged & High-Performing Organization

Self-Assessment:
If you prefer Radar-Maps, try this one
But, refer to the leadership matrix

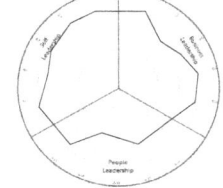

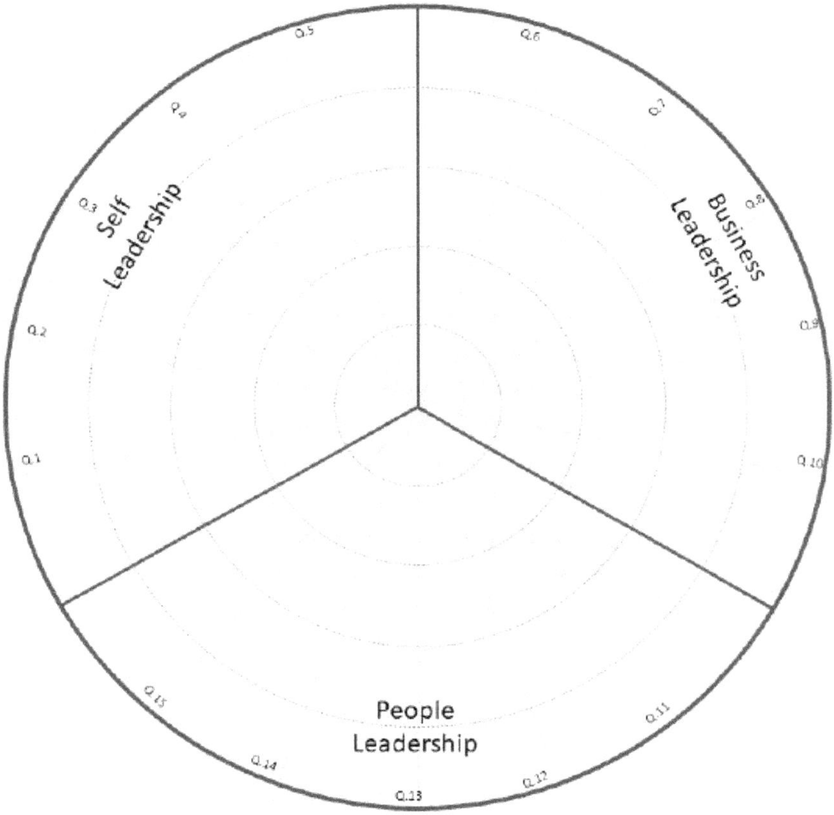

Self Leadership — Q.1, Q.2, Q.3, Q.4, Q.5

Business Leadership — Q.6, Q.7, Q.8, Q.9, Q.10

People Leadership — Q.11, Q.12, Q.13, Q.14, Q.15

"If your actions inspire others to dream more, learn more, do more and become more, you are a leader."
John Quincy Adams

SELF-LEADERSHIP

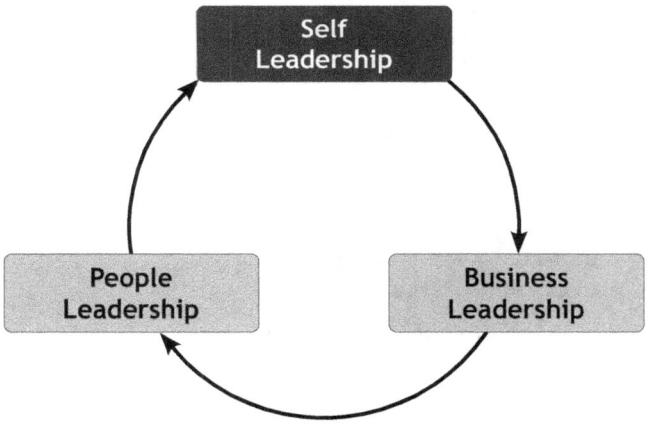

You Can't Lead Others Unless
You First Lead Yourself

Self-Leadership

From the Leadership Self-Assessment

Self-Leadership
1. I am highly engaged in my role. → Highly Engaged In Role
2. I have a high level of self-awareness (behaviours, strengths, weaknesses, etc.). → High Level Of Self-Awareness
3. I am a Role-Model for company and team values. → Values Role-Model
4. I have a clear sense of purpose. → Clear Sense Of Purpose
5. I'm clear about my philosophy of leadership. → Clear Philosophy of Leadership

Business-Leadership
6. I make sure people in my group understand the organization's vision. → Ensure All Understand Vision
7. I ensure other people understand how their work is connected to the strategy. → Connect to Strategy
8. I have built a strong organization to implement the strategy. → Build Strong Organization
9. I ensure people in my group have a sense of urgency to achieve the objectives. → Ensure Sense of Urgency
10. I regularly talk to my direct reports about their performance. → Regular Performance Discussions

People-Leadership
11. I create a high-trust environment. → Create High Trust Environment
12. I encourage and empower other people to deal with issues and develop solutions. → Encourage & Empower
13. I schedule time with my direct reports to discuss their career development plans. → Discuss Career Development
14. I actively coach people to develop their skills and grow in their job. → Actively Coach Others
15. I create high-performing teams. → Build High-Performing Teams

Self-Leadership

Highly Engaged In Role

Your Leadership Challenge
- What is your current challenge as a leader?

High Level of Self-Awareness

Know Yourself
- Your personal focus.
- Evaluate where you focus your time and energy.

Values Role-Model

Values
- What values are important to you?

Clear Sense of Purpose

Life Purpose
- What do you love to do?
- Who do you do it for?
- How do they benefit as a result of what you do for them?

Clear Philosophy of Leadership

Leadership Philosophy
- What are the values that guide your decisions?
- How do you handle mistakes, disappointments, setbacks?
- How much do people trust you, and trust each other?
- How good are you at sharing credit and saying thank you?

Self-Leadership

> ## Highly-Engaged in the Role

Some common challenges faced by leaders at all levels

- I am not getting enough from my people.
- It's hard to deal with international colleagues.
- I need to change this culture, but everyone resists.
- I have a lot to say, but can't get my ideas heard.
- We can't seem to get things done quickly and effectively.
- We have a strategy, but no one is making it happen.
- How can I engage my staff?
- My 360 feedback results were not good – I need to improve.
- My career seems to be at a standstill, I need help to move forward.
- I need to have a difficult conversation with a colleague.
- I can't trust anyone else to get this done, but I don't have time to keep doing this myself.
- We don't have enough leaders in the middle of the organization to achieve our growth targets.
- There is so much to do that I can't focus on what really matters.
- I'm doing OK, but I want to be a better Leader.

"It always seems impossible until it's done."
Nelson Mandela

Your Leadership Challenge

What's your Leadership Challenge?
Points to Consider:
- As a leader/member of your local team
- As a country, working with colleagues in other depts/BUs
- As a region, working with regional teams

Use your answer(s) to help evaluate your current level of engagement in your role. Do you relish the challenge, or are things starting to become too difficult, perhaps even overwhelming?

Note: if things are tough going just now, consider working with a Coach to help you through this phase.

| Values Role-Model | Clear Sense Of Purpose | Clear Philosophy of Leadership |

Self-Leadership

Use this page for notes

Your Personal Focus

> # A High Level of Self-Awareness

The Self-Assessment on page 26 provides a quick and useful method of evaluating where you are in terms of Self-Leadership, Business-Leadership and People-Leadership.

The Personal Focus assessment below will give you an opportunity for a deeper dive and to know yourself, your reactions and general behavioural patterns, in order to be able to modify your behaviour according to the needs of the situation.

What to do:
Go through the two tables on the following pages, then plot your 'profile' on page 38. Note that is the simplified version of the full Garuda Focus Profile, which you can read more about here: https://garuda.no/en/about-garuda/focusprofile/

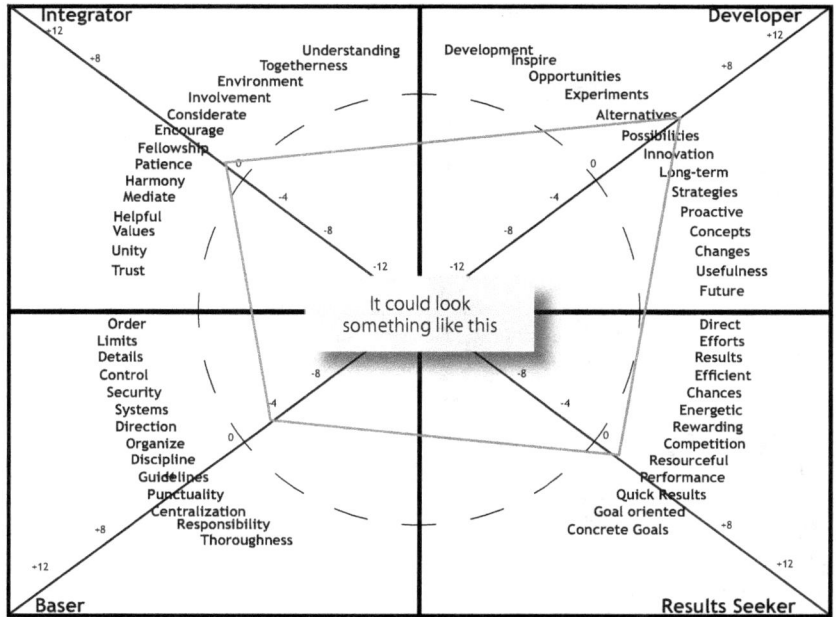

The Leader's Mental Scorecard © Finn Lavalaschka, Garuda Research Institute

| Values Role-Model | Clear Sense Of Purpose | Clear Philosophy of Leadership |

Self-Leadership

Check (or use "X") how important each statement is to you in your role as a leader.

	In my daily decisions and in my role as a leader, I put emphasis on:	Very Important	Fairly Important	Neutral	Less important	Not Important
1	Helping and supporting employees who are having difficulty and may have a hard time managing.					
2	Organizing matters so employees can solve their tasks thoroughly and systematically.					
3	Acting and being perceived as an active, energetic and goal oriented leader.					
4	Leading the way when changes and modifications are to be carried out.					
5	Formulating clear guidelines for responsibility and assignments.					
6	Creating an environment that provides room and time for social togetherness and small-talk.					
7	Inspiring employees to come up with creative solutions.					
8	Assuring myself that everyone always uses their time and resources efficiently and with a goal orientation.					
9	Encouraging, commending, supporting and motivating all employees.					
10	Having systems that allow me to check and see where employees are in regards to plans and given instructions.					
11	Always leading the way and rendering an efficient and result oriented effort.					
12	Ensuring that everyone has space, facilities and opportunities to independently solve tasks.					
13	Making my decisions based on clear and sure facts.					
14	Knowing my employees' background, values and positions.					
15	Playing a central role in the development of concepts and strategies.					
16	Ensuring that people do not waste time, and instead concentrate on creating visible results & getting things done.					

Your Personal Focus

If you indicated "Very important" in the first statement, then circle the number in the "Very important" field. Then, add up your points in each of the four focus areas.

		Very Important	Fairly Important	Neutral	Less important	Not Important		Integrator	Baser	Results	Developer
1	Integrator Focus	4	2	0	-2	-4	=				
2	Baser Focus	4	2	0	-2	-4	=				
3	Results Seeker Focus	4	2	0	-2	-4	=				
4	Developer Focus	4	2	0	-2	-4	=				
5	Baser Focus	4	2	0	-2	-4	=				
6	Integrator Focus	4	2	0	-2	-4	=				
7	Developer Focus	4	2	0	-2	-4	=				
8	Results Seeker Focus	4	2	0	-2	-4	=				
9	Integrator Focus	4	2	0	-2	-4	=				
10	Baser Focus	4	2	0	-2	-4	=				
11	Results Seeker Focus	4	2	0	-2	-4	=				
12	Developer Focus	4	2	0	-2	-4	=				
13	Baser Focus	4	2	0	-2	-4	=				
14	Integrator Focus	4	2	0	-2	-4	=				
15	Developer Focus	4	2	0	-2	-4	=				
16	Results Seeker focus	4	2	0	-2	-4	=				
						Integrator Points					
						Baser Points					
						Results Seeker Points					
						Developer Points					

Now plot your "scores" on the next page

Values Role-Model   **Clear Sense Of Purpose**   **Clear Philosophy of Leadership**

Self-Leadership

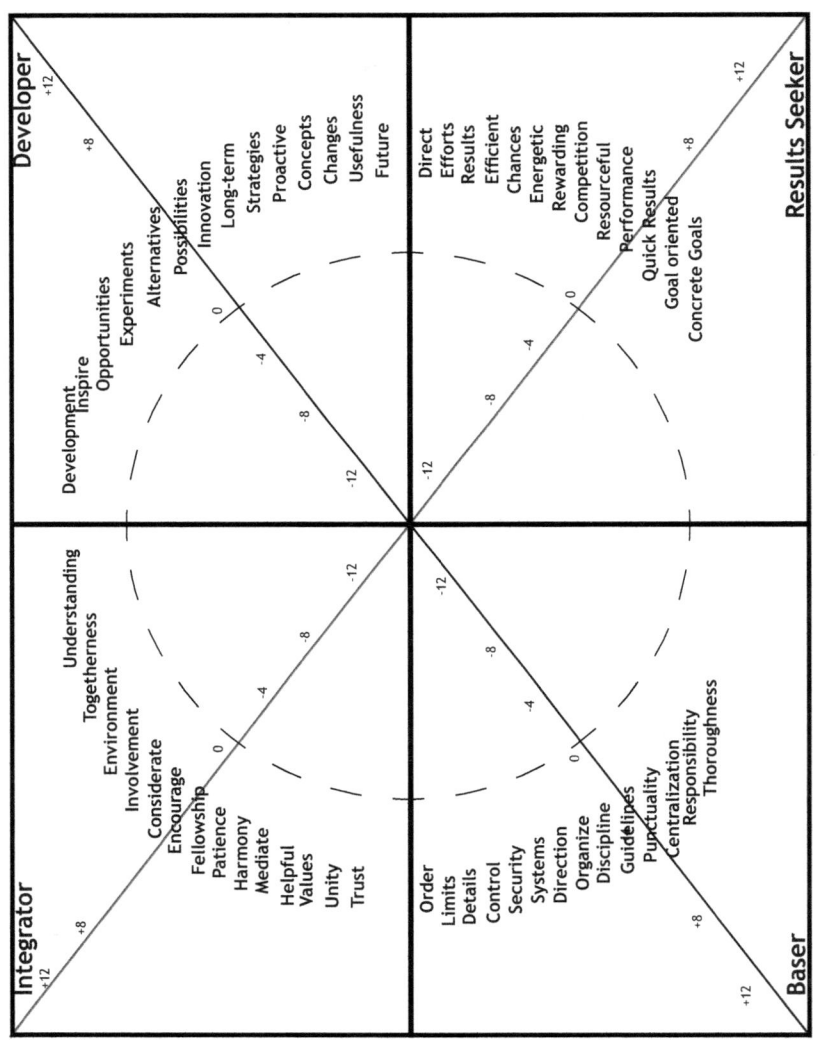

The tool is the simplified version of the full Garuda Personal Focus, which you can read more about here: https://garuda.no/en/about-garuda/focusprofile/

Your Personal Focus

Strengths and Challenges

As an additional step, underline 2 or 3 words in each quadrant that are your strengths, and put an X next to 2 or 3 that are difficult for you.

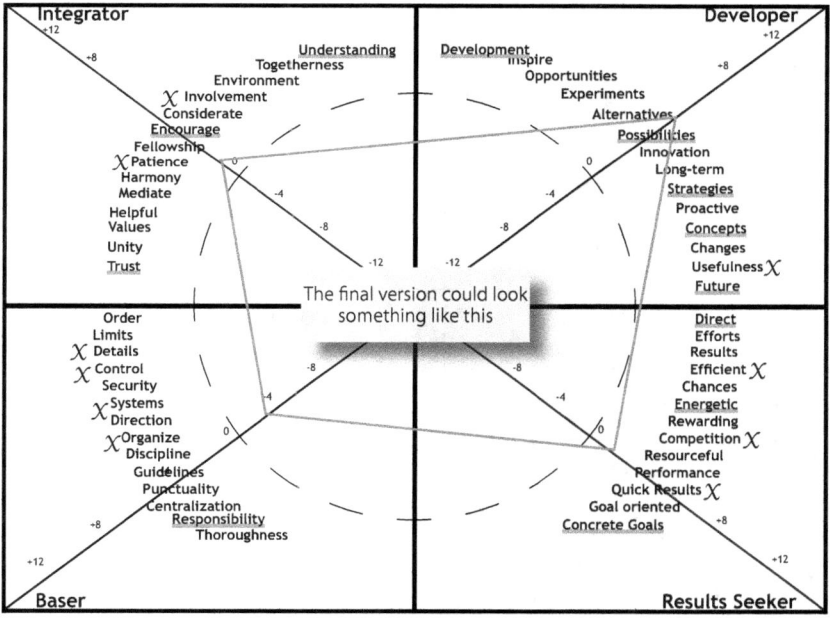

Next, go through the descriptions and "Positive/ Not-so Positive" aspects on the following pages. As this is in a self-assessment format, there are no clear instructions regarding 'what to do if...' - we'll leave that for you to consider.

However, if you would like to dig deeper than we suggest working with a Coach and taking a full profile in Garuda (or DiSC, PI, Saville Wave, Hogan, BehavioralOS, etc.).

| Values Role-Model | Clear Sense Of Purpose | Clear Philosophy of Leadership |

Self-Leadership

The Garuda Focus Profile uncovers 4 different work-styles and is especially useful for individual coaching & development, team-building, team-evaluations and person/position "best fit for the role" assessments.

Integrator	Developer
"Leadership is about communication, understanding and avoiding disagreement and conflicts."	"Leadership is about looking forward, creating opportunities and eliminating outdated structures and rules."
Focus on Integration Likes Working with People & Prefers Working in a Team	**Focus on Future and Vision** Loves New Ideas & Strategies
Baser	**Results Seeker**
"Leadership is about having everything under control, avoiding risk, and guarding against the unexpected."	"Leadership is about creating results, avoiding losing and having the courage to take a chance."
Focus on Structure Prefers to Look at Structuring, Planning & Organization	**Focus on Achieving Results** Motivated by Achieving Goals & Targets

Some example Focus Profiles

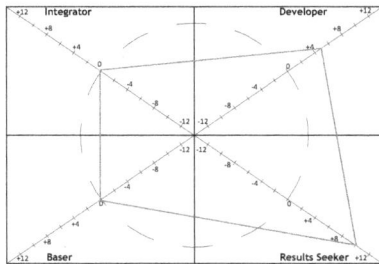 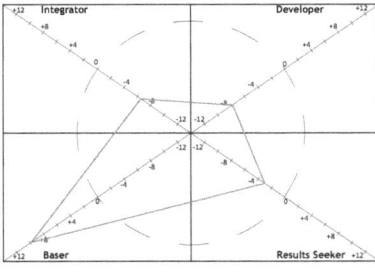

Predominantly "Results Seeker"   Predominantly "Baser"

Your Personal Focus

Understanding of tendencies helps both managers and individual contributors to adapt their styles according to the needs of situation and/or role.

Integrator		Developer	
Positive	Not so Positive	Positive	Not so Positive
• Coordinates • Listens • Responsive • Understanding • Creates connections • Mediates	• Too understanding • Avoids conflict • Time consuming • Too Tolerant • More talk, less action • Too long-winded	• Ingenious • Enthusiastic • Improvising • Holistic • Innovative • Curious • Intuitive	• Careless • Too optimistic • Ignores rules/regulations • Unrealistic ideas • Unclear boundaries • No control
Baser		Results Seeker	
Positive	Not so Positive	Positive	Not so Positive
• Proper • Structured • Planning • Controlling • Quality awareness • Matter-of-fact • Analytical	• No "Big-Picture" view • Too high demands • Too slow • Structure instead of content • Too controlling	• Energetic • Active • Competitive • Focus on competition • Efficient • Hands-on	• No sustainability • No coordination • Walks over other people • Careless

Some example Focus Profiles

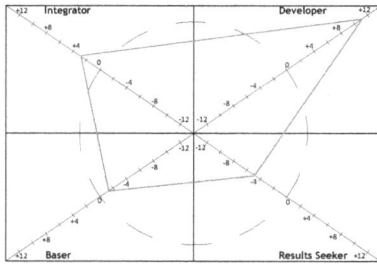

Predominantly "Developer"

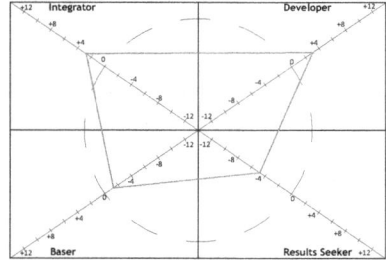

Balance, but with reduced "Results Seeker"

| Values Role-Model | Clear Sense Of Purpose | Clear Philosophy of Leadership |

Self-Leadership

Adjusting Your Focus for Someone Else

Begin by considering one of your employees or stakeholders (if you are not yet a manager, then choose someone you know or work with). Then select 3-5 key words in each quadrant that describe how the person **is,** and how the person is **not.**

What to do (*next page*)
- For each word that describes how the person *IS,* ....count +1
- For each word that describes how the person is *NOT* ....count -1
- *Note: count +/-2 if it is strongly like/unlike that person*
- For each area, plot the total score on the diagonal line (*next page*)

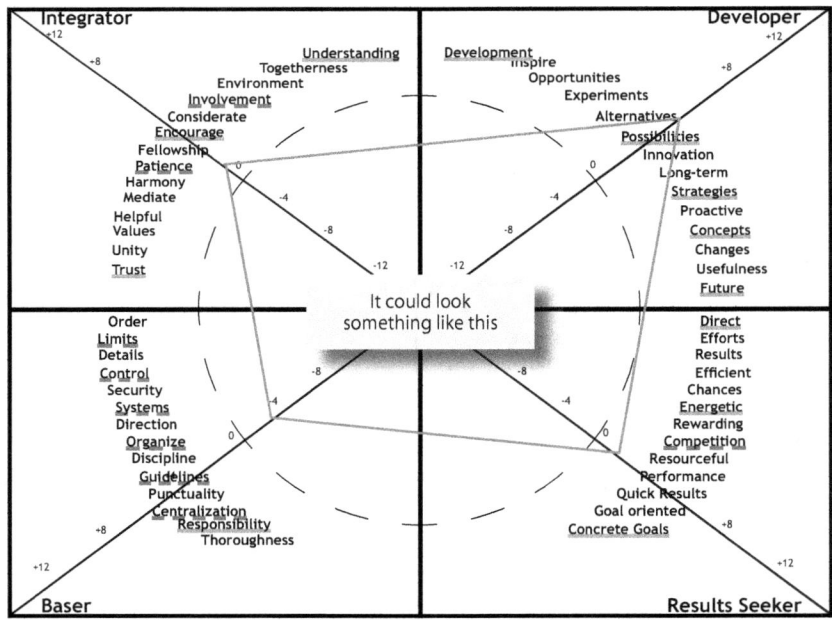

It could look something like this

For this person:

Aim for Motivating Leadership:
- New projects, but not long-term
- Work Independently

Avoid Demotivating Leadership
- Don't give too many instructions
- Best to avoid tasks that require attention to detail

Adjusting Your Focus

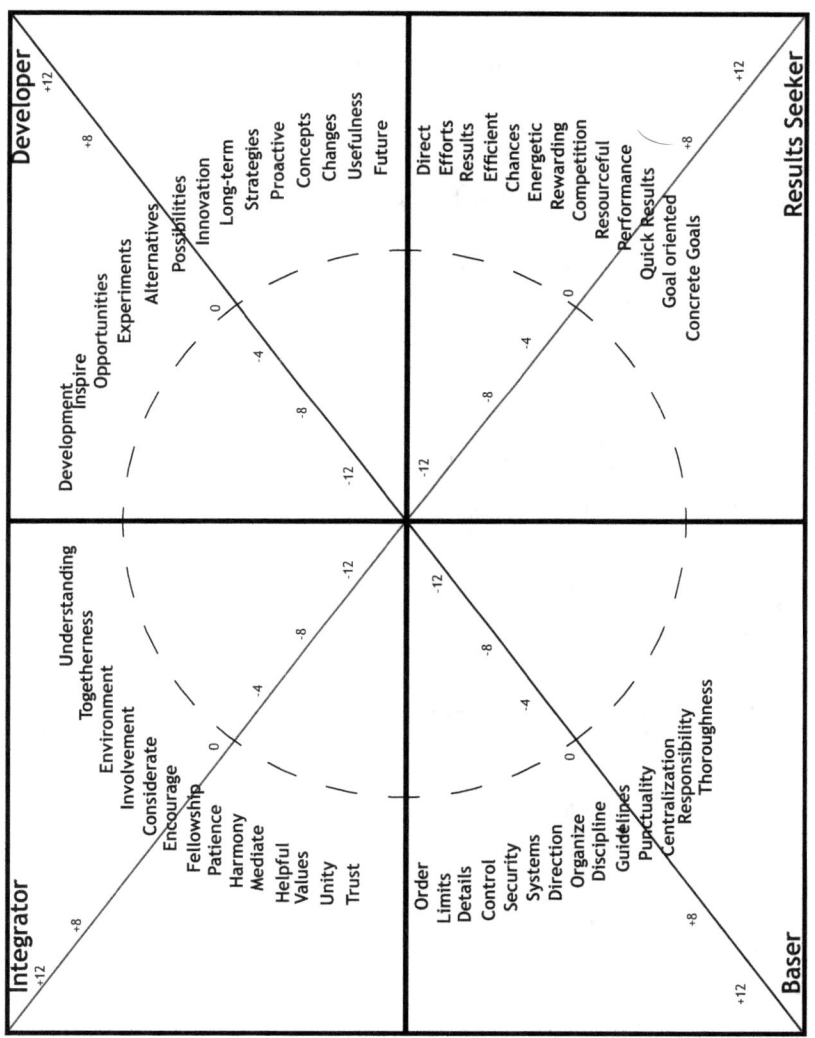

Look for areas of difference/ conflict. For example, a "Baser" might get frustrated with a "Developer" for having hundreds of ideas but no structure to implement them. On the other hand, a "Developer" might get upset with a "Baser" for a perceived 'inability' to brainstorm/ think creatively in group meetings, etc.

Try this method for everyone in your team, and compare their profiles to see if you can spot any possible areas that might need your attention!

| Values Role-Model | Clear Sense Of Purpose | Clear Philosophy of Leadership |

Self-Leadership

Your Personal Priorities

Where do you focus your time & energy?
- List your responsibilities, tasks, activities, projects
- Decide which quadrant they fit into
- What does this tell you about where you focus your time & energy?

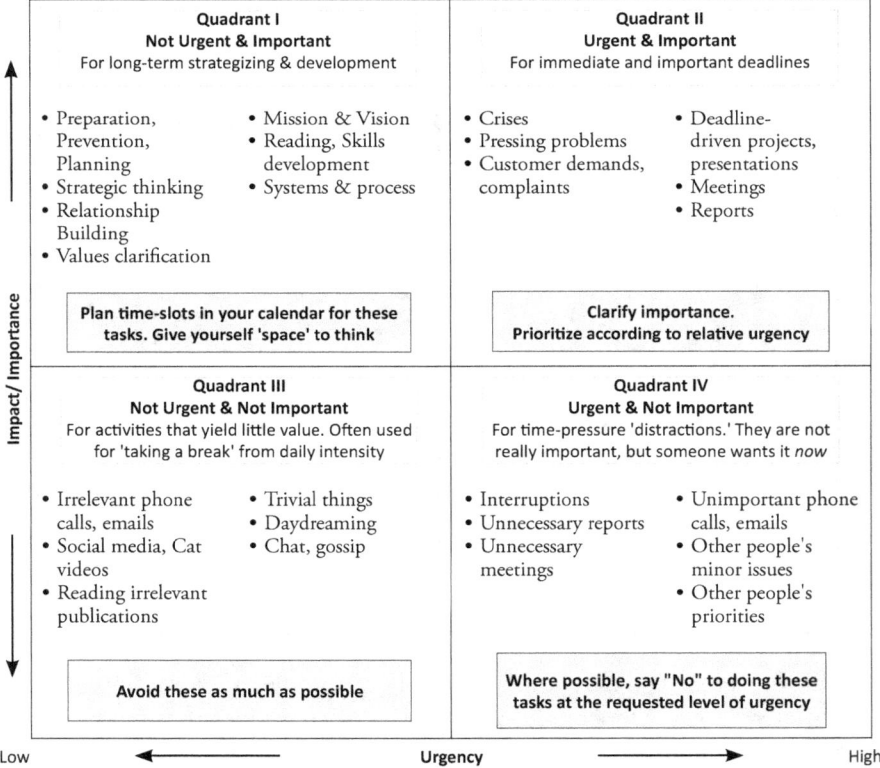

"How you spend your time is the single clearest indicator of what is important to you."

Adapted from the Franklin-Covey Time Management Grid

How You Prioritize

The Prioritization Matrix

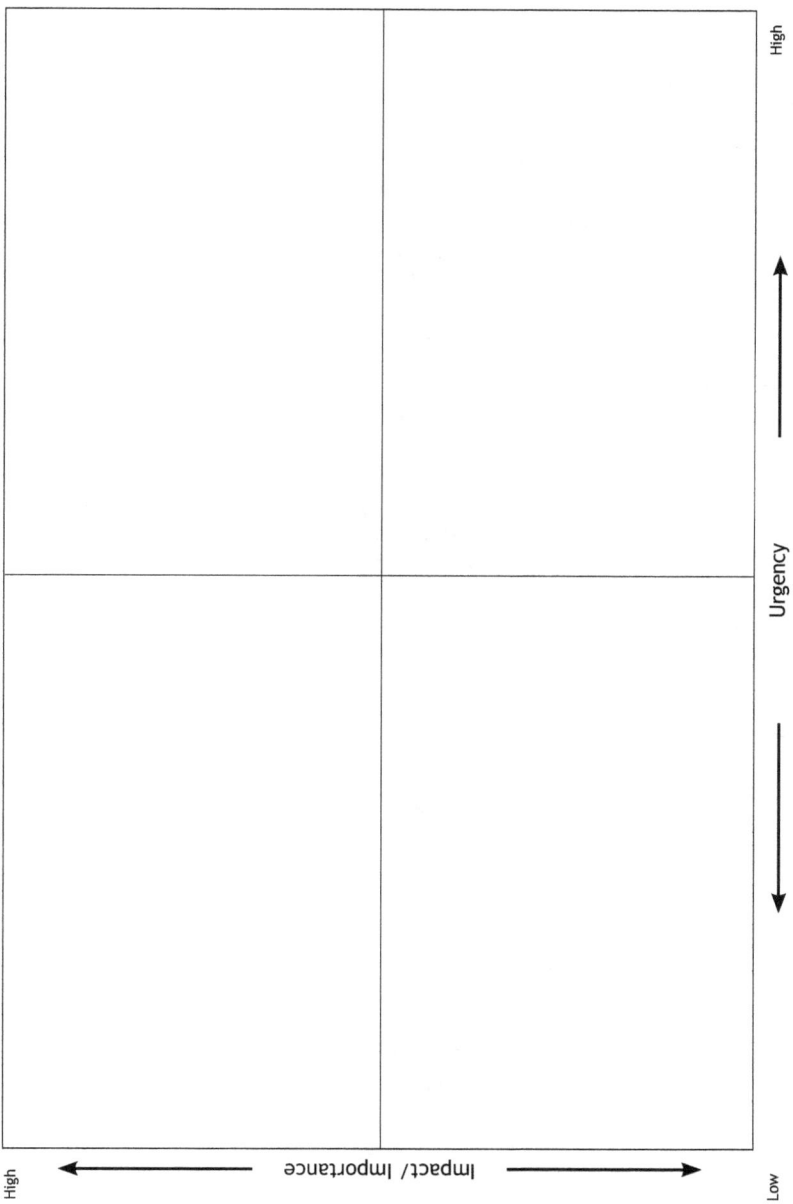

What does this tell you about where you focus your time and energy? Are you spending enough time in Quadrant I?

| Values Role-Model | Clear Sense Of Purpose | Clear Philosophy of Leadership |

Self-Leadership

How Productive Are You?

Use the self-assessment (next page) to figure out your personal productivity level
- Circe the number that is the closest to how you operate (treat #3 as 'neutral')
- Add up your total score - then check the result in the table below
- Not happy with the result, or have "Work to do"? - see the Personal Productivity section on page 148 for some ideas

<35	You have a lot of work to do to become more productive!
35 - 49	You are doing OK in some areas, but falling behind in others. Focus on improving in those areas that you feel will make the biggest difference
50-62	You are doing well. However, keep looking at ways to improve your productivity even further
63+	Congratulations. You are a productivity role model!

The 4W System
Do the Right Thing at the Right Time, with the Right Result.

See page 148

How Productive Are You?

Most like me ←→						Most like me
I do work as it comes to me.	1	2	3	4	5	I use a prioritized list to complete my work.
I'm very busy, and am often late to meetings or appointments.	1	2	3	4	5	I am always on time for meetings or appointments, no matter how busy I am.
I'm too busy to plan projects.	1	2	3	4	5	I use a step-by-step method for planning a project.
It's hard to focus due to constant interruptions, so often I get behind on work.	1	2	3	4	5	I complete work quickly, because I focus on what I am doing.
It's hard to say "No" to an urgent request, even if it isn't so important.	1	2	3	4	5	I politely say "No" to urgent, but unimportant, requests.
I'm too busy to plan ahead for the next day.	1	2	3	4	5	I always plan ahead for the next day.
I don't keep an overview of my projects.	1	2	3	4	5	If anybody asks, I can quickly show an overview of all my projects, with time-lines.
I'm often late on achieving deadlines.	1	2	3	4	5	I meet required deadlines.
I do work when I have time between meetings.	1	2	3	4	5	I block off time on my calendar to complete work.
I rarely think about project outcomes and goals.	1	2	3	4	5	When I plan a project, I think about the outcome and goal to be achieved.
I respond to emails immediately.	1	2	3	4	5	I schedule time every day for email review.
My desk and filing systems are a bit messy.	1	2	3	4	5	My desk and filing systems are tidy and well-organized.
I never go home until all my work is done.	1	2	3	4	5	I re-schedule work for tomorrow if I can not completed it during normal working hours.
Customer requests are always my number one priority.	1	2	3	4	5	My business group's objectives are my number one priority.

| Values Role-Model | Clear Sense Of Purpose | Clear Philosophy of Leadership |

Self-Leadership

Be a Values Role-Model

Values
When individual, group and organizational values are in synch, people will *want* to do something and achieve great results. Organizations with a strong culture based on shared values outperform other firms.

Your Values
- What are your top five values? *(use the table below for some ideas)*.
- What values are important to you in your work?
- What values are important to your personal or family life?

Accountability	Creativity	Fulfillment	Integrity	Prestige
Adventurism	Curiosity	Happiness	Leadership	Respect
Authority	Development	Harmony	Learning	Security
Challenge	Dignity	Health	Leisure	Spontaneity
Comfort	Enterprise	Honesty	Openness	Stability
Compassion	Excellence	Humour	Optimism	Success
Competition	Fame	Independence	Peace	Teamwork
Control	Family	Influence	Persistence	Tolerance
Cooperation	Freedom	Initiative	Possibilities	Tradition
Consideration	Friendship	Innovation	Power	Trust

Your Personal Values

What are your 5 Values?

How do your personal values relate to the Company Values?

Company Values ⟵⟶ **My Values**

How to build shared values in your team.
- Schedule a series of meeting to discuss values - yours, theirs and the organization's.
- Use the Values chart - get your people to do their own values exercise.
- Find areas of overlap.
- Document the agreed "shared values" list, and display it somewhere for all to see.

Self-Leadership

Clear Sense of Purpose

What do you love to do?
- Who do you do it for?
- What do they want or need?
- How do they benefit as a result of what you do for them?

Kevin Reynolds	*"I help people and organizations be the best they can be."*

Brent Conkle	*"I coach Global leaders to achieve great things in their career so they can make the world a better place."*

> **Food for Thought**
>
> How well do you:
> - Set a personal example of what is expected?
> - Follow through on promises and commitments?
> - Ask for feedback on how your actions affect people's performance?

Kevin, Brent: The authors

Your Life Role/ Purpose

Create your personal Life Role/ Purpose statement

Values Role-Model | Clear Sense Of Purpose | Clear Philosophy of Leadership

Self-Leadership

> ## Clear Philosophy of Leadership

What is your leadership philosophy?
How would you describe your leadership philosophy? Imagine you have 30 seconds to describe this to someone (the elevator test). What would you say?

Ask yourself:
- What are the values that guide my decisions?
- What are my beliefs?
- What is my Personal Focus?
- How do I handle mistakes, disappointments, setbacks?
- How much do the people around me trust me and trust each other?
- How good am I at sharing credit and saying thank you?

Here's an example from a Leader that we know:

"Your Success is My Success"

His explanation:
"Success comes through my people, not through me. My job is to ensure they are successful in whatever they do, and give them credit for it, too. If they are successful and <u>feel</u> successful too, then my job is done - basically speaking!"

Create Your Leadership Philosophy

Create your leadership philosophy "30-second elevator pitch"

Values Role-Model | Clear Sense Of Purpose | Clear Philosophy of Leadership

Self-Leadership

Self-Leadership Action Plan

	Action Area	How this Impacts Team Engagement & Performance
1	I am highly engaged in my role.	
2	I have a high level of self-awareness (behaviours, strengths, weaknesses, etc.).	
3	I am a Role-Model for company and team values.	
4	I have a clear sense of purpose.	
5	I'm clear about my philosophy of leadership.	

Review the exercises for Self-Leadership, then create an action plan for steps you will take in the next 6-9 months.

Build Your Self-Leadership Action Plan

	Actions I'll Take in The Next 6-9 months
1	
2	
3	
4	
5	

Values Role-Model Clear Sense Of Purpose Clear Philosophy of Leadership

Business-Leadership

Use this page for notes

BUSINESS-LEADERSHIP

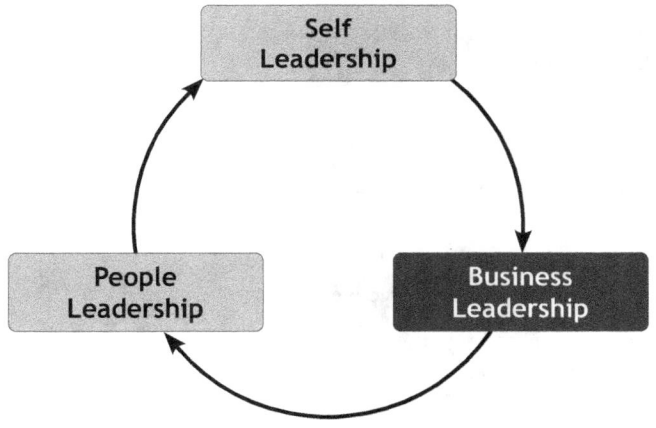

Leaders Need to Inspire Others to
Take Part in a "Shared Vision," and
Translate that Vision into Action

Business-Leadership

From the Leadership Self-Assessment

Self-Leadership

1. I am highly engaged in my role. → Highly Engaged In Role
2. I have a high level of self-awareness (behaviours, strengths, weaknesses, etc.). → High Level Of Self-Awareness
3. I am a Role-Model for company and team values. → Values Role-Model
4. I have a clear sense of purpose. → Clear Sense Of Purpose
5. I'm clear about my philosophy of leadership. → Clear Philosophy of Leadership

Business-Leadership

6. I make sure people in my group understand the organization's vision. → Ensure All Understand Vision
7. I ensure other people understand how their work is connected to the strategy. → Connect to Strategy
8. I have built a strong organization to implement the strategy. → Build Strong Organization
9. I ensure people in my group have a sense of urgency to achieve the objectives. → Ensure Sense of Urgency
10. I regularly talk to my direct reports about their performance. → Regular Performance Discussions

People-Leadership

11. I create a high-trust environment. → Create High Trust Environment
12. I encourage and empower other people to deal with issues and develop solutions. → Encourage & Empower
13. I schedule time with my direct reports to discuss their career development plans. → Discuss Career Development
14. I actively coach people to develop their skills and grow in their job. → Actively Coach Others
15. I create high-performing teams. → Build High-Performing Teams

Business-Leadership

Ensure All Understand the Vision

Vision & Mission
- What you do and why you do it.

Connect to Strategy

Link Team & Organizational Mission
- Overall objectives for your company, your business unit and your dept./team.

Build a Strong Organization

Organizational Capabilities
- The skills, knowledge and competencies needed to achieve your strategy.

Ensure a Sense of Urgency

Doing the Right Thing at the Right Time
- Focusing on the objectives of the company, organization, team.

Regular Performance Conversations

Performance Conversations
- Manage individual performance through on-going "Performance Conversations."

Ensure Everyone Understands the Vision

Whether you call it "Purpose," "Vision" or Mission" (or all 3!), you and the people around you will want to know "What we do and Why we do it."

To keep things simple, we'll use "Vision" - although an on-line search will reveal that companies tend use the above three terminologies somewhat interchangeably on their "About Us" pages.

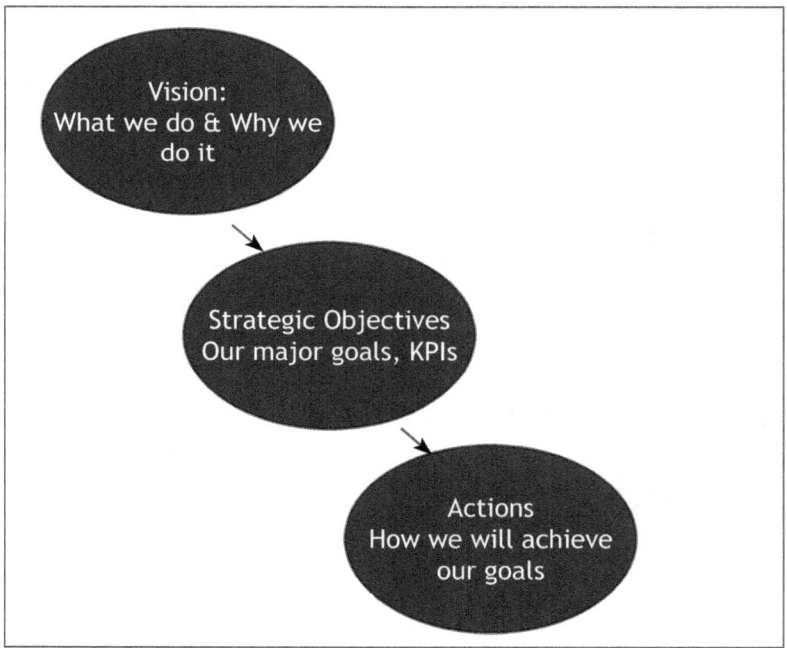

For example
- "Be the safest and most customer focused transportation company."
- "$500 million revenue by 2020."
- "Be the No.1 Data Transfer Company."
- "Aiming to halve cancer deaths within 10 years."
- "Promote and develop the growth of tennis."
- "To organize the world's information and make it universally accessible & useful."
- "I have a dream…"

Ensure All Understand the Vision

Some examples

Fast Retailing (Uniqlo)

Corporate Statement	Group Mission
Changing clothes. Changing conventional wisdom. Change the world.	To create truly great clothing with new and unique value, and to enable people all over the world to experience the joy, happiness and satisfaction of wearing such great clothes. To enrich people's lives through our unique corporate activities, and to seek to grow and develop our company in unity with society.

Intel

Purpose	Vision	Mission
We create world-changing technology that enriches the lives of every person on earth.	To be the trusted performance leader that unleashes the potential of data.	We engineer solutions for our customers' greatest challenges with reliable, cloud to edge computing, inspired by Moore's Law.

Ely Lilly	Lilly unites caring with discovery to create medicines that make life better for people around the world.
Starbucks	Our mission: to inspire and nurture the human spirit – one person, one cup and one neighbourhood at a time.
Honda	Serve people worldwide with the "joy of expanding their life's potential"
Nike	To bring inspiration and innovation to every athlete in the world.
Microsoft	Our mission is to empower every person and every organization on the planet to achieve more.
General Electric	We rise to the challenge of building a world that works.

Creating Your Vision

1 **Take some time to think about:**
- What do you think about the future?
- What's important to you, your team, your organization?
- What will you do to achieve that future?

2 **Then**
Create a 30-60 second "elevator pitch" for your "Vision." It can cover one or more of:
- Your team
- Your department
- Your organization

What's your vision?

Points to consider:
- Keep it short & simple
- Make it "Action Oriented" - driving behaviours; things that people can do

Creating The Team Vision

1

1) **List products/ services**
   - What themes do we see?
   - What's unique? What differentiates us from others?

2) **List customers/ customer types**
   - Who are our customers?
   - What do they really want/need from us?

3) **Describe our business from the viewpoint of customers**
   - To them, what is the purpose of our organization/ our team?

4) **What is the end result we offer?**
   - What result do we offer, not just products and services?

2 In ~25 words, create the purpose of your organization/ team.

For example:
"We help leaders create highly-engaged and high-performing organizations that achieve extraordinary results"

Note: This is best done using a whiteboard

Business-Leadership

Team not Feeling Connected to the Vision?

If you feel the team is not connected to the vision, or if your employee engagement survey results are indicating that this is a problem area, they try conducting one or both parts of this team exercise.

What to do:
- Prepare a white board, as per the next page.

Then ask the team:
- What does it (the vision) mean for you?
- Do some areas mean more to you than others?
- How connected do you feel to the Mission/Vision?
- How does it affect you?
- How is the organization performing with respect to the Mission/Vision?

Also consider trying this version:
- Ask everyone to map their current activities to the mission/vision, using Post-It notes or maker pens
- Then discuss how aligned their actual activities are - and if there are areas where better alignment or clarification needed.

Food for Thought

How well do you:
- Ask group members to share their own vision for the future?
- Show how individual interests can be achieved as part of the group?
- Ensure people in my group understand what is expected of them?
- Make certain that goals, plans, and milestones are set?

Connecting the Team to the Vision

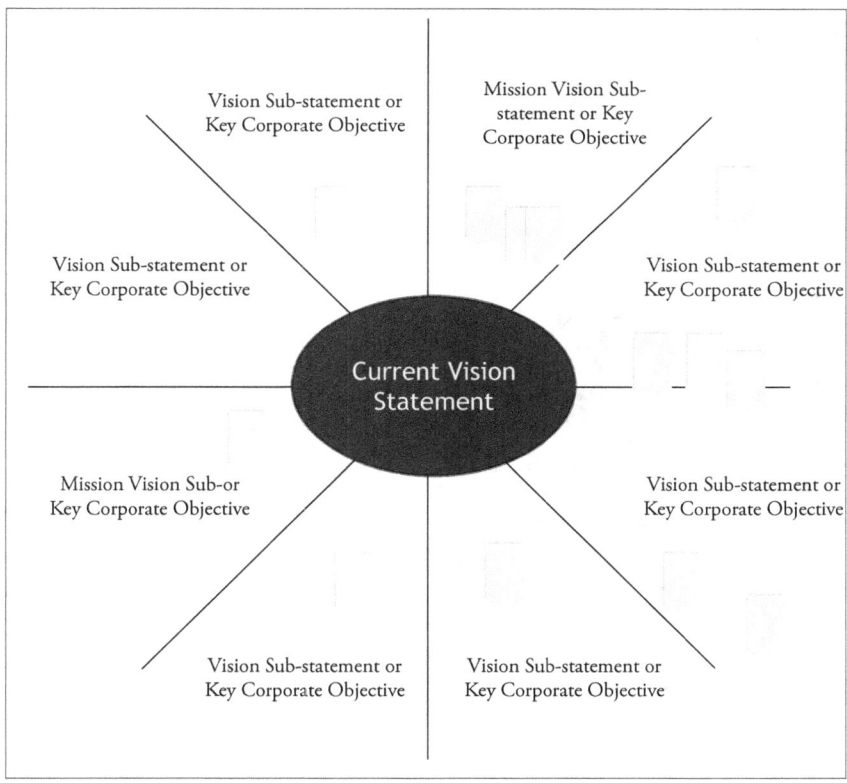

Note: This is similar to the team activity on page 163

Business-Leadership

Connect to the Organization's Strategy

"Line of Sight"
Team Vision/ Mission & Objectives should be linked, as best possible, to the Organizational Vision/ Mission and Objectives.

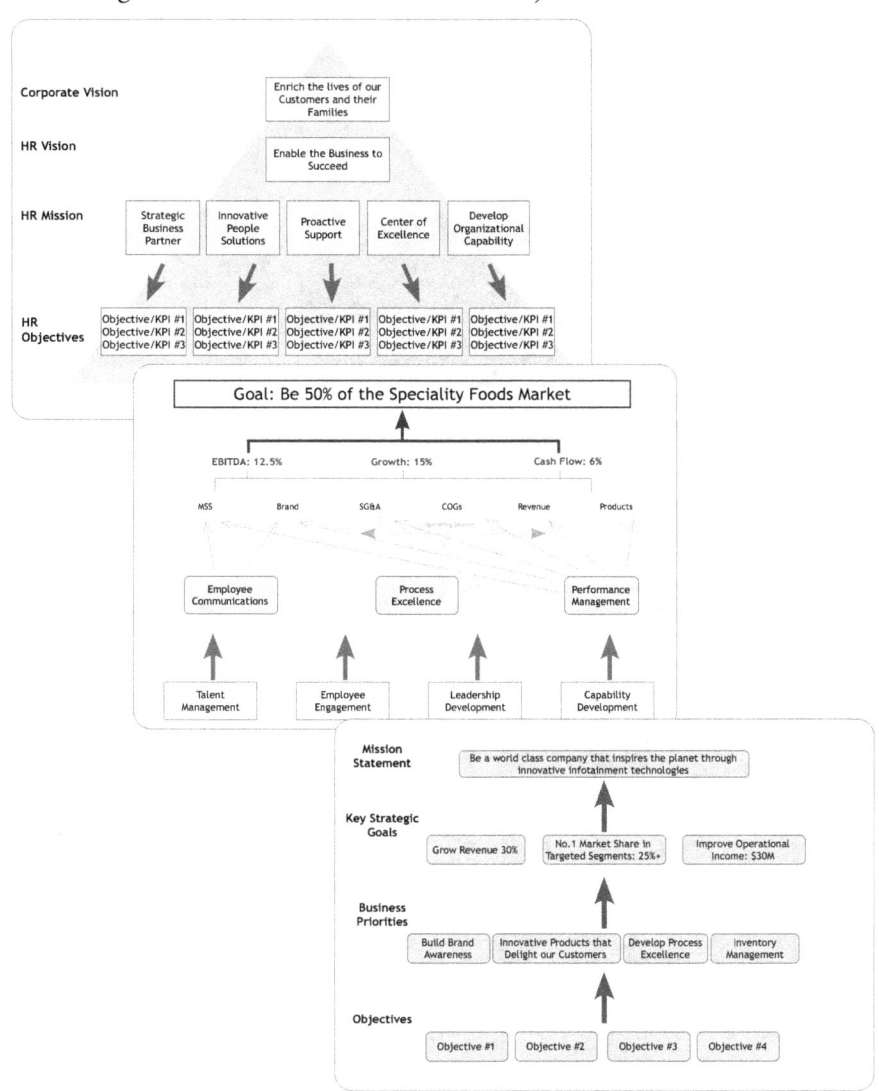

Link to Organizational Objectives

"Line of Sight"
- Try this for one (or more) of your own objectives. How well are they aligned to the corporate mission and objectives?
- Grab a sheet of paper and do the same for each of your direct reports. How does it look? Are things well-aligned, or is there work to be done?

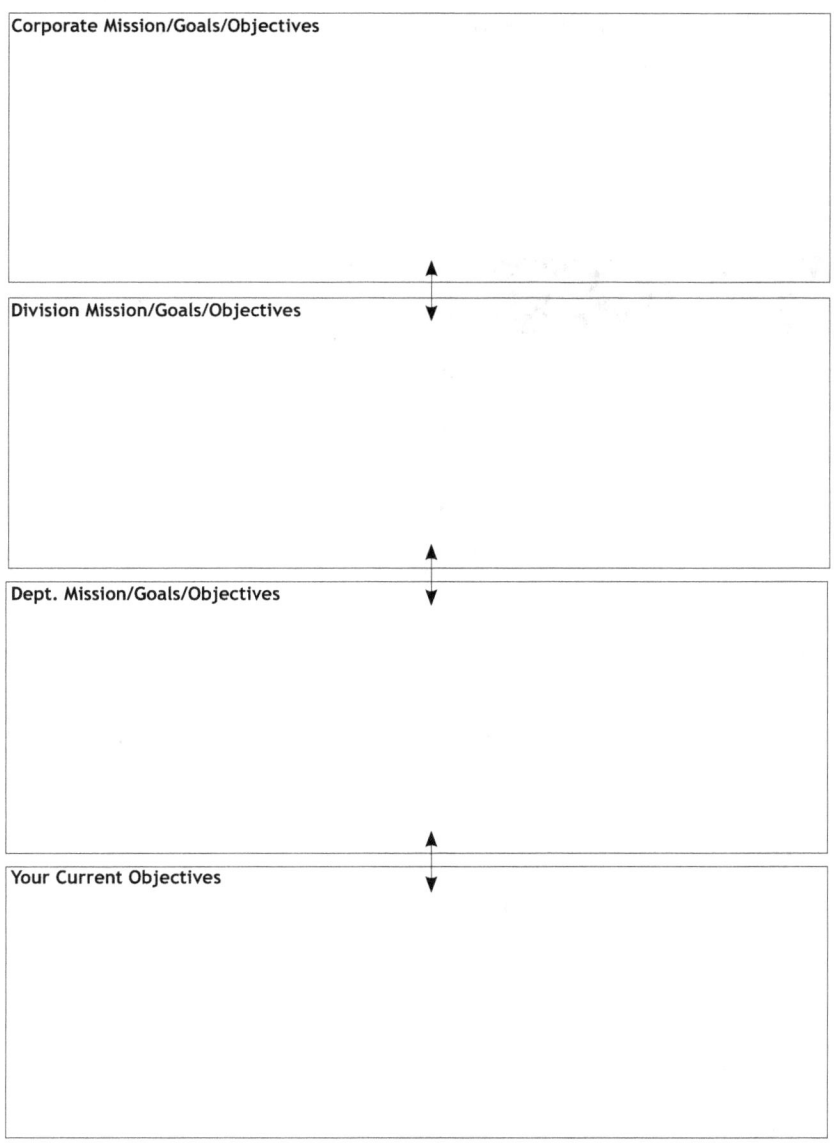

Business-Leadership

Make it SMART

You are probably already familiar with the idea of SMART objectives (see below if not). Even so, the important thing for both you and your people is to make sure everything is linked, as best possible, to the Company and BU goals/ objectives.

SMART

Specific – it's easy to tell exactly what is being produced.
Measurable – there are concrete success indicators.
Achievable – it can reasonably be accomplished.
Relevant – it fits with our business objectives.
Time-bound – the completion date and conditions are clear.

For example:

"Leaders are responsible for creating an environment in which people can be their best."
Simon Sinek

Make it SMART

Company Goal	BU Goal	Manager/Department Objectives	Individual Objectives: (KPI)	Weight
New Product Introductions that delight our customers	New Products that Inspire and Perform	Launch 10 innovative New "A" class Products, by end year, with: a) Customer response = 75% "delighted", b) Sales Traction & Profitability 100% of goal.	Develop and launch 2 "A" products that a) delight customers and b) on track to achieve launch sales projections, by end of fiscal year.	40%
New Product Introductions that delight our customers	New Products that Inspire and Perform	Launch 10 innovative New "A" class Products, by end year, with: a) Customer response = 75% "delighted", b) Sales Traction & Profitability 100% of goal.	Complete product Roadmap for 2018-2020, including 5 Pro-Level products, by end Q2.	30%
New Product Introductions that delight our customers	New Products that Inspire and Perform	Launch 10 innovative New "A" class Products, by end year, with: a) Customer response = 75% "delighted", b) Sales Traction & Profitability 100% of goal.	Sound quality evaluation of "phase-two products" --> All meet or beat phase one product levels.	20%
Build a highly engaged and innovative organization that achieves extraordinary results	Personal Competency Development: Leadership Competency Development	Personal Competency Development: Leadership Competency Development.	Improve Prioritization and Time-management, so that projects delivered on time. Visible improvements: Managers evaluation.	10%

Business-Leadership

Weight				
Individual Objectives: (KPI)				
Manager/Department Objectives				
BU Goal				
Company Goal				

See page 186 for a useful method when setting team objectives

Align Job Descriptions to Mission/Goals

Organizations/ Business Units are responsible for producing Division/ Dept. & Team results, while contributing to the overall corporate goals and objectives.

Accordingly, roles/ positions should ideally be designed to fulfill team, dept., & division mission/objectives, and also be aligned to the overall corporate mission/objectives.

Job Descriptions must clearly describe & explain:
- Role description and purpose.
- What the person is accountable for.
- Why this role/position is important.
- The impact of the role?
- Key responsibilities.
- Required competency levels.
- Required experience, technical skills, education.
- General Performance expectations.

> Note: Not all organizations use Job Descriptions - so skip this section if not relevant

For example ⟶

Business-Leadership

Business Title: Junior HR Business Partner
Department or Business Unit: HR
Direct supervisory Responsibilities: No
Overtime Eligible : Yes
Reports To: Senior HR Business Partner

Example Job Description

Overall purpose: "To build a high-performing and highly engaged organization that achieves extraordinary results"

Role Description
In your role as Junior HR Business Partner you will assist the senior HRBP in providing HR solutions to Business Unit Heads to enable the organization to better implement its strategy and achieve business and organizational goals. You will need to be able to understand & discuss business issues & also people/organizational issues. Internally, within HR you will coordinate with the other members of Japan HR to ensure provision of a full range of services to your internal customers.

Key Responsibilities

	Key Roles and Responsibilities	Main Deliverables/Outcomes
1	Act as an HR consultant and partner to assigned BUs/Depts. on all HR related issues – and internally coordinate within HR to provide relevant solutions.	Internal customers show "Meets or Exceeds Expectations" on HR Performance Satisfaction Survey.
2	Support the implementation of Performance Management Initiatives, including supporting the Performance Appraisal process to ensure true performance management is taking place.	All Assigned BUs hit performance distribution curve expectations. Engagement scores for "Rewards and Recognition" meet agreed targets.
3	Coordinate with Japan C&B on internal and external salary benchmarking to ensure fair/competitive pay scales are maintained, whilst taking proper account of individual performance.	Smooth implementation of the Japan compensation plan in the BU – salaries consistent and aligned accordingly.
4	Coordinate with Talent Development Manager to ensure organization and people development is implemented, including talent assessment and development, succession planning.	Succession Planning plan in place as per agreed schedule. Employee Engagement scores for "Growth and Development" meet agreed targets.
5	Work with Corporate HR/Data Management function to ensure each BU's Job Descriptions, Learning Descriptions, Personal Development Plans and Employee records are updated and properly utilized by department managers.	All employees have updated JD/IDP, as per schedule.
6	Employee Engagement: Assist the Senior HRBP in the overall coordination of the EES program. Provide required overview of EES results and recommendations to the management team.	Employee Engagement scores in the BU reach agreed targets - though accountability is with the BU head.

Example Job Description

Competency Requirements

Technical Expertise	• HR Knowledge: Understand Corporate HR goals and mission and local HR policies and procedures. • Understand business practice in Japan. Learn how to coordinate effectively between departments. • Be completely familiar with new systems, specifically HRIS, LMS, and Performance Appraisal system. • Strong analytical skills and proficiency in MS office application.	Level 4: Advanced
Customer Focus	• Understand the individual business goals and needs of each department.	Level 3: Intermediate
Influence	• Influence without authority: learn how to discuss and reach agreement (and also drive agreement) without direct authority.	Level 3: Intermediate
Problem Solving	• Solve various commercial and operation challenges under time pressure. Develop own innovative and creative skills.	Level 3: Intermediate
Strategic Capability	• Create action plans for each individual department and continually update based on new developments. • Think strategically regarding how to formulate solutions.	Level 2: Basic
Communication	• Be an efficient communicator with department management, HR staff, and corporate HR.	Level 4: Advanced

Additional Requirements

- Degree holder
- Can work independently with minimum supervision, with a proactive approach.
- Enjoys interacting with people with good interpersonal skills, along with the ability to work effectively with senior management.
- Strong command of English and excellent Japanese language skills.
- Business experience in a range of functional areas, or alternatively strong HR experience if joining Japan HR from outside the group.

Business-Leadership

Build a Strong Organization

When building a strong organization, there's a useful idea to keep in mind, which we call 7R, and looks like this:

7R

- Right Person
- Right Position
- Right Time
- Right Capability
- Right Mindset
- Right Organization
- Right Cost *(suggested by a CEO - but a good add!)*

A good place to start with 7R is by asking yourself, "Are the best people in the most important/impactful Roles?"

Or, to put it another way:
- Which are the key positions in the organization for implementing the strategy and achieving our objectives?
- Who are the key people in the organization - the High-Performers who will lead the company to the future?

> Note:
> - A position could be a high contributor to immediate business results, but only a mid/low level contribution to overall strategy, e.g., sales of existing or legacy "cash cow" products.
> - Conversely, a position could make a low contribution to business results, but be strategically important due to developments of a new product/business area that will not see short-term business results.

Note: We teach the full 7R method in our Strategic HRBP program - this section is designed to give you an overview of some of the useful tools.

The 7R Model

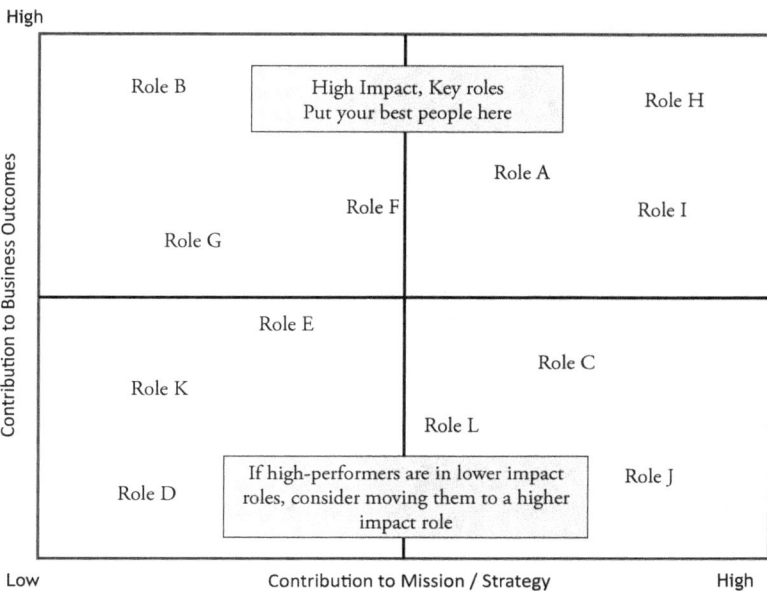

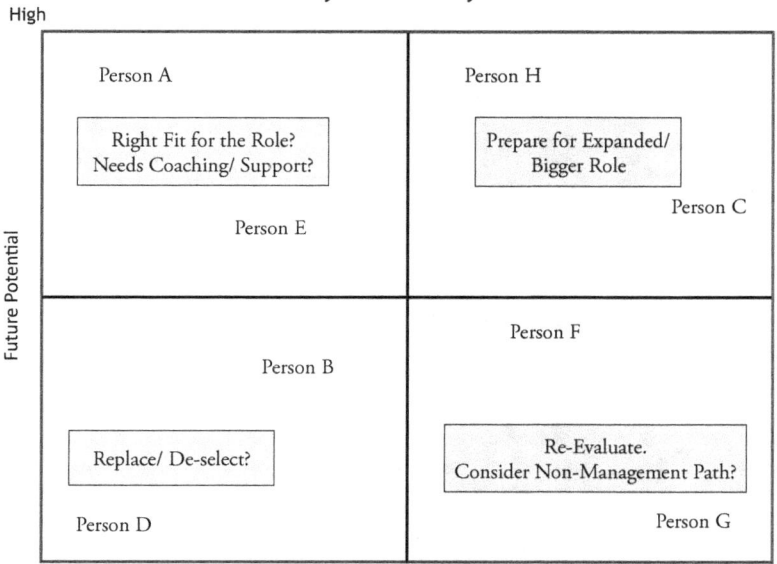

Business-Leadership

Key Role Analysis

Key Role/ Key Person Analysis

Key Person Analysis

Key Role/ Key Person Matrix

Key Role/ Key Person Matrix
This is a good discussion framework for evaluating if key people are in key roles.

The Position		The Person		
Critical/ Highly Impactful Role	Move to less critical role	Consider a) development or b) replacement with higher performer	The best people should be in the most critical roles. Consider next development actions
Impactful Role	Move to less Impactful role		Consider move to more critical role
Less Impactful Role			Move to more impactful role
	Less Effective Performer	Successful Performer	High Performer

Key Role/ Key Person Matrix
You can transfer the discussion results to an Excel sheet, like this:
Note: colour-coding can help to quickly identify role-impact and people-performance.

Key Role/ Key Person Matrix

Role	Person in Role	Actions to take	Owner	Timing
Sales Role A	David	Consider move to Less Critical role/ replace with High Performer		
R&D Role E	Maki	Develop in role		
Online Role G	Shohei	Move to Less Critical role/ replace with HIgh Performer		
Sales Role B	Kento	Develop in role		
Fin Role C	Shota	Develop in role		
Mkt Role F	Yuko	Promote?		
G&A Role H	Mark	Move to more impactful role		

Build a Strong Organization | Sense of Urgency | Performance Conversations

Business-Leadership

> # Right Person for the Role?

Psychometric profiles such as DiSC, PI, Hogan Assessments, Saville Wave, etc., will give you another way of understanding your leadership personal profile - we used a simplified Garuda profile (page 35).

We're not covering any of these specifically here, but we do want to mention one usage method that is sometimes overlooked - namely matching individual profiles to the role profile.

What's a role profile?
Some of these tools allow you to do an assessment of the requirements for the role itself. For example, an Accountant's role might look like the profile on the left, whereas a Sales Executive profile might look like the one on the right.

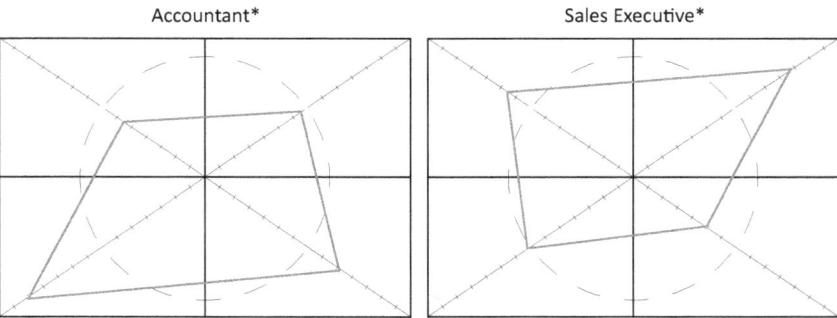

If an individual person's profile is matched to the requirements of the role, then there is a higher likelihood of better performance in that role. Likewise, if the profiles don't match, then there is a lower likelihood of better performance.

Of course, this is not a 100% "works every time" method, but overall you'll get better individual results if you match people to their natural roles.

Alternatively, you might want to put someone into a non-matching role as a developmental challenge, or as a change agent to drive new ideas and processes, etc.

* Not actual profiles - for illustration only. See next page for how to do a role profile

Right Person for the Role?

That said, don't fall into the trap of *not* putting someone into a role just because they have the "wrong profile." There's a lot more to good performance than simply having the right "shape!"

Matching/ Non-Matching Profiles

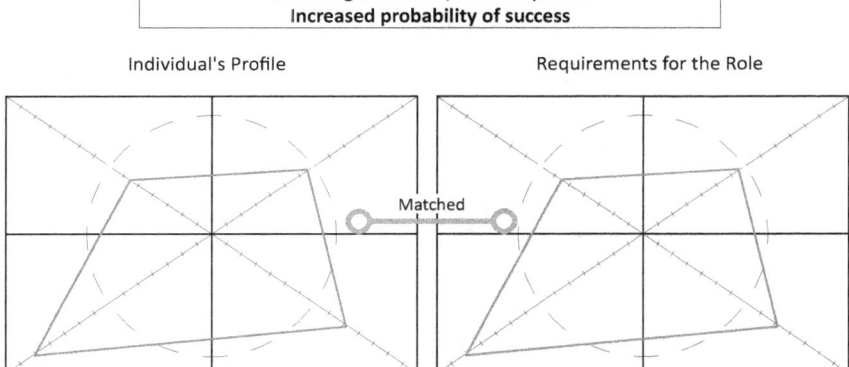

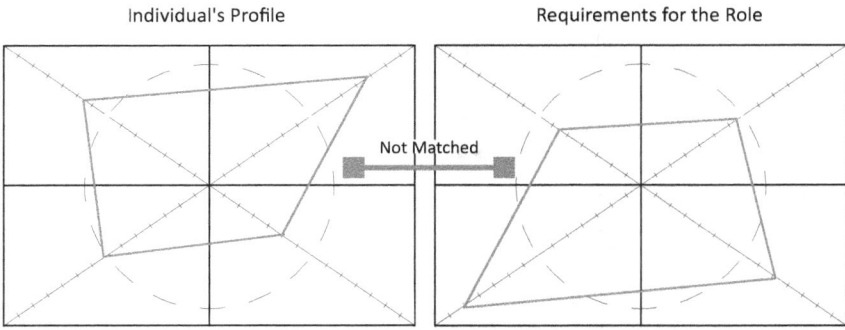

Business-Leadership

Creating a Position Profile
Try For Yourself

	To be successful in this position, the following are required for/ by the person in the role. Note: Consider the requirements for the <u>Role</u>, not the actual person currently in the role.	Agree	Partly Agree	Neutral	Partly Disagree	Disagree
1	Be organized, and solve tasks in an orderly and systematic way.	2	1	0	-1	-2
2	Maintain his/her tasks and activities in order, and under control.	2	1	0	-1	-2
3	Prefer following fixed routines, systems and processes in his/her daily work.	2	1	0	-1	-2
4	Work most efficiently under a clear a framework, within guidelines.	2	1	0	-1	-2
5	Prefer performing tasks that require a systematic and detail-oriented approach.	2	1	0	-1	-2
6	Must be self-disciplined, punctual and accurate.	2	1	0	-1	-2
7	Feel it is important that everybody follows rules/ guidelines for performing their duties.	2	1	0	-1	-2
8	Stay within given guidelines/ direction.	2	1	0	-1	-2
	Baser: Overall Score					
9	Should feel best when he/she can see specific results from his/her efforts.	2	1	0	-1	-2
10	Go for goals quickly, directly and without need for further discussion.	2	1	0	-1	-2
11	Direct his/her efforts towards achieving efficient and quick results.	2	1	0	-1	-2
12	Prefer tasks that he/she is able to finish and see the results of right away.	2	1	0	-1	-2
13	Use his/her time efficiently and in a goal-oriented way.	2	1	0	-1	-2
14	Prefer situations where his/her own personal efforts create results.	2	1	0	-1	-2
15	Should be an impatient and results oriented person.	2	1	0	-1	-2
16	Produce good results regardless of how difficult the conditions are.	2	1	0	-1	-2

Right Person for the Role?

	Results Seeker: Overall Score					
17	Be a patient and tolerant mediator.	2	1	0	-1	-2
18	Create agreement and common understanding when collaborating with other people.	2	1	0	-1	-2
19	Good at mediating and creating unity when different interests and people need to be brought together.	2	1	0	-1	-2
20	Can reach agreement with others, rather than promoting his/her own viewpoints.	2	1	0	-1	-2
21	Should be patient and tolerant when together with other people.	2	1	0	-1	-2
22	Be good at integrating people with different social attitudes, opinions and values.	2	1	0	-1	-2
23	Create agreement and solidarity about solutions to issues/challenges/problems/tasks.	2	1	0	-1	-2
24	Help people who are in difficulties, either of a professional or personal nature.	2	1	0	-1	-2
	Integrator: Overall Score					
25	Prefer to be at the forefront when new ideas, visions and changes are to be implemented.	2	1	0	-1	-2
26	Develop creative and efficient strategies and methods for reaching Team/BU goals.	2	1	0	-1	-2
27	Leave daily routines and tasks to others, so as to able to think more about the goal and the meaning of "what we do."	2	1	0	-1	-2
28	Make a significant contribution when new business strategies and visions are planned and formulated.	2	1	0	-1	-2
29	See and utilize new opportunities before everybody else does.	2	1	0	-1	-2
30	Be a driving force when renewals and change initiatives are started.	2	1	0	-1	-2
31	Good at seeing everything from a comprehensive and long-term perspective.	2	1	0	-1	-2
32	Trust his/her intuition and feelings when he/she makes decisions.	2	1	0	-1	-2
	Developer: Overall Score					

Now plot the results on the next page

Points to Consider
- How well do the profiles match?
- What gaps do you see?
- What issues could develop as a result?

Business-Leadership

Requirements for the Role

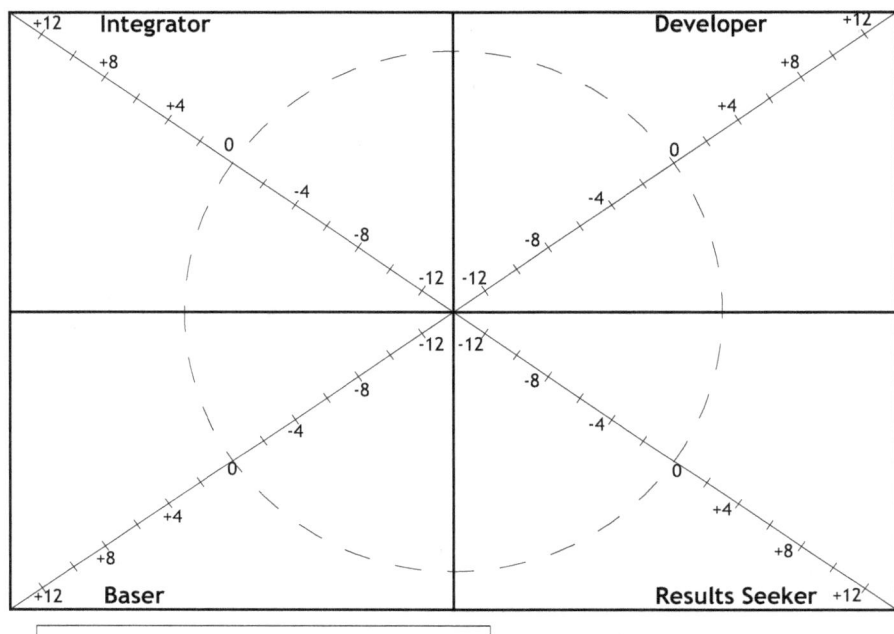

Person in the Role
(see page 42)

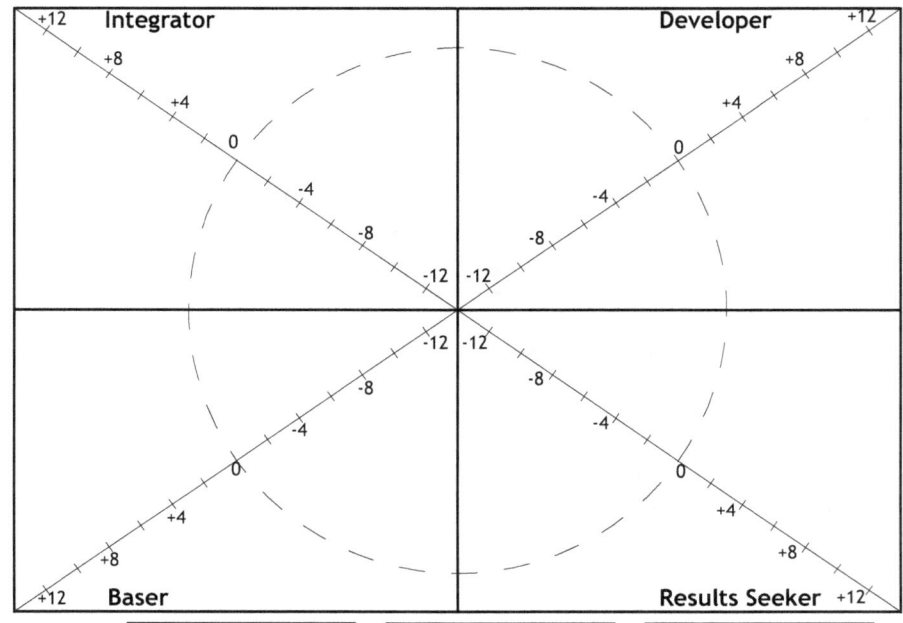

Right Person for the Role?

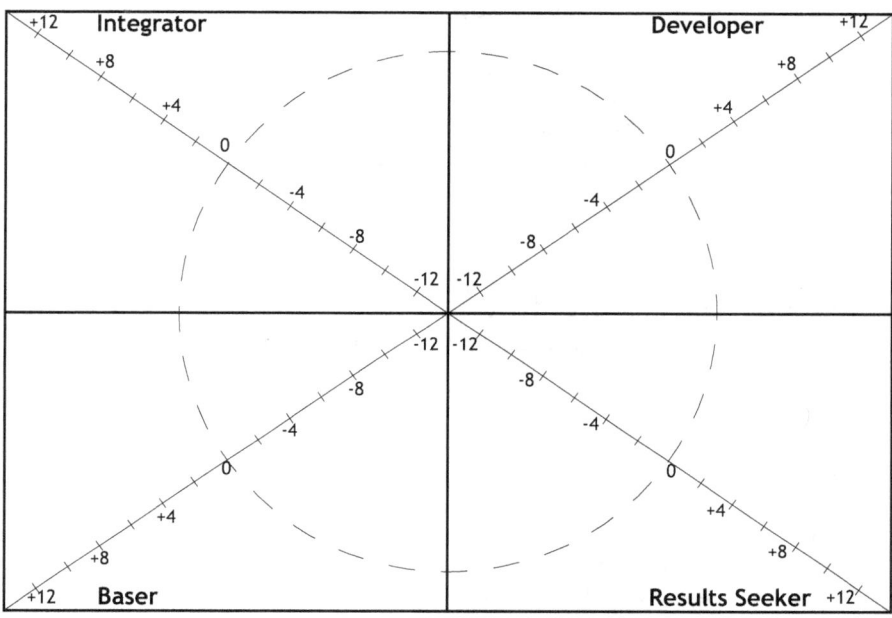

Requirements for the Role

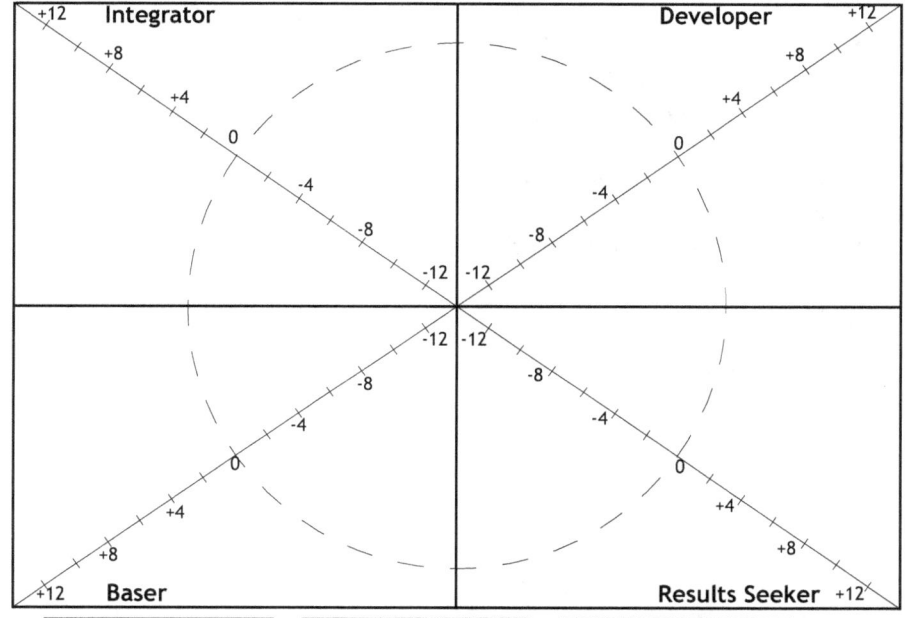

Person in the Role
(see page 42)

Business-Leadership

Right Capabilities

"Organizational Capability" is the ability of the organization to implement the strategy and achieve its objectives. For this, the essential question is: Do we have the right capabilities to achieve our objectives?

Or, to put it another way → *"In order to achieve our strategy, our organization needs to be able to..."*

For example:

- Create new products faster than our competitors.
- Build depth of expertise, particularly in research and development.
- Produce leading edge products.
- Offer a diverse product line.
- Encourage innovation.
- Create common standards.
- Become a low cost producer.
- Continually increase process efficiency.
- Build long relationships with customers and grow repeat business.
- Deliver high levels of customer satisfaction.
- Customize products at a customer's request.
- Cross-sell and bundle products.
- Create preferred sourcing relationships with customers.
- Exploit multiple distribution channels.
- Create alliances with other organizations in order to deliver comprehensive solutions.
- Work together.
- Move fast.
- Take the right risks.
- Focus on the right things.

Assess Organizational Capabilities

Use a 4x4 Matrix to Assess Current & Required Capabilities

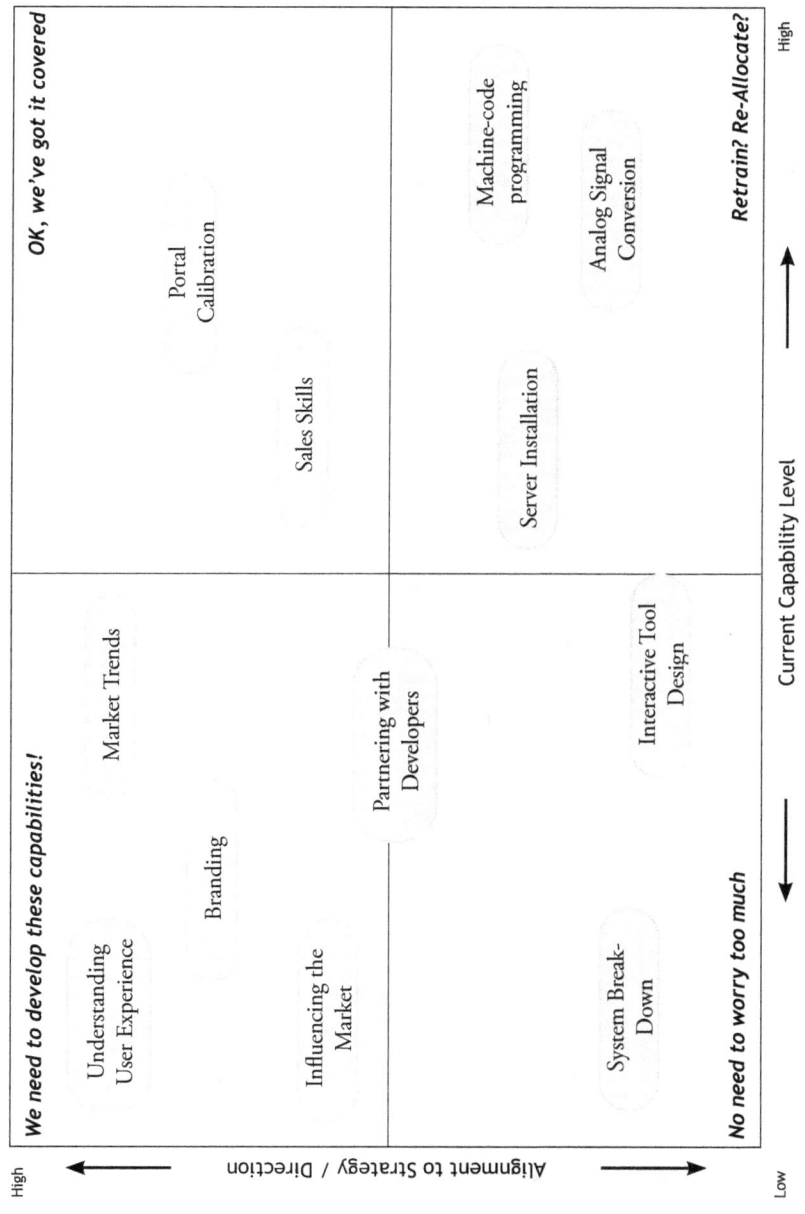

You'll find a blank template on the next page

Business-Leadership

Try it Yourself

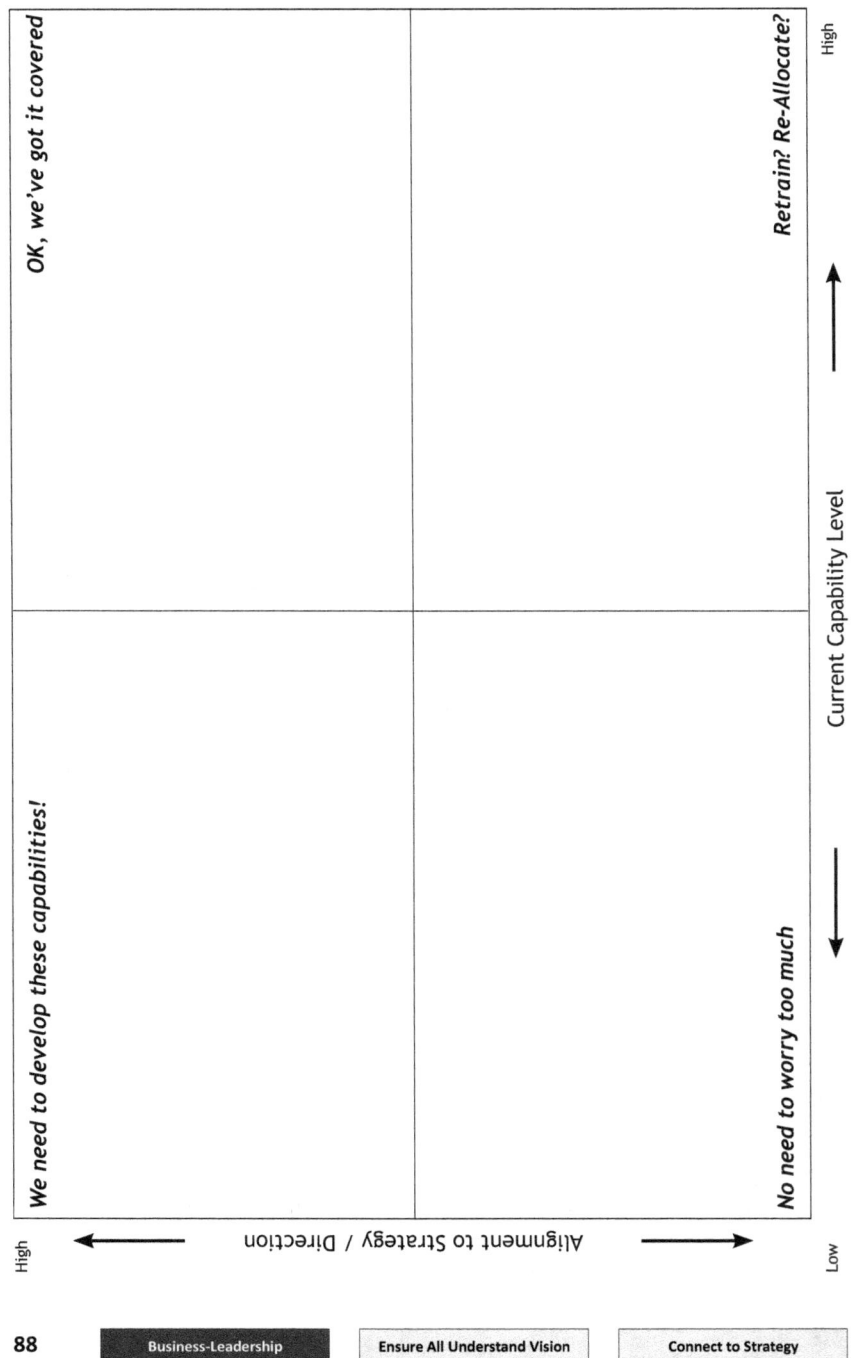

Bridging the Capability Gaps
(usually found in the top left-hand quadrant)

Capabilities Needing Development	Actions to Fill the Gap

Business-Leadership

Succession Planning - A Brief Introduction

Succession Planning is the process of identifying and developing new leaders who can replace the current leaders when they move on, e.g., when they retire or return to HQ from an assignment, etc. It is also is something that all leaders should do, but disappointingly not all of them do! (the better leaders are, of course, role models for this).

Usually this is done together with your HR Business Partner - but here we'd like to (very) briefly show you a commonly method you can use to get started, although we recommend you engage with your HRBP in order to do this more effectively.

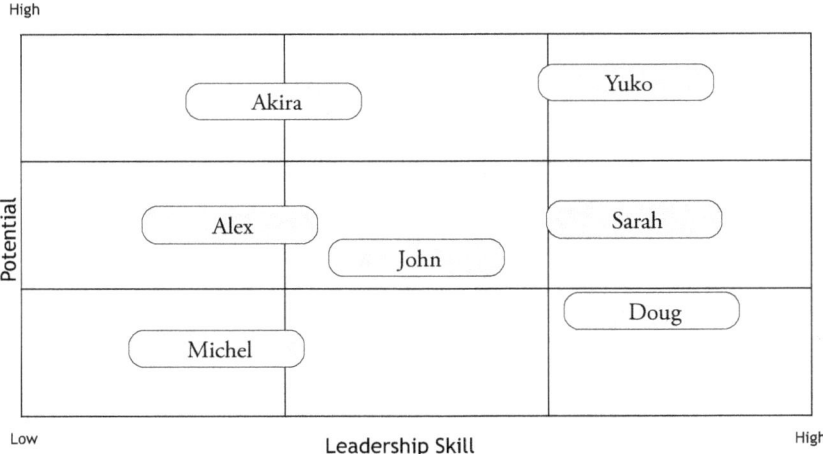

The X and Y axes can be anything of your choice. For example, instead of "Potential" you could have "Performance," or "Level of current contribution to the business," - with "Future Growth Potential" instead of "Leadership Skill."

Also, in this example, "Leadership Skill" could be a combined KPI of 360 Feedback, Engagement, etc.

Using the 9-Box for Succession Planning

Typical Succession Planning template. Usually HR will manage this, but senior leaders will also need to be involved. For example, in this case "O-san," the current position holder, would probably share responsibility for developing "A-san" so that she is ready to take on the role when he retires.

Position	General Comments	Person Currently in Role	Candidate	Ready	Comment	Development Need	Action Plan
CHRO	Vision/Focus: 1. Reduction of expenses, through office move, h/count change, etc. 2. Retraining of employees needed, as can't afford to hire new ones. 3. Current org structure makes people too busy for skill development. Will need to re-organize and provide clearer responsibility and focused job-scope. 4. Negotiation becomes increasingly important M&A, contracts, etc. 5. General Org; Combine Customer Support and Customer Service into one for better efficiency and focus."	O-san	A-san	3-5 years	Will need English if he can succeed O-san as HR, especially for US HQ communications and future "M&A activity" likely to happen.	1. English program → raise level to international business English standard. 2. People Developer: become an in-house trainer for management and I/C development.	WIP

Business-Leadership

> # Right Organization

Right Organization

It's beyond the scope of this book to discuss organizational design, but we've included a few common structures for your reference.

If you'd like to know more, then there are plenty of resources available, including the work of Jacob Morgan, which you can see here: https://thefutureorganization.com/

Process Organization

Process
- Alternative to functional structure
- Potential for new/changed processes

```
                    General
                    Manager
         ┌─────────────┼─────────────┐
     New Product   Order Fulfillment   Customer
     Dev. Process      Process      Acquisition &
                                    Maintenance
         │             │             │
    New Product    Order Teams    Customer Teams
      Teams
```

Functional Organization

Functional
- Small, single product line
- Undifferentiated market
- Expertise within function
- Long product development and life-cycles
- Common standards

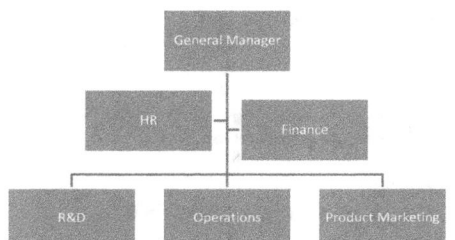

Flatter Organization

Flatter Organizations
A "flatter" structure seeks to open up the lines of communication and collaboration while removing layers within the organization
- There are fewer layers, arrows point both ways
- For larger organizations this is the most practical, scalable, and logical approach to deploy across an entire company.
- This is the model that most large (and many mid-size) organizations around the world are moving towards

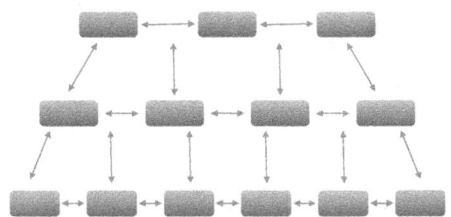

Business-Leadership

Hierarchical Organization

Hierarchical Organizations
Communication typically flows from the top to the bottom
- innovation slows
- engagement decreases
- almost no collaboration
- Heavy bureaucracy
- Extremely slow to react
- Opens space for competitors and new players to quickly take over the market
- Difficult to attract and retain top talent

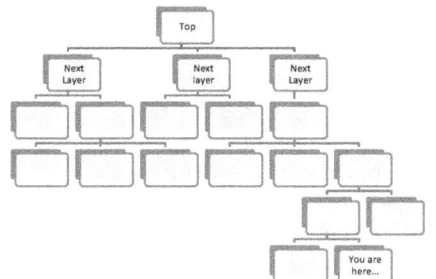

Hybrid Organization

Hybrid
- Combines Product and Function
- May require each group to have own support BUs (HR, Finance, etc)

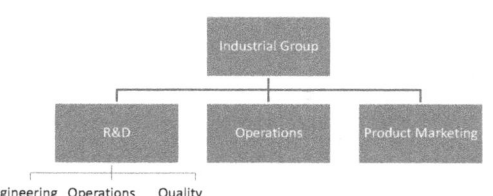

Right Organization

Matrix Organization

Matrix Structure
- Employees may be part of a functional group (i.e., engineering) but may serve on a team that supports new product development (i.e., new album)
- For example, a recording engineer who works for a music publisher, may have engineers who report to him but may also use his expertise and work with teams to develop new music albums.

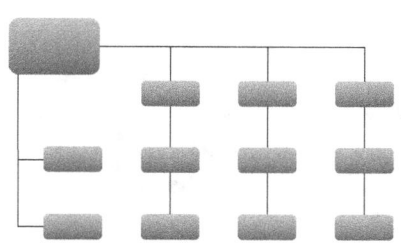

Advantage
- Employees have responsibility not only for their department but for organizational projects.
- Sharing of human resources across products
- Meets both demands of environment: innovation and product quality
- Opportunity for functional and product skill development
- new music albums.

Challenge
- Employees some get direction/instruction from two different managers
- Dual authority can be frustrating and confusing for employee
- Employees need interpersonal skills and training
- Time-consuming coordination needed
- Dual pressure for power balance needed

Product Organization

Product
- Product focus
- Multiple products, separate customers
- Short product development and life cycle

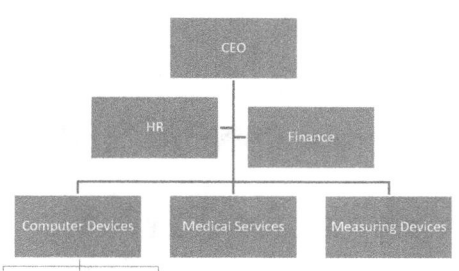

Right Cost

What's the total "people" cost of the organization?
It was always surprising - and concerning - to find managers/ leaders who were not fully aware of the total costs of their organizations, particularly the people-related costs.

In such cases, training budgets would be held in check (when owned by the business, not HR) but recruiting costs would spiral, and yet nobody seemed to mind - hopefully this isn't you!

Of course, there are managers/ leaders who are very aware of these kinds of issues.

So, what kind of "cost" are we talking about? Basically, everything related to headcount/ people in the organization: salary, bonuses, health insurance, social insurance, pension costs, home mortgage support (in Japan, at least), monthly commuting (also in Japan), overtime, sick leave, cars, turnover, training, recruitment, etc. And you can add in IT and other office-related costs, too.

Your HRBP and/ or HRIS information systems should be able to help you to gain a clear cost picture for your organization.

See the example opposite for a typical Overview, which inlcudes some high-level costs.

Right Cost

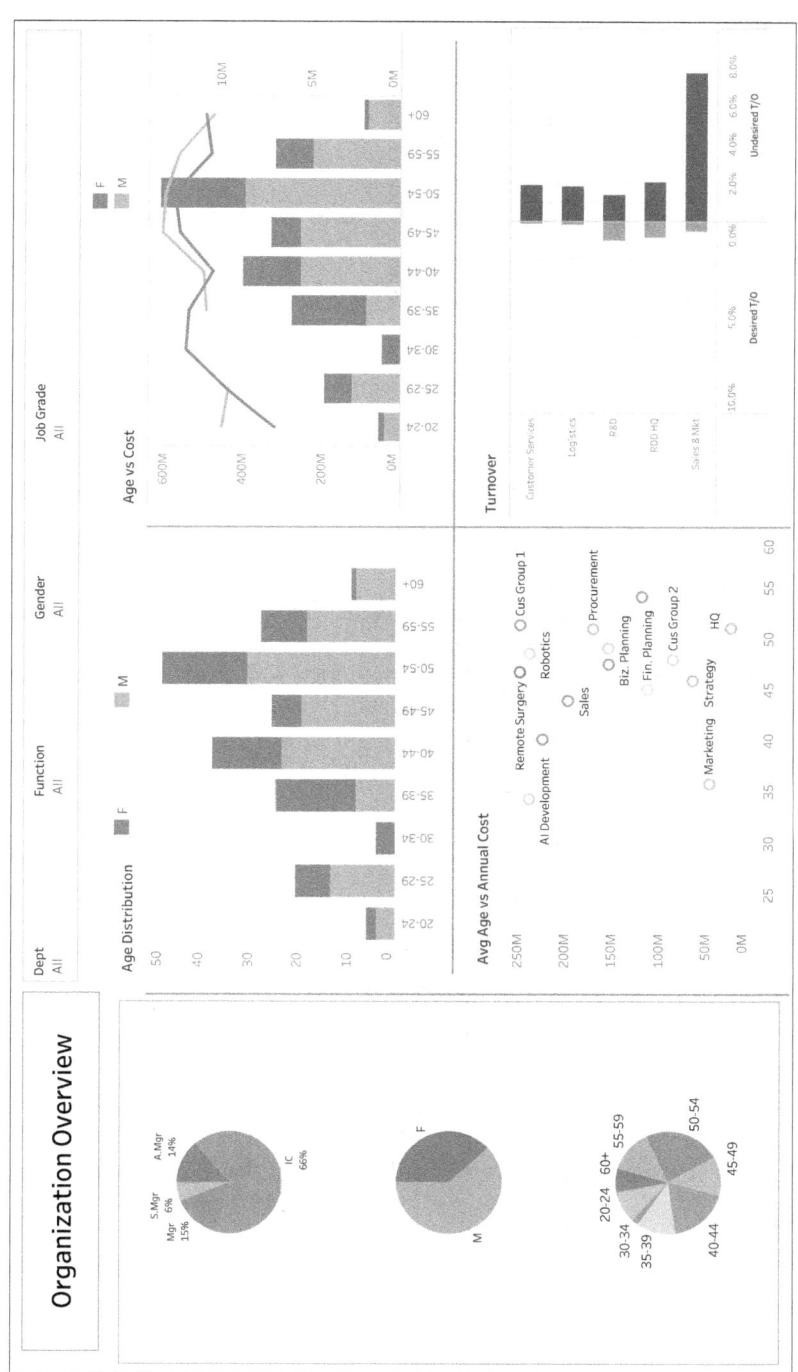

Create a Sense of Urgency

Of all the concepts and ideas that we cover in our leadership classes & 1:1 coaching sessions, having a "Sense of Urgency" has created the most confusion and/ or mis-understanding.

Many participants focus on the 'urgent' part and feel it means: "do things quickly, right now, within today, don't go home until it's done..." Actually, this is pretty close to the complete opposite of the actual meaning!

Yes, things should be done promptly wherever possible, but they need to be the *right* things. So, here's our definition:

Sense of Urgency

Doing the Right Thing at the Right Time for the Right Reasons, by:
- Focusing on the objectives of the company, organization, team.
- Focusing on important priorities.
- Saying "No" to unnecessary tasks / activities.

To Achieve a True Sense of Urgency

Make sure you have/ do the following:
- Clear Vision & Mission.
- Individual objectives aligned to Team, Department, Division & Company objectives.
- Consider using the Prioritization Matrix with your direct reports.
- Consider running the 'How Aligned Are We?" activity *(see the Resources section, page 163)*.

Do the Right Thing at the Right Time for the Right Reasons

Individual objectives aligned to company objectives - page 69

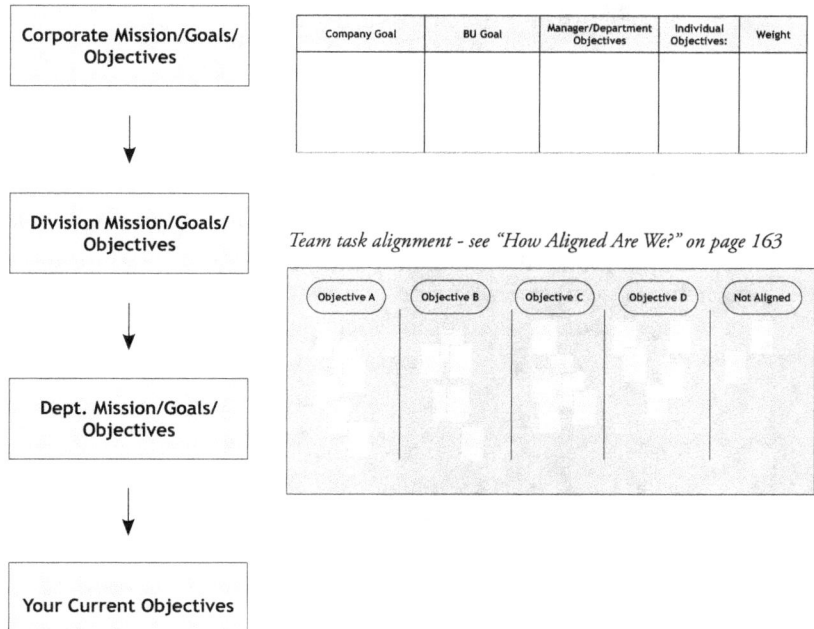

Team task alignment - see "How Aligned Are We?" on page 163

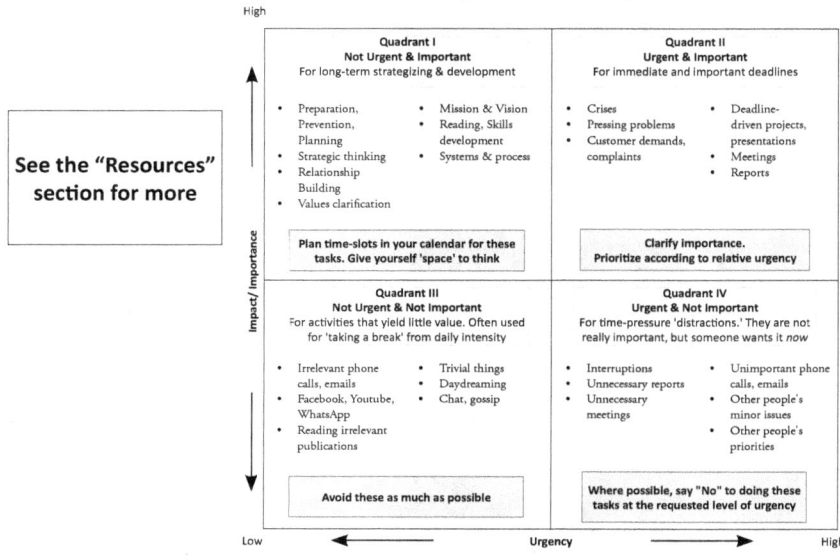

Use the prioritization matrix with your direct reports - page 45
Note - this is also a good exercise to do together as a team

Business-Leadership

Hold Regular Performance Conversations

Discuss Goals and Projects
- Focus on progress to goals.
- Examine project status.
- Be supportive - you are there to help the person achieve her/his goals. Offer help and guidance where necessary.
- Meet often, e.g., once a month for a scheduled "Performance Conversation."

Goals
- "How do you feel you are progressing?"
- "Are any of your goals causing concern?"
- "What could I stop or start doing to help you achieve your goals?"
- "What barriers are preventing you from achieving your goals?"
- "What skill gaps do you feel you have that might prevent you from achieving your goals?"

Projects
- "What is most challenging in your current/recent project?"
- "Do you think the project is/was successful?"
- "For your current/past project, where do you think there are opportunities to improve?"
- "What would you do differently next time?"

For More Difficult Situations

Telling someone they are doing well is fairly straightforward and not particularly challenging. But what if things are not going well?

How can you have *that* conversation and still maintain the relationship? You'll find some ideas below.

Preparation

- Does the employee understand what the problem is?
- Does the employee really understand the expected level of performance?
- Does the employee fully understand what will happen if performance standards are not met?
- Do you (the manager) have all the relevant facts and information? Who, What, Where, When, Why and How?

In the Meeting

- Discuss performance issues, not the person.
- Make the discussion based on facts, not assumptions.
- Be objective: bring data, documentation, records.
- Listen.
- Focus on the future, not the past.
- Summarize what has been said and what has been agreed to.
- Put it in writing, if necessary.
- End positively.
- Set a time and place for follow-up.

Use the Three-Step Assertive Communication Method

- Step One: Show Understanding.
- Step Two: Express Your Opinion.
- Step Three: Propose a Solution.

More on this ⟶

Assertive Communication Technique
An Overview of the General Method

Step One: Show Understanding
Before disagreeing, you must show the other person that you really do understand and respect their opinion or feeling.
- "I understand that..."
- "I recognize that this issue is very important for you."
- "I hear you saying that you're frustrated about the way this situation has been handled."
- "I appreciate that you feel..."
- "So if I understand correctly, you're mainly concerned about..."
- "I can understand why you'd be upset about the way that our sales department made promises that we can't deliver – I'm not happy about it either."
- "I know how you feel – the regulations are a problem for us too."
- "So you're upset about..."
- "So you're worried about..."

Step Two: Express Your Opinion
Respect your own opinion and feelings by clearly communicating them. Try to use appropriate linking words to avoid sounding aggressive.
- "However, I feel that..."
- "Nevertheless, in our situation we need to..."
- "On the other hand, we must consider..."
- "Even so, it is important that..."

Step Three: Propose a Solution
Try to move the discussion forward by presenting your idea or asking for a suggestion.
- "Therefore, I would like to suggest that we .... How do you feel about this idea?"
- "I feel it would be better if we... Could you agree to this?"
- "So, one possible solution could be... Would that work for you?"
- "Do you have any suggestions?"

Applying the method to a Performance Conversation

Applying the Assertive Communication Method

Applying the Method

Step One: Show Understanding
"I do understand that you have been under a lot of pressure, especially regarding the heavy workload you have. And this was the main reason why the contracts were not completed on time."

Step Two: Express Your Opinion
"However, the delay in completing those contracts resulted in a five thousand-dollar penalty that we had to pay to the client. That's a significant amount of money. I think this situation could have been avoided if you had made better use of your available time.

I feel that you tend to go from one urgent issue to the next, without structuring your time effectively. This results in you getting behind on the important issues, and then you try to complete them at the last minute - which in this case was the customer contracts."

Step Three: Propose a Solution
"You are a valuable member of the team and I'd like to help you improve in this area. So, let's do two things. First, we'll get you on a time management class, run by the company in-house training department. And secondly we'll put in place a regular weekly 1:1 review meeting.

We'll use that meeting to go over your task list and make sure you're focusing on the key items. How does that sound?"

You'll find more on Annual Performance Meetings on page 197

Business-Leadership Action Plan

	Action Area	How this Impacts Team Engagement & Performance
6	I make sure people in my group understand the organization's vision.	
7	I ensure other people understand how their work is connected to the strategy.	
8	I have built a strong organization to implement the strategy.	
9	I ensure people in my group have a sense of urgency to achieve the objectives.	
10	I regularly talk to my direct reports about their performance.	

Review the exercises for Business-Leadership, then create an action plan for steps you will take in the next 6-9 months.

Build Your Business-Leadership Action Plan

	Actions I'll Take in The Next 6-9 months
6	
7	
8	
9	
10	

Build a Strong Organization   Sense of Urgency   Performance Conversations

People-Leadership

Use this page for notes

PEOPLE-LEADERSHIP

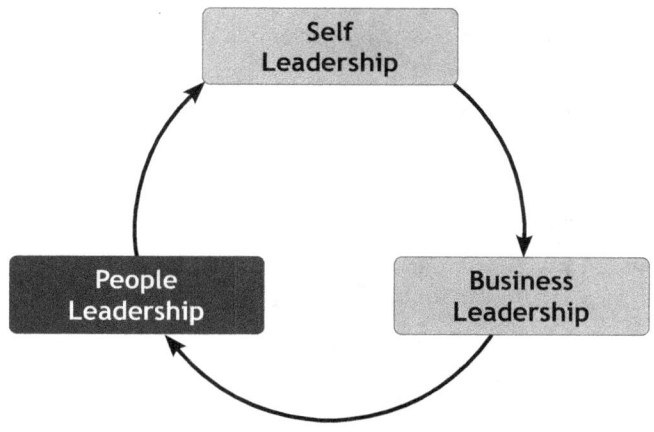

Your Success Comes from the
Success of the People Around You

People-Leadership

From the Leadership Self-Assessment

Self-Leadership

1. I am highly engaged in my role. → Highly Engaged In Role
2. I have a high level of self-awareness (behaviours, strengths, weaknesses, etc.). → High Level Of Self-Awareness
3. I am a Role-Model for company and team values. → Values Role-Model
4. I have a clear sense of purpose. → Clear Sense Of Purpose
5. I'm clear about my philosophy of leadership. → Clear Philosophy of Leadership

Business-Leadership

6. I make sure people in my group understand the organization's vision. → Ensure All Understand Vision
7. I ensure other people understand how their work is connected to the strategy. → Connect to Strategy
8. I have built a strong organization to implement the strategy. → Build Strong Organization
9. I ensure people in my group have a sense of urgency to achieve the objectives. → Ensure Sense of Urgency
10. I regularly talk to my direct reports about their performance. → Regular Performance Discussions

People-Leadership

11. I create a high-trust environment. → Create High Trust Environment
12. I encourage and empower other people to deal with issues and develop solutions. → Encourage & Empower
13. I schedule time with my direct reports to discuss their career development plans. → Discuss Career Development
14. I actively coach people to develop their skills and grow in their job. → Actively Coach Others
15. I create high-performing teams. → Build High-Performing Teams

People-Leadership

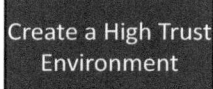

Build Trust
- Improving Trust with people around you.

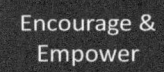

Empower Others
- Empowering people to make decisions, solve problems and improve performance.

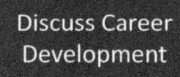

One-on-One Development Conversations
- Set regular 1:1 meetings to discuss personal engagement, progress to goals/projects, career & learning.

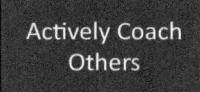

Give Feedback
- Give both positive & corrective feedback.

Be a Coach
- Coaching other people using the GROW model.

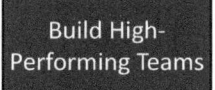

Build High-Performing Teams
- Creating High-Performing teams.

Create a High Trust Environment

Who trusts you?
- Include people from work, family, your social life, organizations you belong to, etc. List actual names. (*no need to show anybody!*)

Behaviours:
- How do you know they trust you?
- What have you done to build a trusting relationship?
- Have you had obstacles to building trust?
- Would they agree with your assumption that they trust you?

People Who Trust Me	My Behaviours - What I Did to Create Trust

"Don't find fault, find a remedy."
Henry Ford

Building Trust

People I Would Like to Trust Me More	What is Missing?

How to Build Trust

- Say to others: "I trust you.' – and mean it, too.
- Give people trust, even if they haven't yet given it to you.
- Find out about other people – who are they, their dreams, their hopes. Learn about them and what they do.
- Take a colleague to lunch.
- Listen, listen, listen.
- Frequently talk about the common goal you are trying to achieve.
- Make sure people understand how they are independent.
- Get people together face-to-face.

People-Leadership

Encourage & Empower

Delegating is possibly the most important thing you can do to become a more effective leader. It will help your direct reports to grow, and will also help you to grow as a leader.

Overall, delegating effectively will help you to get results through people, instead of doing it all yourself.

Start by trying this delegation Self-Assessment. Do you:

Delegate tasks to ease the workload.	1	2	3	4	5	Prefer to do the work yourself.
Show confidence in staff to complete tasks.	1	2	3	4	5	Lack confidence in staff to complete tasks.
Allow staff to undertake delegated work in their own way.	1	2	3	4	5	Prefer to check on how staff complete the task.
Know everyone in your team well in terms of their strengths and weaknesses.	1	2	3	4	5	Not know people in your team well.
Give clear instructions when delegating.	1	2	3	4	5	Find that people come back to you with questions after you have delegated a task.
View delegation as an opportunity to develop individuals.	1	2	3	4	5	View delegation as means of getting the task done.
Provide training to inexperienced staff in new skills to undertake a task.	1	2	3	4	5	Prefer not to delegate tasks to inexperienced staff.
Agree a completion time for the task and review as appropriate.	1	2	3	4	5	Expect staff to complete the task as soon as possible.

Delegation Self-Assessment

Delegate the required authority to the staff to make appropriate decisions.	1	2	3	4	5	Keep decision making authority for yourself.
Tolerate mistakes, recognizing that people learn through them.	1	2	3	4	5	Expect delegated work to be error-free.
Balance the workload of your staff.	1	2	3	4	5	Delegate work to certain individuals in the team more than others.
Identify the tasks you should not delegate.	1	2	3	4	5	Prefer to delegate as much work as possible.
Think about the amount you should delegate to your staff in terms of their workload - and your workload, too.	1	2	3	4	5	Think more about your workload than your staff's.
Give feedback to staff, both positive and corrective.	1	2	3	4	5	Prefer not to give immediate feedback, especially when negative.
Hold regular follow-up meetings.	1	2	3	4	5	Too busy to hold regular meetings.
Take responsibility when a delegated task goes wrong.	1	2	3	4	5	Blame the staff for failing to achieve the delegated task.

32 or under
You delegate tasks well. The balance of your delegated tasks is good. You recognize that delegation provides a learning opportunity for your staff.

33-50
You delegate in some areas, but there is room for improvement. Consider what you are currently doing yourself and how these tasks could be delegated. You may need to develop the ability of your staff so that they can do those tasks.

50+
Your delegation could be improved. Your staff may see you as 'dumping' tasks, rather than delegating. You need to recognize that delegation provides an opportunity for you to be more effective as well as to develop your staff.

People-Leadership

Three Levels of Delegation

Three Levels of Delegation	
Level One	The direct report has full decision making authority. The Leader only defines the objectives - it is up to the direct report to decide the process and make decisions.
Level Two	The direct report has some decision making authority - other decisions are made during discussions with the Leader.
Level Three	The direct report has no decision making authority - and is only responsible for the task itself. The Leader makes all decisions.

How do you delegate?
- Which delegation level do you use most?
- How can you improve from this level?
- What could prevent you from delegating?

Where Can You Delegate More?

Consider your objectives. What tasks can be delegated? What tasks should you do, as leader?

Tasks that can/ should be delegated	Who these tasks should be delegated to

To Delegate Effectively:
- Plan it.
- Clarify what is required.
- Explain what is to be done and why
- Say what authority they have.
- Tell others what authority has been given.
- Allow your staff to decide both time and method.
- Check progress at agreed intervals.
- Be prepared for mistakes.
- Give feedback, both positive and negative.
- Provide support – you are still responsible.

People-Leadership

Discuss Career Development

Set regular 1:1 meetings for discussing your direct reports' individual development and career planning. Below are suggested areas for your next discussion.

Engagement	<ul><li>"What things de-motivate you at work?"</li><li>"What talents or skills do you have that you are not often using in your daily work?"</li><li>"If you could change one thing about your role or your work, what would it be?"</li><li>"What kind of support or assistance do you need to do your job better?"</li><li>"What would make your job easier, or more fulfilling?"</li><li>"What issues or concerns affect your daily work?"</li><li>"What part of your work is worthy of recognition or praise?"</li><li>"What is most rewarding about your current work?"</li><li>"What do you enjoy least about your current role?"</li><li>"What do you need from me that you are not currently getting?"</li></ul>
Career Development	<ul><li>"What is most important for you in terms of your long-term career?"</li><li>"What are your career aspirations, both long and short term?"</li><li>"What do you need me to do to help you on your career path?"</li><li>"What training, skills and development do you see as helping with you career progression?"</li></ul>

One-on-One Development Conversations

| **Learning & Development** | • "In what way do you feel your skills & knowledge are developing?"
• "What would you like to learn more about?"
• "What types of training or development opportunities would interest you in the coming months?" |

If your organization does not already have a template for Individual Development Planning, try using the one below, and link the "Skill/ Capability" to the Capability Gap Analysis we did earlier - page 87.

Skill/ Capability	Why Needed	Plan & Measurement	Time Frame

People-Leadership

Coaching & Feedback

As we noted under "Performance Conversations," giving positive feedback is usually not so challenging. The difficult part comes when you have to say something less than positive. Below are some ideas on how to do both.

Positive Feedback

Be Specific
- "I really like the way you did…"

Describe Benefits
- "By doing that it helped us to…"
- "Because you did that, we could…"

Summarize
- "So, please keep doing…"

Corrective Feedback

Be Specific
- "I noticed that you were late three times this week."
- "When you were talking to our customer in Singapore, I noticed that you forgot to use her name."

Explain Outcome/Result
- "When that happens, we are unable to…"

Plan Improvement
- "Let's talk about the cause of this situation and try to figure out how to correct it."
- "Let's make a plan to ensure these mistakes are avoided in future."
- "Can you think of an action plan that would help you?"

Summarize & Document Agreement (when necessary).
- Send a brief email to summarize.

Giving Both Positive & Corrective Feedback

> Be a Coach

Coaching is used in one-on-one interactions. The purpose is always to "expand the perspective" of the other person and support them in developing greater competence and commitment

As a "coach," you will typically help your team members to solve problems, make better decisions, learn new skills or otherwise progress in their role or career.

Think back to a conversation that broadened your perspective and helped you to see a new solution, or opened doors. What happened in that conversation that created change?

And, how can you do the same for others?

In the next few pages we briefly cover the GROW model of coaching, just to get you started. An on-line search will help you to discover more and to dig deeper, and there are plenty of excellent books which cover GROW and other coaching methods.

As we go through the GROW method - remember that the goal of the Coach is to get the Coachee to come up with their own answers, rather than giving them instructions on how to solve the issues at hand.

Goal
Current Reality
Options
Will

People-Leadership

The GROW Model of Coaching

G — Establish the Goal
- What are you trying to achieve?
- What is your goal?

R — Examine Current Reality
- What's happening now?
- What is the current situation?

O — Explore Options
- What choices do you have?
- What alternatives have you considered?

W — Establish the Will
- What will you do now?
- What's the next step for you?

> **Ask Questions, Listen well**
> - Ask open questions such as "What effect did that have?" This creates a discussion.
> - Try to avoid 'closed' questions such as "Did that cause a problem?" where the answer could simply be 'Yes/No,' which might stop a discussion.

The GROW Model of Coaching

 Establish the Goal

Example Questions:
- "What is the current challenge you are facing?"
- "What are you trying to achieve?"
- "How will you know that you have achieved that goal?"
- "How will you know if the problem is solved?"
- "What are the goals you want to achieve?"
- "Why are you hoping to achieve this goal?"
- "What would you try now if you knew you couldn't fail?"

 Examine Current Reality

Example Questions:
- "What is happening now?"
- "What is the result of that?"
- "Why haven't you reached that goal already? What do you think is stopping you?"
- "What do you think ...'s perception of the situation was/is?"
- "Do you know other people who have achieved that goal?"
- "What did you learn from...?"
- "What have you already tried?"
- "How could you turn this around this time?"
- "What could you do better this time?"
- "On a scale of 1-10 how severe/serious/urgent is the situation?"

Example Questions

 Explore Options

Example Questions:
- "What else could you do?"
- "What if this constraint was removed?"
- "What are the benefits and drawbacks of each option?"
- "What else could you do? What else? Anything else?"
- "What could be your first step?"
- "What would happen if you did that?"
- "What would happen if you did nothing?"
- "What has worked for you already?"
- "What would you gain/lose by doing that?"
- "Which option do you feel ready to act on?

 Establish the Will

Example Questions:
- "So what will you do now?"
- "What could stop you moving forward? And how will you overcome it?"
- "What else will you do?"
- "What support do you need to get that done?"
- "What do you need from me/others to help you achieve this?"
- "How will you know when you have done it?"
- "Who do you need to talk to first? Who needs to know?"
- "What are 3 actions you can take that would make sense this week?"
- "What will happen (what is the cost) of you NOT doing this?"

GROW - Example Questions

What if.....
If you don't have time/ space for the whole GROW method, then just try using "What if...?"
- "What if you tried...?"
- "What if you could...?"
- "What if you changed...?"

What kind of leader are your team looking for?
Here's an idea we picked up from a coachee - useful for working with leaders and their teams, for example in response to a 360 survey. It's best to have HR facilitate the discussion.

- Get your team in a room - with the leader.
- Prepare a whiteboard (right).
- Have each person write their name on a post-it, and position the post-it on their individual expectation/ need from their leader.
- Then, engage the group in a discussion about how the leader can (or can not) fulfill all of these expectations!

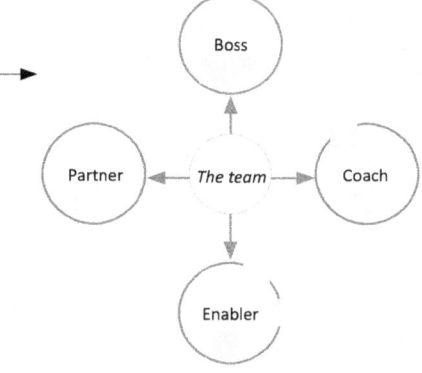

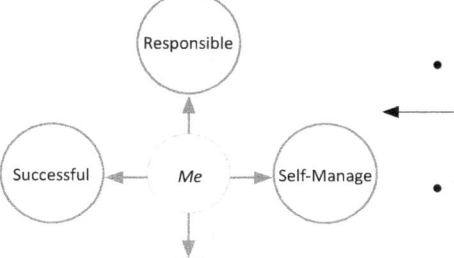

- The leader (i.e., you) can do something similar - setting the expectations of her/his staff (left).
- The leader can share this with the group, in response to the group's expectations.

Note: Use as many circles as you wish.

People-Leadership

Build High-Performing Teams

Definitions of what constitutes a 'High-Performing Team' may vary between individual managers and leaders, but this one seems to be close enough:

> "A high-performing team (HPT) refers to teams, organizations, or virtual groups that are highly focused on their goals and that achieve superior business results. High-performing teams outperform all other similar teams and they outperform expectations given their composition."

Although this is a great definition, it's not going to be easy (or possible) for all teams in an organization to achieve this goal - as they can't all outperform each other! That said, the team from the quick case-study on page 25 is a good example of a team that went from under-performing to achieving great results.

In this section we'll look at some specific techniques and tools that you can use. That said, the best way to create an HPT is to utilize all the methods in this book, not just the ones listed in this section

7 Categories of High-Performing Teams
These 7 categories are a useful way of evaluating the status of a team. Hopefully each category is self-explanatory, but I'll leave it up to you to create your own definitions!

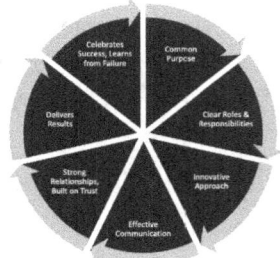

What to do:
- Run the assessment with a team
- Share the results with everyone
- Discuss areas where the team would like to improve
- Create an action plan.

High-Performing Team Assessment

How to score the assessment (next page)
- Take the average of each category and plot the result on the chart

	High-Performing Team Assessment	Your Team
1	Clear Team vision, mission, goals and objectives	4
2	Good Team plan/strategy	4
3	Individual goals and objectives are linked to Team goals & objectives	3
4	Strong customer focus (internal or external)	5
5	Every Team member feels he/she is necessary	5
	Common Purpose Average-->	**4.2**
6	Clear roles & responsibilities	4
7	Fair distribution of workload	2
	Roles & Responsibilities Average-->	**3.0**

Common Purpose

Clear Roles & Responsibilities

1= Strongly Disagree, 2= Disagree, 3= Neutral, 4= Agree, 5= Strongly Agree

People-Leadership

	High-Performing Team Assessment	Your Team
1	Clear Team vision, mission, goals and objectives	
2	Good Team plan/strategy	
3	Individual goals and objectives are linked to Team goals & objectives	
4	Strong customer focus (internal or external)	
5	Every Team member feels he/she is necessary	
	Common Purpose Average-->	
6	Clear roles & responsibilities	
7	Fair distribution of workload	
	Clear Roles & Responsibilities Average-->	
8	The Team is creative	
9	Team members are self-motivated	
	Innovative Approach Average-->	
10	Information is shared - Team members do not "hide" things	
11	Interactive communication between Team members is strong	
	Effective Communications Average-->	
12	Good atmosphere in the Team	
13	High trust among Team members	
14	The Team listens to each other	
15	The Team uses "We" instead of "I"	
16	OK to risk confrontation, because people focus on the problem, not the person	
17	The Team can work through people and technical/business problems	
	Strong Relationships Average-->	
18	The Team delivers excellent results	
19	The Team shares responsibility for results	
	Delivers Results Average-->	

High-Performing Team Assessment

	High-Performing Team Assessment	Your Team
20	Individuals celebrate Team wins, even if they were not directly involved	
21	The Team uses "failure" as a learning opportunity to find better ways of doing things.	
	Celebrates Success, Learns from Failure Average-->	

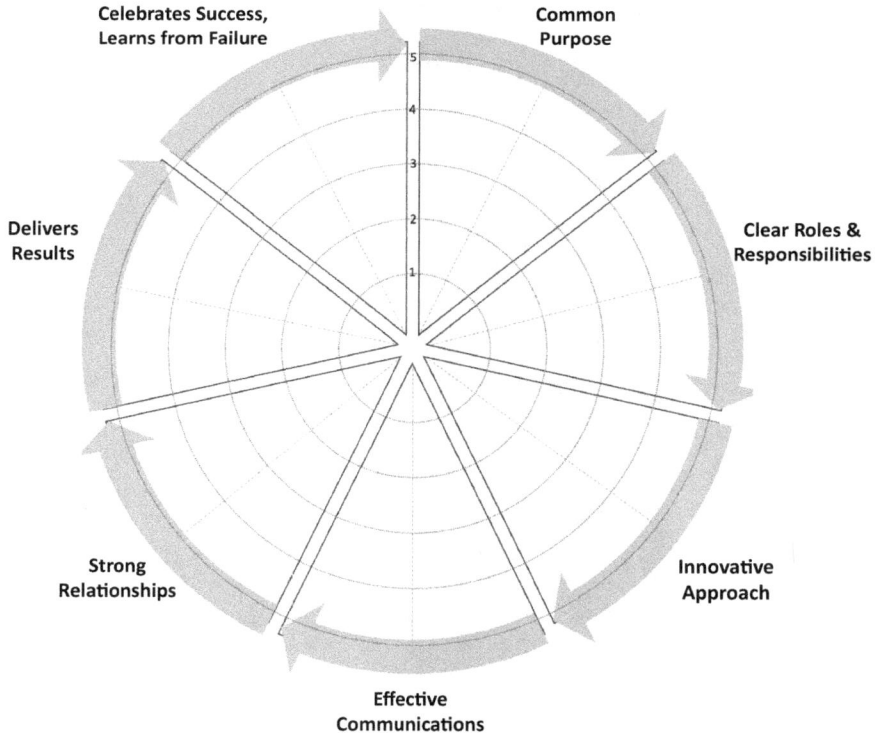

1= Strongly Disagree, 2= Disagree, 3= Neutral, 4= Agree, 5= Strongly Agree

People-Leadership

Next page
- Some high-level ideas for ways of developing / improving team performance in the 7 Categories.
- You can also do this on a whiteboard as a brainstorm method with the team --> share the results and ask "where can we do better?"

High-Performing Team Assessment

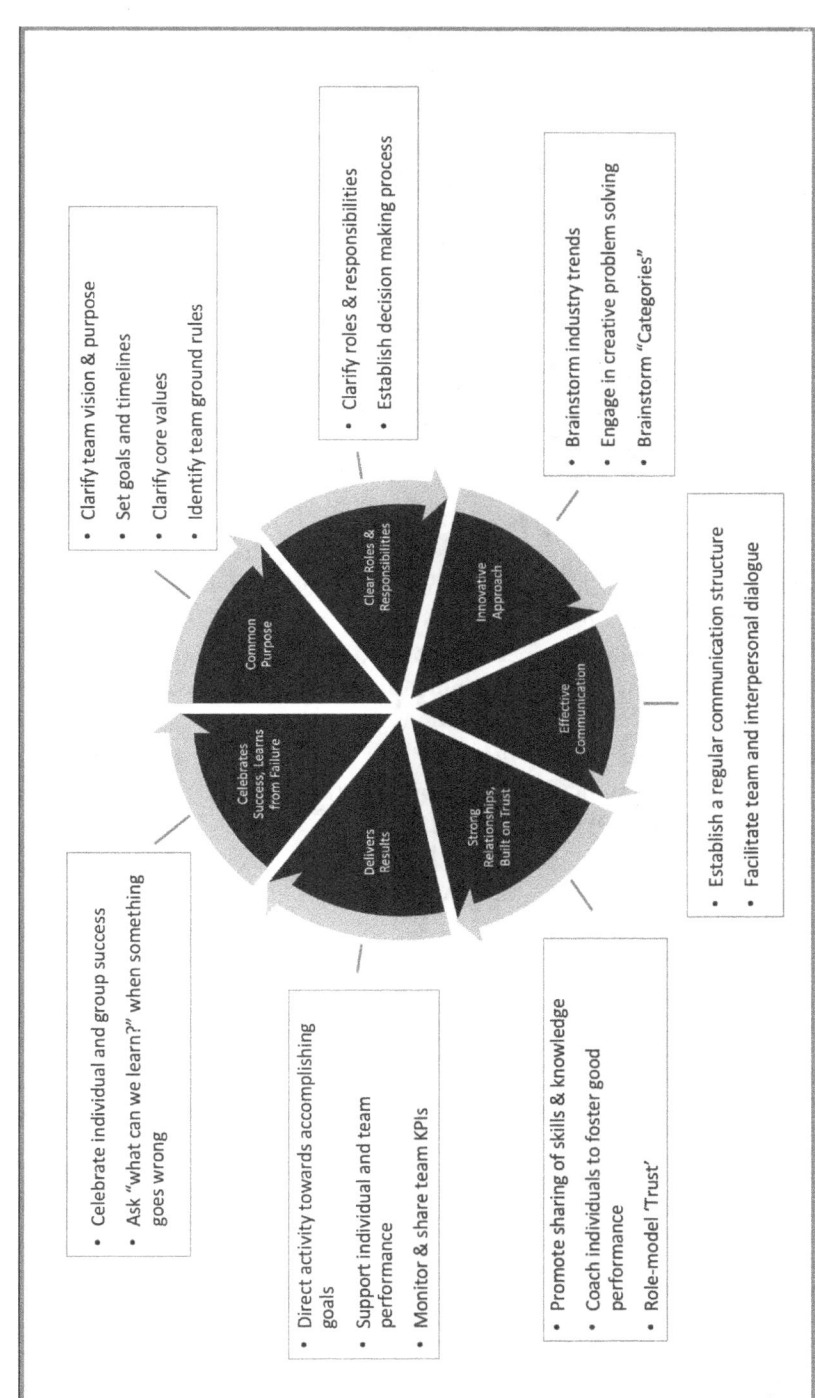

The Tuckman Model

The Forming, Storming, Norming, Performing model of group development was first proposed by Bruce Tuckman in 1965. He found that these phases are all necessary in order for a team to grow, face up to challenges, tackle problems, find solutions, plan work, and deliver results.

(See Wikipedia for more.)

It's a well-known and useful way of looking at teams and their development, particularly for teams that are stuck in the "Storming" phase, even while they have moved into the "Norming" phase. In other words, teams are delivering results, but there is still conflict, disagreement and lack of alignment to the vision, etc.

When working with managers who are having "problems with my team," we've often found that this is due to a gap (or complete lack) of "Forming" activities, which often happens when new members join, or there is a new strategy/ direction, or the team splits into different groups, etc.

You can think of this as "Re-Forming" - something has changed, so you'll need to do some Forming work, such as re-setting the team vision, introducing new members, etc.

The Tuckman Model

Forming	Storming	Norming	Performing
Team meets each other, establishes ground rules. Quite formal- members are treated as strangers.	Members start to communicate feelings. They still see themselves as individuals rather than part of a team. They resist control by group leaders and can show hostility.	People feel part of the team. They realize they can achieve more if they accept other viewpoints.	The team works in an open and trusting atmosphere. Flexibility is the key. Hierarchy is not so important.
• Individuals are not clear on what they're supposed to do. • The mission isn't owned by the group. • Wondering where we are going. • No trust yet. • High learning. • No group history; Unfamiliar with members. • Norms of the team are not established. • People check one another out. • People are not committed to the team.	• Roles and responsibilities are articulated. • Agendas are displayed. • Problem solving doesn't work well. • People want to modify the team's mission. • Trying new ideas. • People set boundaries. • Anxiety abounds. • People push for position and power. • Competition is high. • Lots of personal attacks. • Level of participation by members is at its highest (for some) and its lowest (for some).	• Success happens! • Team has all the resources for doing the job. • Appreciation and trust build. • Purpose is well-defined. • Feedback is high, well received and objective. • Team confidence is high. • Leader reinforces team behaviour. • Members self-reinforce team norms. • Team is creative. • More individual motivation. • Team gains commitment from all members on direction and goals.	• Team members feel very motivated. • Individuals defer to team needs. • No surprises. • Little waste. Very efficient team operations. • Individuals take pleasure in the success of the team-big wins. • "We" versus "I" orientation. • High pride in the team. • High openness / support. • High trust in everyone. • Superior team performance. • OK to risk confrontation.

Planning to overcome gaps →

Building a High-Performing Team - Actions to Take

High-Performing Team - What's Missing?	Actions to Fill the Gap

Actions to Build a High-Performing Team

Unsure of what actions to take?
If you're unsure how to overcome some of those issues you identified under "What's Missing?," try referring to the various team development and other activities in the Additional Resources section.

Additional Resources - page 147

- Activities for Building High-Performing Teams
- Team Facilitation
- Root Cause Analysis
- Making Transparent Decisions
- Risk Analysis
- Developing Innovative Business Ideas
- Developing the Strategy
- Leading Change Initiatives

Food for Thought

How well do you:
- Give feedback in a constructive way?
- Find ways to celebrate team accomplishments?
- Ask "What can we learn from this?" when something goes wrong?
- Let others choose how to do their work?
- Support decisions that others make?
- Ensure your direct reports have a personal development plan?
- Guide others on their career choices?
- Find ways to let others use their strengths?
- Thank people for their contributions?
- Praise others for a job well done?
- Give others appreciation and support?
- Actively listen to diverse points of view?

People-Leadership

Celebrate Success

Getting things done is not easy. Leaders encourage others to carry on. They inspire people with courage and hope. Performance improves when leaders publicly honour/ praise those who have excelled. Leaders set the example by getting personally involved in celebration and recognition.

To be that kind of leader, make sure you...
- Create occasions to bring others together.
- Find out about people's stories – what they are doing to make the organization successful.
- Tell stories about how people went "the extra mile."
- Use hallways, elevators, cafeterias as venues, too.
- Make sure people understand how they are part of the whole.
- Celebrate smaller milestones – don't just wait for the big one!
- End each team meeting by publicly praising people.
- Have fun!

> If you want to create a community, then use language that gives a feeling of community:
> - Don't say "Employee," "Boss," "Manager," "Subordinate."
> - Instead, say "Associates," "Crew," "Team members," "Partners," "Colleagues."

How does your team celebrate success?

Celebrate Success, Learn From failure

Learn from Failure

Leaders use "failure" as a learning opportunity. They are willing to experiment to find better ways of doing things. They create safe environments for people to learn from their failures as well as their successes.

They ask: "What can be learned from this experience?"

Think of failure as a gift on the road to getting better and better.

> *"I've missed more than 9000 shots in my career. I've lost almost 300 games. 26 times, I've been trusted to take the game winning shot and missed. I've failed over and over and over again in my life. And that is why I succeed."*
> Michael Jordan

**Think of a business project that did not work out as planned......
what were the learning points from that?**

People-Leadership

People-Leadership Action Plan

	Action Area	How this Impacts Team Engagement & Performance
11	I create a high-trust environment.	
12	I encourage and empower other people to deal with issues and develop solutions.	
13	I schedule time with my direct reports to discuss their career development plans.	
14	I actively coach people to develop their skills and grow in their job.	
15	I create high-performing teams.	

Review the exercises for People-Leadership, then create an action plan for steps you will take in the next 6-9 months.

Build Your People-Leadership Action Plan

	Actions I'll Take in The Next 6-9 months
11	
12	
13	
14	
15	

Integrated Leadership

> ## Integrated Leadership - Quick Summary

1
- Where are you now on the Leadership Matrix?
- Where do you want to be in 3 months from now, 1 year from now?

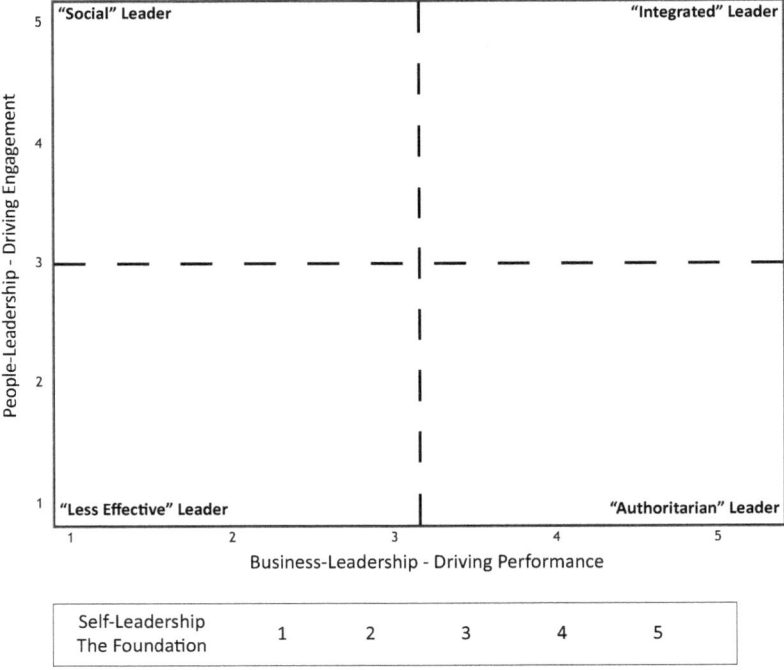

2
- Consider where you can take action for areas of improvement.
- Build action plans based on the Leadership Self-Assessment (see next page for a reminder).

3
- Ok, so that covers the basics. But what if you need to do something "more" than the areas included on the Self-Assessment?
- If so, see the Resources Section for some ideas, on page 147.

From the Leadership Self-Assessment

Self-Leadership

1. I am highly engaged in my role. → Highly Engaged In Role
2. I have a high level of self-awareness (behaviours, strengths, weaknesses, etc.). → High Level Of Self-Awareness
3. I am a Role-Model for company and team values. → Values Role-Model
4. I have a clear sense of purpose. → Clear Sense Of Purpose
5. I'm clear about my philosophy of leadership. → Clear Philosophy of Leadership

Business-Leadership

6. I make sure people in my group understand the organization's vision. → Ensure All Understand Vision
7. I ensure other people understand how their work is connected to the strategy. → Connect to Strategy
8. I have built a strong organization to implement the strategy. → Build Strong Organization
9. I ensure people in my group have a sense of urgency to achieve the objectives. → Ensure Sense of Urgency
10. I regularly talk to my direct reports about their performance. → Regular Performance Discussions

People-Leadership

11. I create a high-trust environment. → Create High Trust Environment
12. I encourage and empower other people to deal with issues and develop solutions. → Encourage & Empower
13. I schedule time with my direct reports to discuss their career development plans. → Discuss Career Development
14. I actively coach people to develop their skills and grow in their job. → Actively Coach Others
15. I create high-performing teams. → Build High-Performing Teams

Measuring Leadership Outcomes

Measuring Outcomes

There are many ways to evaluate the results of leadership actions or an HR-related intervention, and at the risk of some repetition from other sections, below are some ideas for measuring the results of your efforts and programs. The actual goals & targets, we'll leave up to you.

Things to consider for your program measures:
- Business Results/ Performance to Organizational Objectives
- Individual Performance Improvement
- Employee Engagement Survey improvement
- 360 improvements
- Retention
- Productivity
- Sick leave
- Cost savings/ Reductions in that division/ dept./ team
- Cost of Program vs all the above

	Considerations
Business Performance	• What is the current level of performance to team / organizational /company objectives? • Is this improving, decreasing?
Retention	• How many people are leaving the organization per year? • What is the total cost of replacing them? Including recruiting agencies, training, etc. • Is this number increasing, decreasing?
Productivity	• How much overtime is being done? • What other productivity measures do you use? (e.g., no. of contracts created by by legal team, etc.) • Is this number increasing, decreasing?
Sick Leave	• How many sick days, or other days? (not holidays). • Is this number increasing, decreasing?

Combine HR and Business Measures

Combine HR and Business Performance measures (i.e., cost savings)

Issue / Situation	Year One Solution	Year Two Solution	Program Outcome

Organization
• 27 FTEs with imbalance of foreign mgmt. & leaders
  – 9 Japanese assistant mgr. & mgrs. vs 6 Non-Japanese sr. mgrs. & director.
 	
Engagement & Performance
• Lowest Engagement scores in org;
  – 56%
• Lowest performance score average in org.
  – 8 below, 17 meet, 2 exceed expectations
 	
Staff & Cost Impact
• Turnover ratio: 4 FTE left dept.
  – 14.8%
  – 22.5M yen 'cost to replace'
• High overtime
  – 42M yen annually
• High amount of sick leave
  – 21 days individual average annually
	Assessments
	• 360 Global Leadership survey :
	  – Assistant mgrs. up to director
	
	Workshops
	• 3 day leadership workshop x 2
	• 1 day performance management workshop x 2
	• 2 days inter-cultural training workshop
	• 2 days presentation skills training x 4
	• 1 day change management workshop x 2
	
	Coaching
	• 9 months coaching - core topics:
	  – leadership, performance, W/L balance, career development, others
	
	Note: Workshops & coaching were for Individual Contributor up to director
		Assessments
		• 360 Global Leadership survey :
		  – Assistant mgrs. up to director
		
		Workshops / Projects
		• Change management project
		  – Bottom up approach
		• 4 half day change management workshops
		• 2hr. twice a month Change Management team mtg.
		• Change initiative categories:
		  – Employee value proposition, performance management, authority, resources, training, collaboration & work structures
		• 1.5hr. monthly performance management meeting
		
		Coaching
		• 9 months coaching - core topics:
		  – leadership, performance, W/L balance, career development, others
			Organization
			• Department Growth: Increased headcount from 27 to 32 FTEs
			  – 1 local staff promoted to assistant mgr.
			  – 2 local staff promoted to mgr.
			
			Engagement & Performance
			• Engagement score increased
			  – From 56% to 83%
			• Improved performance scores
			  – 20 'Meet Expectations'
			  – 12 'Exceed Expectations',
			  – (vs. 8 below, 17 meet, 2 exceed expectations at start)
			
			Staff & Cost Impact
			• Turnover ratio; 1 FTE left dept.
			  – From 14.8% to 3.1%
			  – 'Cost to replace' reduced from 22.5M yen to 4.8m yen
			• Overtime reduction
			  – From 42m yen to 21m yen annually
			• Sick leave reduction
			  – 21 days to 11 days average annually

~39M JPY (~360K USD) annual cost reduction at program end

Integrated Leadership

Link to Business Priorities

Business Objective	HR Objective	Description	KPIs/measurements	Time-frame
Eliminate Unjustified Costs	Outsource Payroll Processes	Develop and implement plan for outsourcing payroll	• Costs of providing payroll: Overall saving of 5.0M JPY	End Q2
Be the recognized Market Leader in AI Development	Attract & keep the best talent by being a recognized Employer of Choice	Provide a positive image of the company, through: Recruitment fairs, Effective web site design, University visits, etc.	• Employer of Choice survey result: Increase score from 3.75 to 4.10	Mid Q3
Be a High Performing and Efficient Organization	Deliver on Customer Service Operational Excellence	Implement full sales and customer service training program to maximize effectiveness at the customer interface	• Organizational Productivity: • 3,000 units/month per employee	End Q4
Be a High Performing and Efficient Organization	Revise and Renew Performance Management System	Implement new performance management program, deliver training to all relevant managers, evaluate results through PM survey	• Performance Management Survey result: Increase score from 3.10 to 3.50	Mid Q1
Be a High Performing and Efficient Organization	Best-in-class leadership at all levels in the organization	Develop and implement leadership skills program. Focus on: improving coaching for performance; developing leadership competency; dealing with low performers.	• "My Manager" survey result: • Increase score from 2.90 to 3.40	Start Q2

Link to Business Priorities/ Employee Engagement

Changes in Employee Engagement Survey results

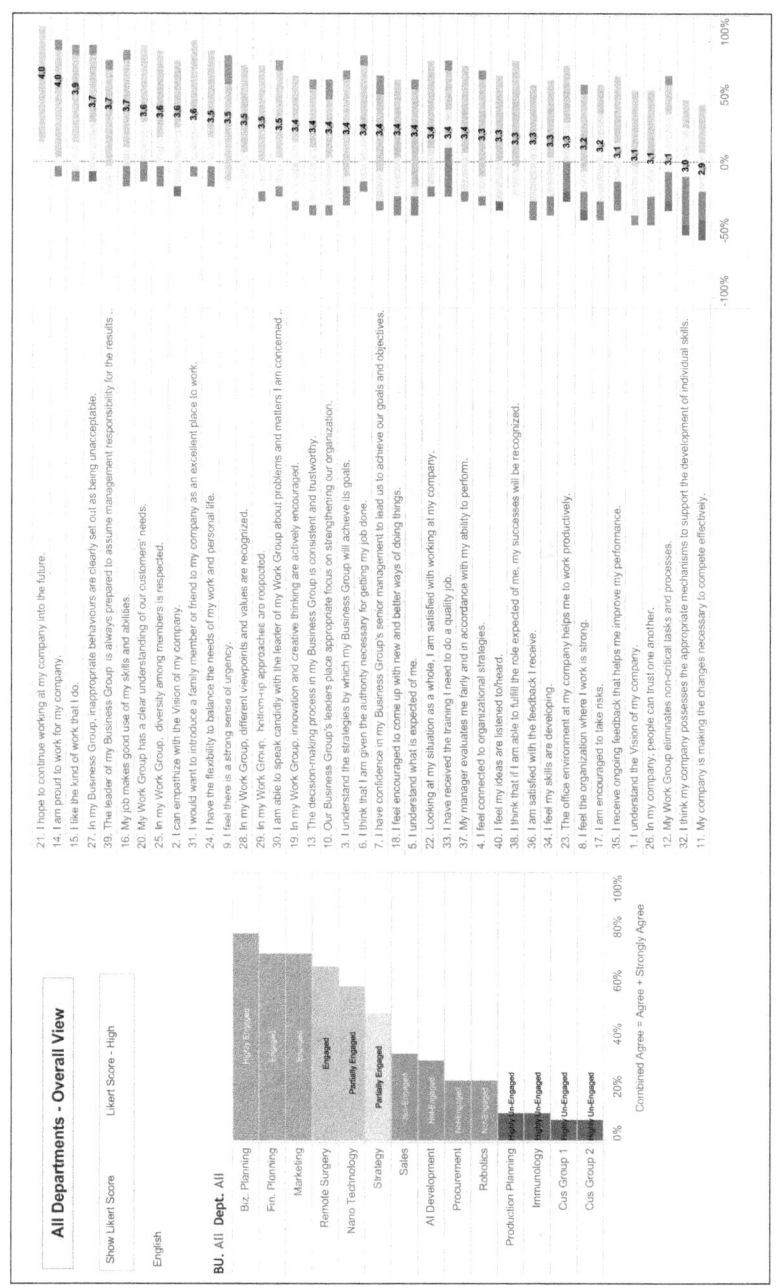

143

Integrated Leadership

Changes in Overtime and Retention *(hopefully better than these results!)*

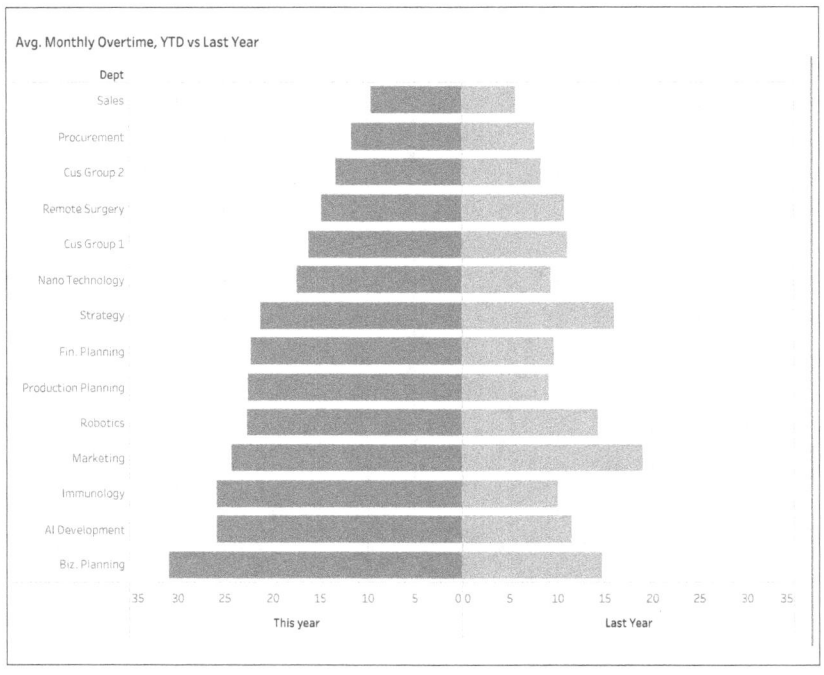

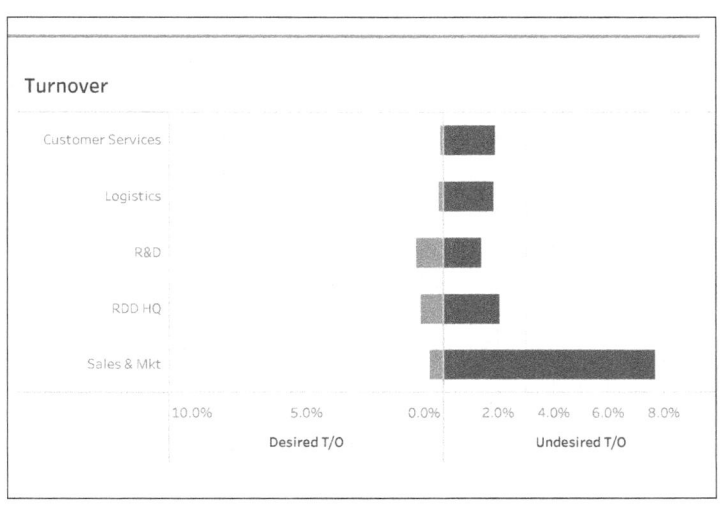

Changes in Overtime, Retention, 360 Surveys

Changes in 360 feedback

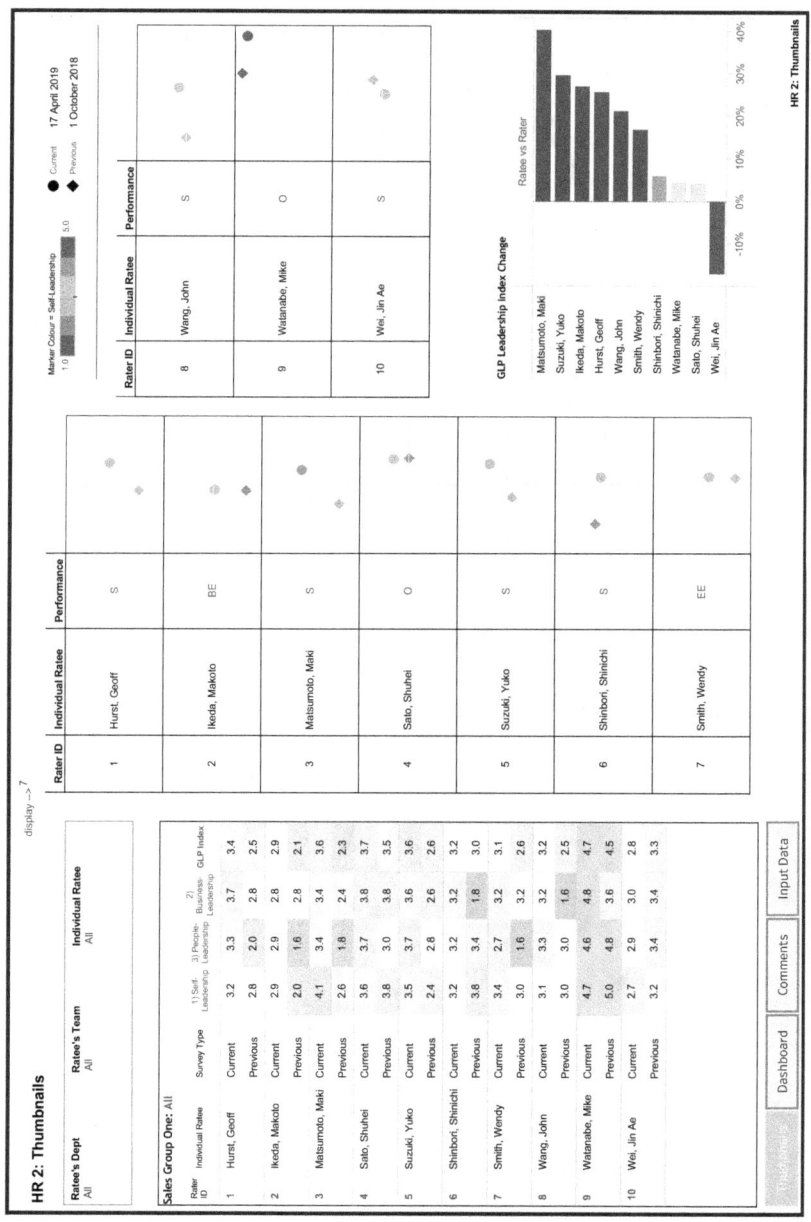

The Highly-Engaged & High-Performing Organization

Use this page for notes

Additional Resources

Improving Your Personal Productivity

There a many great books and on-line resources for improving individual productivity - most of them far more complete than the **4W** method we are about to look at now!

That said, the **4W** method will hopefully give you enough ideas to get started. From there, it's probably best to do your own research, as new tools and ideas are constantly being developed.

Stress comes from having many things to do, but these things are not "organized" in a system that you can trust

The Goal is to get things off your mind, and into a system that works...

...So that your mind will trust that you have everything in a plan and under control...

...So that you can use your mind for creativity and problem solving & 'adding value' - not for keeping "to-do" lists in your head

Do the Right Thing at the Right Time, with the Right Result

With reference to Getting Things Done by David Allen

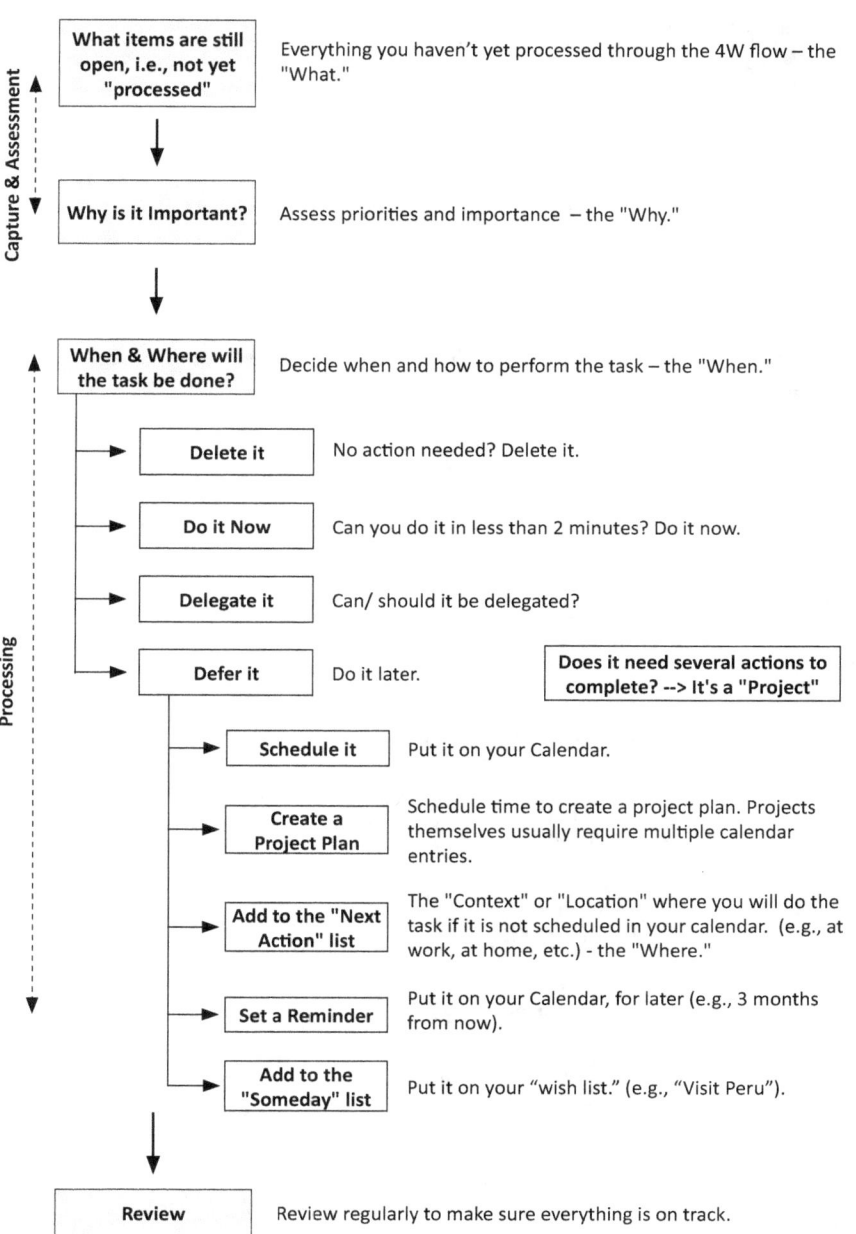

The Highly-Engaged & High-Performing Organization

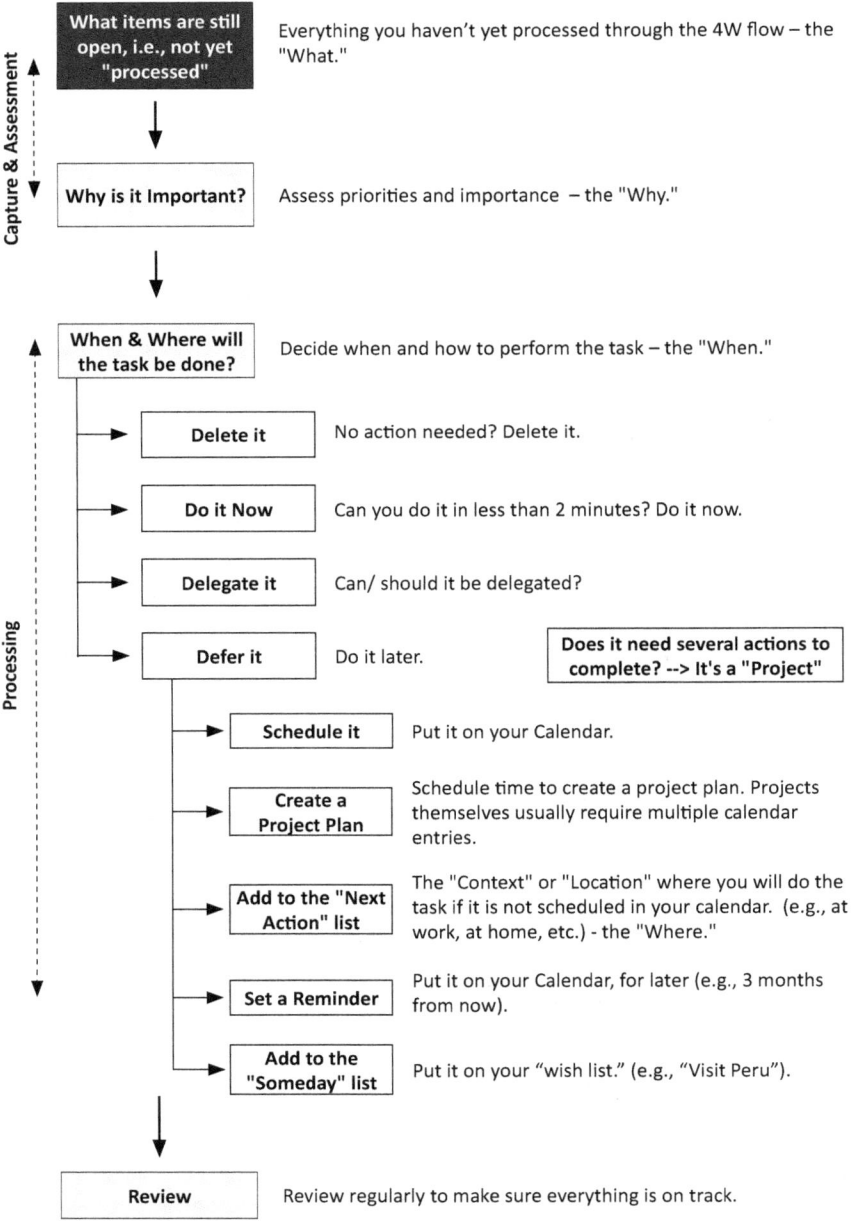

The 4W System

Step One: Capture

"Download" everything you have to do - everything that is on your mind, or on a to-do list somewhere, then move on to your email in-box.

Think about all the things/ activities/ tasks/ actions/ projects that you have to do. Use Post-it notes, write one item per Post-it. Do this for all business-related and personal activities --> i.e., everything that's on your mind. Even things you might do one day, such as "Visit Peru."

For example:

Professional
- Projects not complete
- Phone calls to make
- Emails to reply to
- Reports to read/write
- Proposals
- Expense claims
- Computer update
- Budget planning
- Meetings to set-up
- Product road map
- Training class to attend
- Performance appraisal preparation
- Organizing exhibitions

- Give feedback
- Re-set filing system
- Review production process
- Interview candidates
- Book flights
- Do the 360 survey

Personal
- Book family holiday
- Fix the sink
- Install new windows
- Tommy's birthday
- Cut the grass
- Join the gym

- Buy new laptop
- Change bank accounts
- Change to winter tires
- Buy a new jacket
- Attend that event
- Submit manuscript
- Install LEDs outside
- Clean the furniture
- Change wallpaper
- Visit Peru
- Set up personal blog
- Study Kanji
- Learn to type properly
- Pay those bills

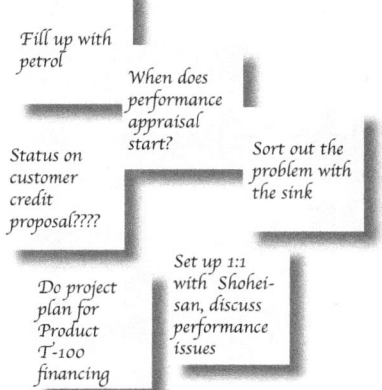

Fill up with petrol

When does performance appraisal start?

Status on customer credit proposal????

Sort out the problem with the sink

Do project plan for Product T-100 financing

Set up 1:1 with Shohei-san, discuss performance issues

Don't be surprised if you use 50 or more Post-it notes!

> **Why start by downloading everything?**
> The goal is to get things off your mind and into the 4W system, so your mind can focus on delivering projects and being creative - not on "keeping lists in your head."
>
> So, start by getting everything out of your head and on to paper. Note: you only need to do this full download once. After this, you can process items on a daily basis.

The Highly-Engaged & High-Performing Organization

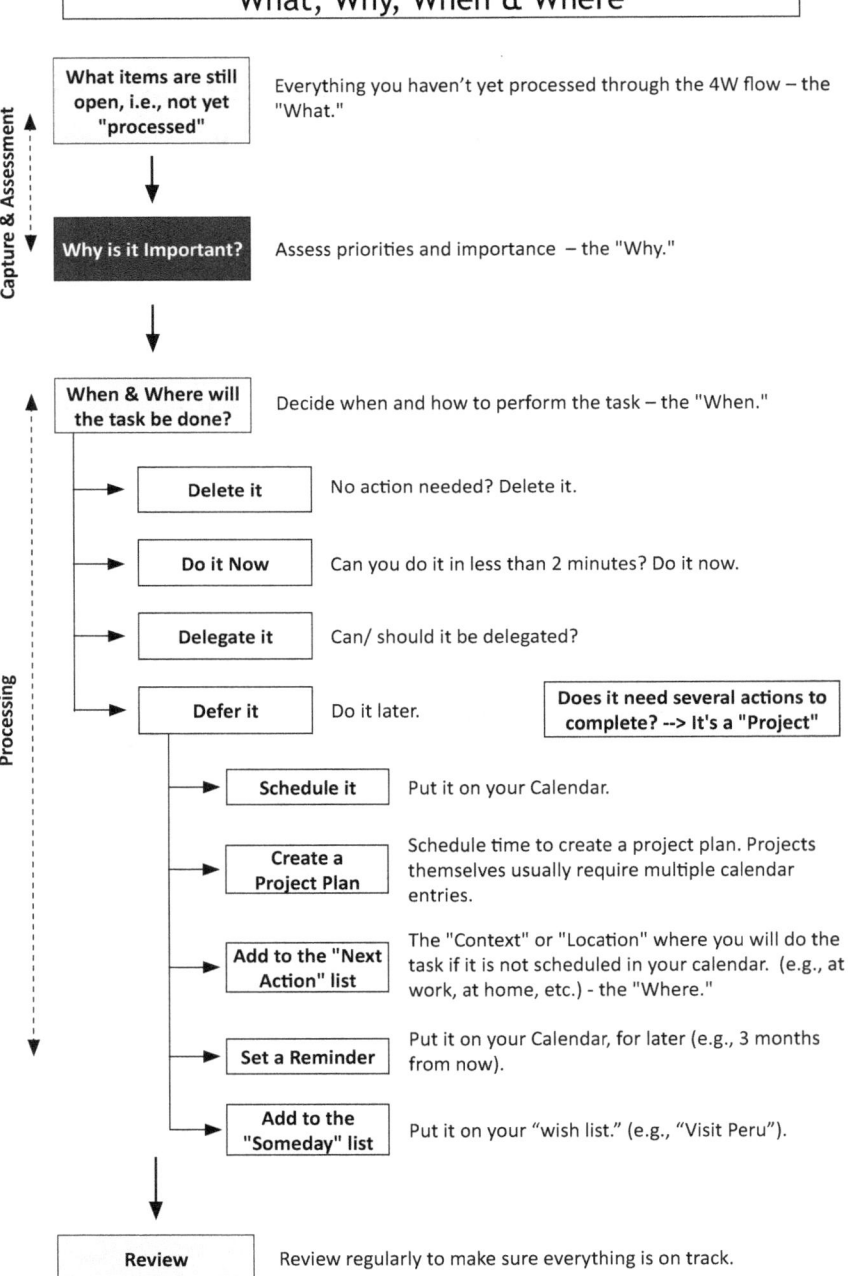

The 4W System

Step Two: Assess Importance
Connect to "Why"

Align "Items" from Step One to Mission/ Vision/ Objectives.

For example:

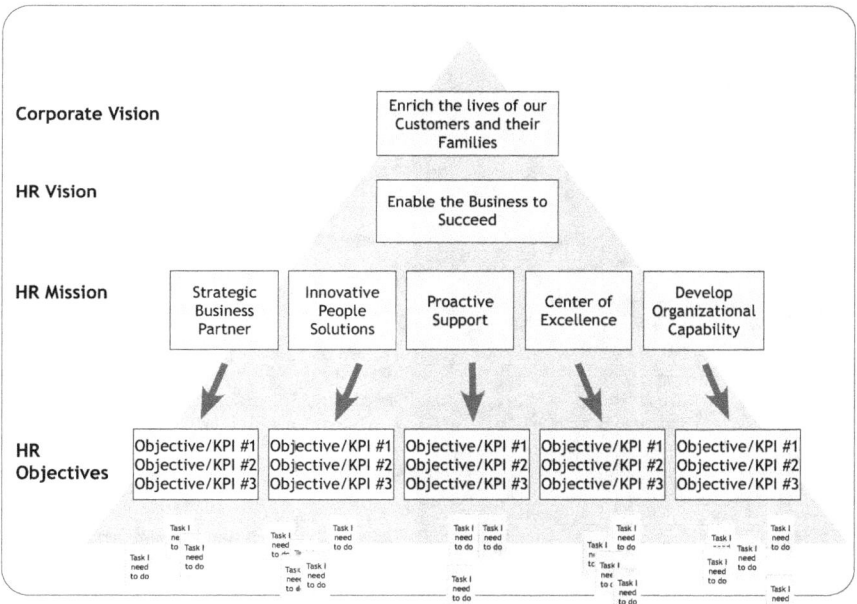

Enable the Business to Succeed	Home & family
Personal development	Contributor to society

Use any format/method that suits you best

153

The Highly-Engaged & High-Performing Organization

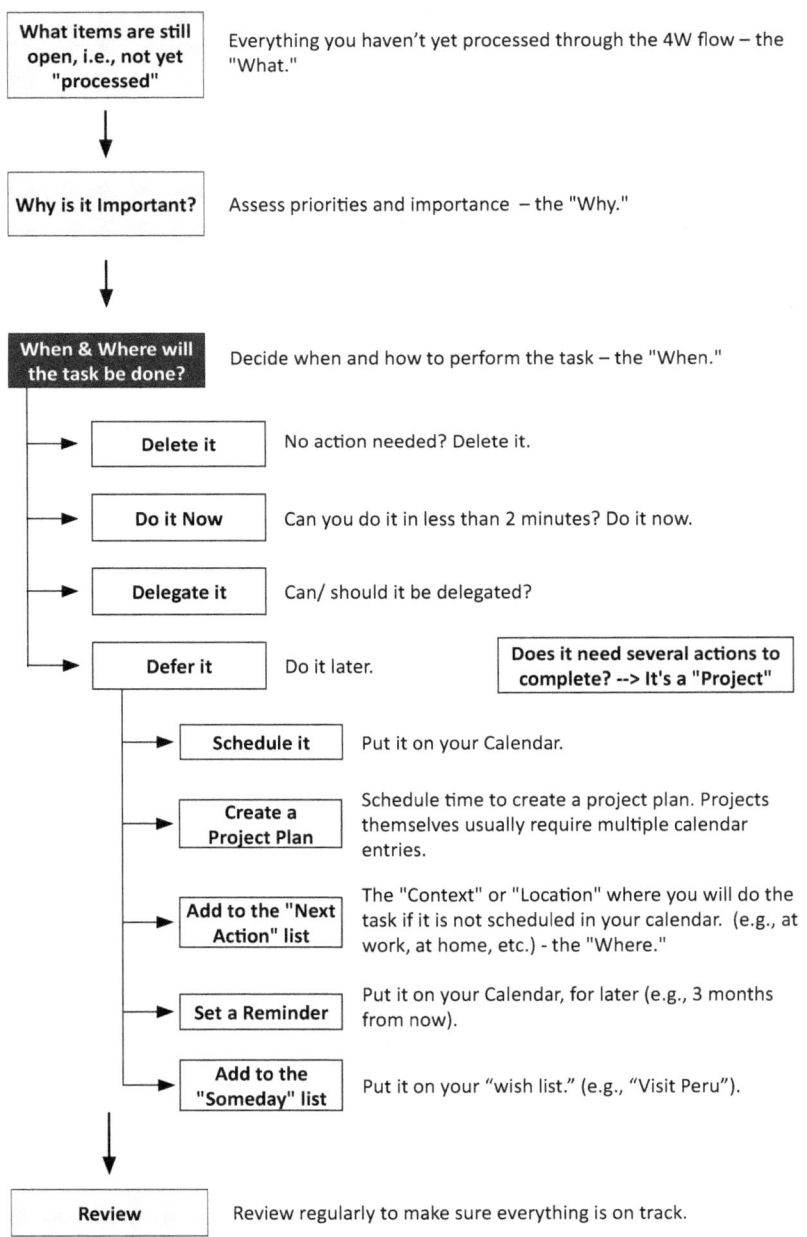

The 4W System

Step Three: Schedule Actions

Use your calendar as your main tool. Schedule as many things as you can, including 'Reminders.'

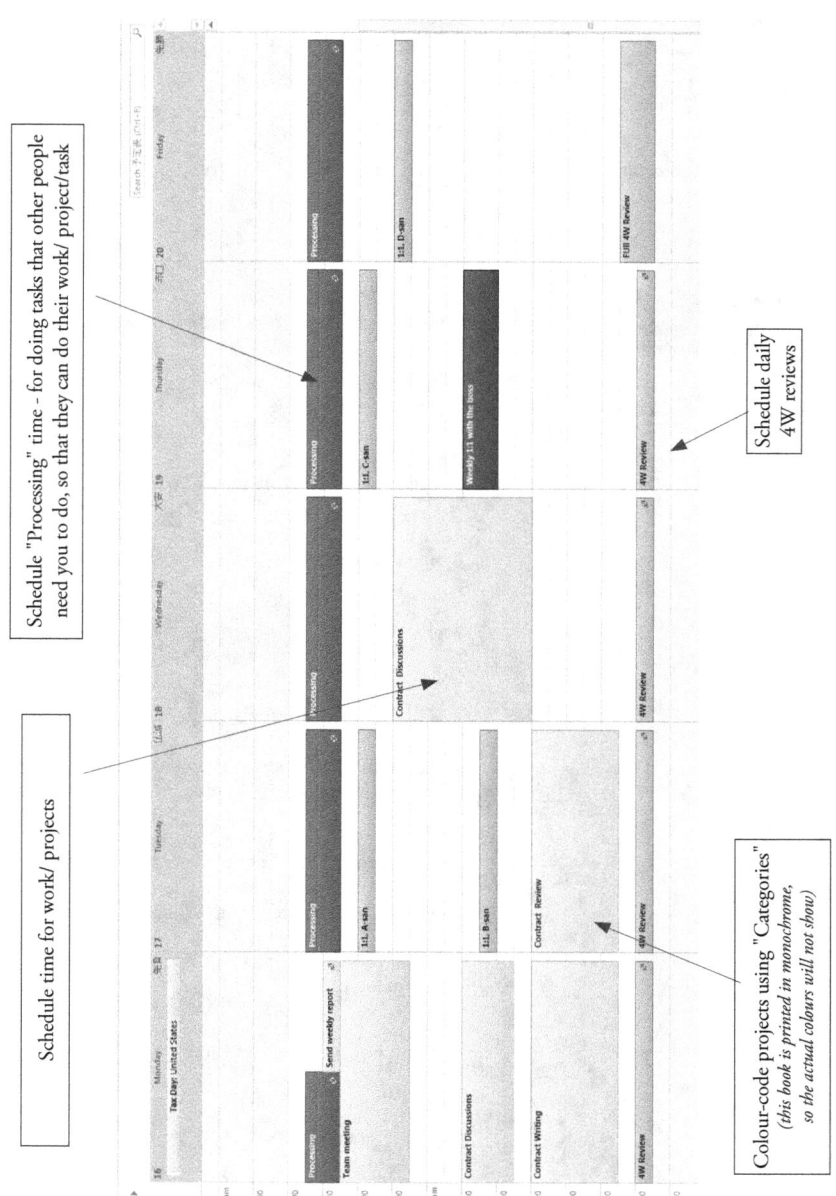

The Highly-Engaged & High-Performing Organization

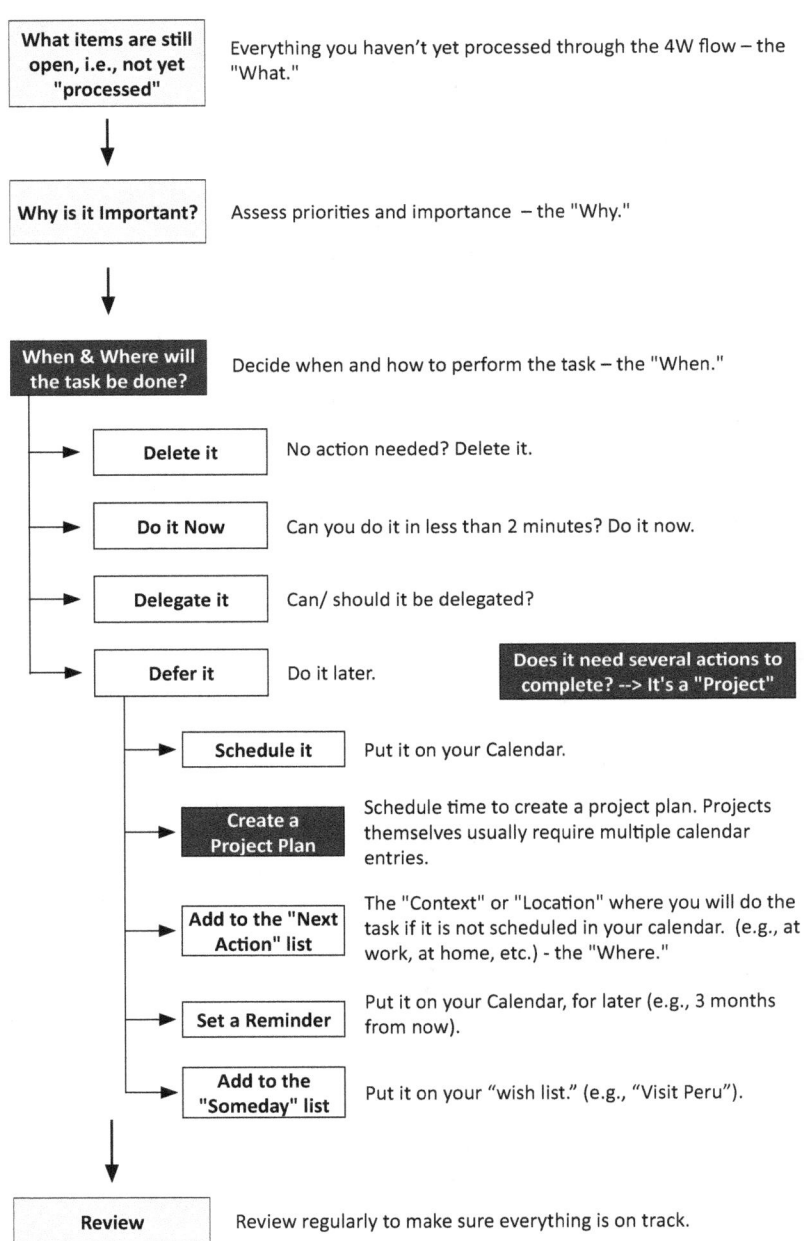

The 4W System

Simplified Project Planning
For non-project managers

| Try this 4 Step Process for Planning Projects | ➡ | 1. Purpose & Outcome
 2. Brainstorming
 3. Organizing
 4. Next Action |

---

1. Purpose & Outcome

- Why are you doing this?
- What result do you want?
- What will success look like?
- How will you measure success?

For example 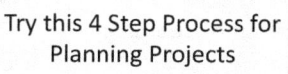 *Productivity*
- *Full workbook and system in place*
- *Workshops delivered to all employees*
- *Relevant EES results + 10%*
- *Projects delivered on time*
- *OT reduced by 25%*

2. Brainstorming

- Generate as many ideas as you can
- Don't evaluate the ideas yet - just get them out of your head

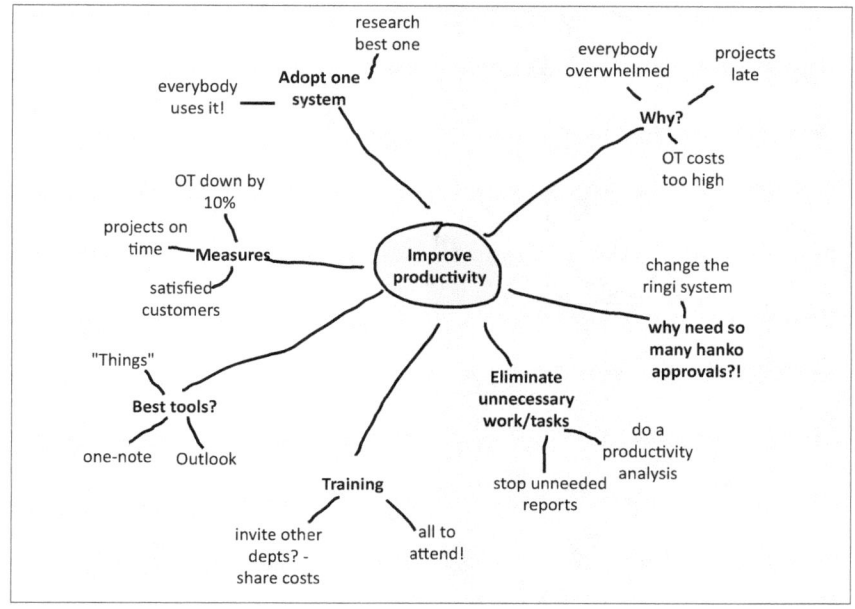

157

The Highly-Engaged & High-Performing Organization

| 3. Organizing | • What must happen to get the outcome you want?
• In what order must they occur?
• Create the project schedule
• Maintain an overall projects schedule |

Maintain a list of Areas of Responsibility/ Projects

Areas of Responsibility/ Projects	
Organization and People Developer	**Home & Family**
Performance Leadership: Workshops	Fix damage on the garden wall
Engagement Survey	Double glaze all windows
HRBP Workshop	Ceiling air con on landing
Performance Leadership: Workshops	Organize CDs
Engagement Survey	Dump - sell Gas fires
Performance Leadership: 360 Survey	Install radiators, floor heating
Talent Management Implementation	
Productivity Expert	**Writer**
Re-set my desk for optimal effectiveness	Finish my novel!
Install One Note to Outlook	
Link to One Note, Outlook	
Organization PEX Project	
Productivity Workshop	

The 4W System

Keep things simple - but add more details if you like:

Project Planner		
Project / Outcome	**Task/ Activity**	**Due**
Performance Coaching Workshop	Develop new materials	Jun 10
	Create Power-point version	Jun 15
	Print full set and proofread	Jun 22
	Print final version, in binder, final check	Jun 30
	Book classrooms	Jun 30
	Send announcement to all managers	Jul 5
	Conduct workshops	Aug-Sept.

Spreadsheet Gantt-style: Gives detailed view of schedule(s), without too much in-depth information found in typical project management software.

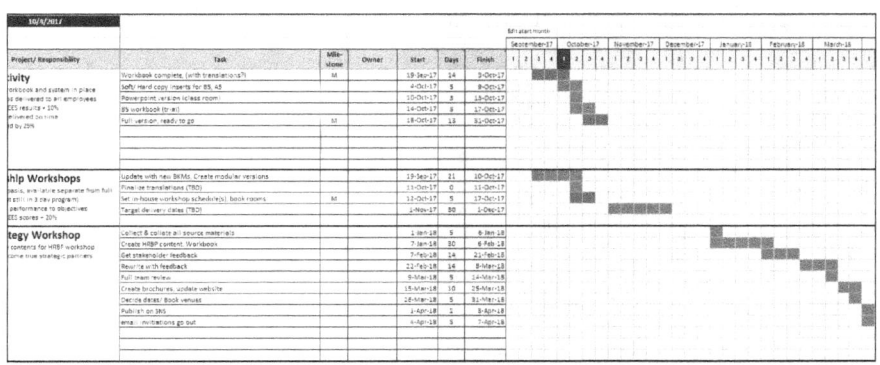

4. Next Actions

- Do it now (if under 2 mins)
- Delegate it
- Defer it - i.e., schedule it in your calendar
- Keep a project schedule

The Highly-Engaged & High-Performing Organization

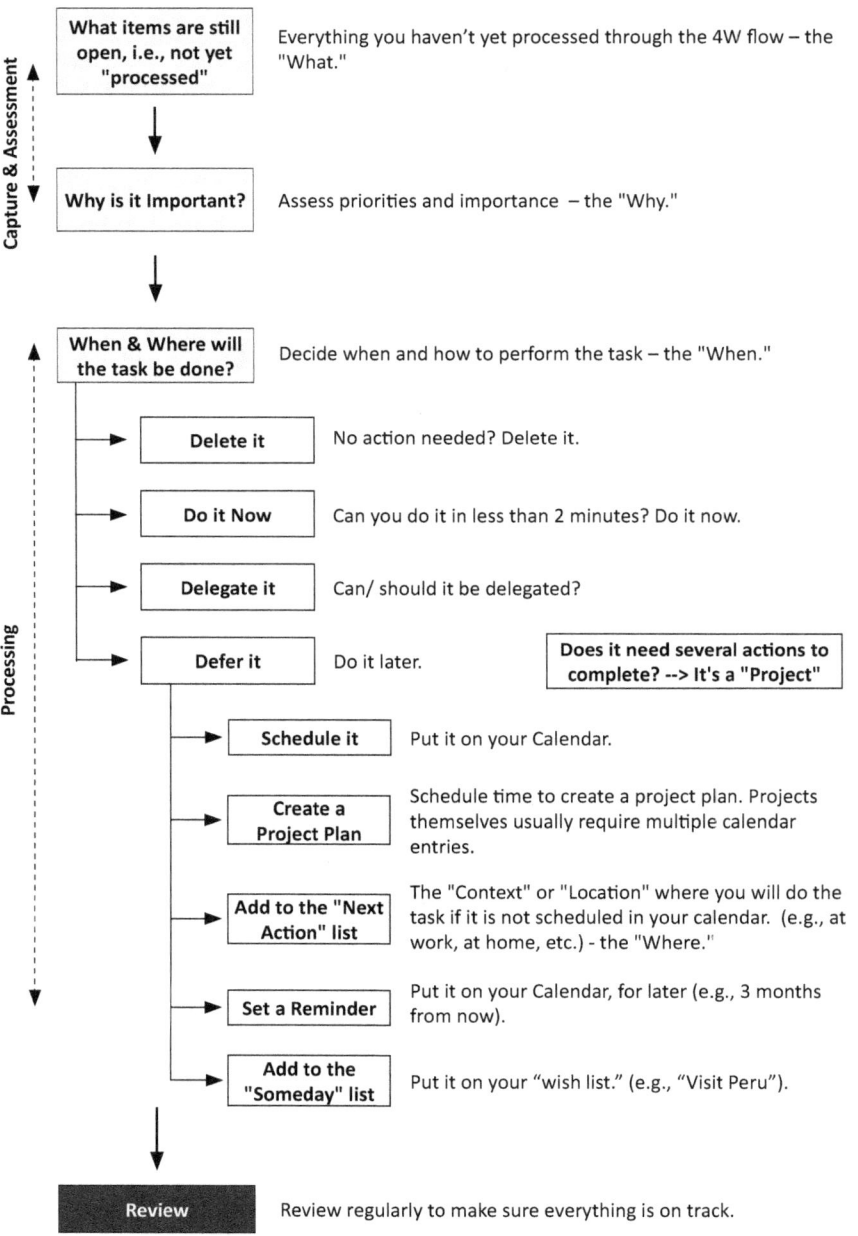

The 4W System

Step Four: Review Regularly

Daily Review

- Morning or evening - up to you
- Empty your "In-Tray"
- Process emails in one batch

Weekly Review

1. Look for past calendar items, over the previous 2-3 weeks
2. Look ahead, 4 weeks
3. Download all ideas, tasks, unfinished items, etc.
4. Go through the Processing part of the process
5. Review Goals, Objectives, Projects, Areas of Responsibility
6. Re-build the Action List
7. Re-set the Project Overview time-line

Your "In-Tray" consists of all things you need to do, but have not yet been processed

Notes taken on slips of paper, or phone   Emails

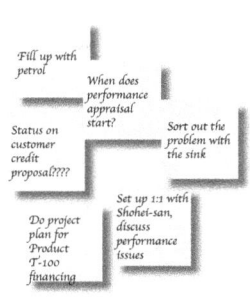

Note book

Capture
Buy an electric pencil sharpener for the office
Set meeting for follow-up with sales team
Buy more note-pad paper
Get back to Bryan on his request
Buy dog food

Whiteboard printouts

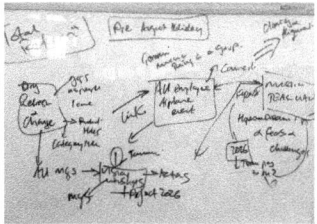

161

Activities for Building High-Performing Teams

These are some activities you can use for helping to build a high-performing team. You could run them yourself, but we recommend working with your HR Business Partner as a facilitator.

There are various different activities, so choose which one suits you best. That said, there are many more resources available, so an on-line search should result in some excellent ideas & tools not listed here.

Giving Feedback/ Post Activity Discussion
Here are 5 questions you can ask at the end of an activity:
1. In general, how do you believe your team functioned during the activity?
2. What behaviors did you observe?
3. What are the general reactions of each team member to the project and what occurred?
4. What did your team do well?
5. What could your group do to improve its effectiveness?

Team Alignment, Vision

1 "How Aligned Are We?"

This is a useful exercise to run with your team
- Think about all the things/ activities/ tasks/ actions that you do.
- Use Post-it notes to see where & how they align to the Mission and Objectives.

Then run a team discussion:
- How well do our activities align to the key objectives?
- What do we need to start, stop doing?
- Do we have the right focus?

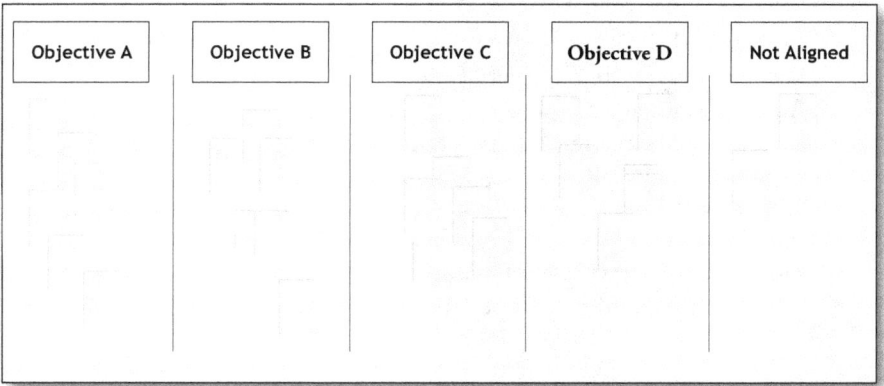

2 "Vision of an Effective Team"

<u>Purpose</u>: Creating focus, passion, and group buy-in. The team finds a common purpose and is more willing to cooperate as an effective team.

<u>Materials needed</u>: Pens, paper, white-board, etc.

<u>Instructions</u>: Each person finishes the sentence, "My vision of a team that works is…"

The entire team now creates one statement or visual that represents the total of these vision statements.

3 "Team CV/ Resume"

<u>Purpose</u>: Improve team members' understanding of each other's knowledge, capabilities and experience.

<u>Instructions</u>: Create a one-page Team Resume that reflects this talent, knowledge, experience, and resources. Write the resume on a flip chart/ PowerPoint, then describe the Team Resume to the rest of the class in 3 minutes or less

<u>Possible contents:</u>
- Education (e.g., team's collective years of education, for example)
- Work experience (collective years)
- First jobs, Other positions held
- Professional skills
- Personality types (e.g., Myers-Briggs)
- Accomplishments and awards
- International experience (e.g., nationalities represented, languages, experiences abroad)
- Special skills
- Publications
- Hobbies/ Interests/ Special talents
- Travel, Family and pets (types and names)

4 "Life Time-line"

<u>Purpose</u>: Improve team communication through sharing life stories.

<u>Materials needed</u>: Large sheets of paper, markers, pens.

<u>Instructions</u>: Distribute a sheet of paper and some writing/drawing utensils to each player. Explain that they will be creating a time-line of their lives: the high points, the low points, and how things have changed over time. Key places, events, and people might be part of the time-line. Each person is free to draw pictures or write anything they like to tell a story about their lives. There is no right or wrong way to do this.

Note:
Each person can share with their group, or if you don't wish to make sharing mandatory, you can ask for some volunteers to come to the front of the room and share their time-line stories with the whole group.

5 "Who we are and what we do"

Purpose: Improve team members' understanding of each other's roles and responsibilities. The team uncovers where their roles overlap, where there are gaps in understanding and how they can work together more effectively - especially in cross-functional teams. This is also good for building virtual teams.

Instructions: Each person (or can be a pair) representing a job role (or department or location) should prepare a short presentation of their role (or department, office, region, sector, etc), which they will give to the group, in turn. The presentations can be informal (flip-chart or discussion style) or more formal (PowerPoint).

Suggested contents
- Here's what we do/can do (including personal introductions)
- Here's why the function is important to our organization and our customers/the project
- Our challenges (for example, inter-departmental, strategic, project aims issues)
- How you can help us (especially looking at connecting and dependent functions)

After each presentation allow time for initial questions and feedback and to quickly identify any actions or opportunities for follow-up.

6 "Story of My Life"

Purpose: Learn personal backgrounds in a fun setting. Team uncovers common interests and opens dialogue.

Materials needed: Decks of cards — picture cards only.

Instructions: Cards represent different stages of life; i.e. Jack is childhood, Queen is teenage years, King is young adult, Ace is now. As each person draws a card, they must tell one story about the period of their life that corresponds to the card.

7 "Let the Ideas Fly"

Purpose: Gather ideas from a group of people, to address an issue or problem. Good for large groups of people, for example an all-employee town-hall meeting.

Materials needed: Each person has a sheet of A5 or B5 paper, used to make a paper plane. Also, prepare 2-3 sheets of flip chart paper for each table team.

Instructions: Decide the theme for the session. For example: "What's wrong with the way we handle customers?" Or maybe: "What do we need to change for our future success?" Arrange the attendees at team tables, 5-7 people per table

- Instruct attendees to write their answer/recommendation/input on the sheet of paper.
- Then, everybody folds their sheet into a paper plane.
- Everybody throws their plane into the air (be careful, it can get chaotic here!).
- The planes fly randomly around the room.
- Each table team collects the paper planes that fall near them.
- Each table team discusses the theme, using the ideas from the paper planes.
- Each team uses the flip chart paper to draw/discuss their thoughts, ideas, recommendations, etc. Note: encourage each person on the team to use their individual creativity and draw their ideas on the flip chart.
- Each table team presents their discussion to the room. It there are too many tables to allow each team to present out, then choose 4 or 5 volunteer teams.

Finally, collect all the flip chart sheets and summarize into an action plan (usually done following the session)

8 "The Marshmallow Challenge"

<u>Purpose</u>: Improve team communication and innovative problem solving.

<u>Materials needed</u>: Each team kit contains twenty sticks of spaghetti, masking tape (one meter), string (one meter) and one marshmallow. These ingredients should be placed into a paper lunch bag, or similar (so people cannot see the contents until the activity starts). You will also need a measuring tape.

<u>Instructions</u>: Build the Tallest Freestanding Structure: The winning team is the one that has the tallest structure measured from the table top surface to the top of the marshmallow.

The Entire Marshmallow must be on top: The entire marshmallow needs to be on the top of the structure. Cutting or eating part of the marshmallow disqualifies the team!

- Use as much or as little of the kit as needed.
- The team cannot use the paper bag.
- Teams are free to break the spaghetti, cut up the tape and string to create new structures.
- The Challenge Lasts 18 minutes
- Teams cannot hold on to the structure when the time runs out. Those touching or supporting the structure at the end of the exercise will be disqualified!

Feedback:
Most people assume that the marshmallows are light and fluffy and easily supported by the spaghetti sticks. However, when they actually try to build the structure, the marshmallows don't seem so light!

The lesson here is:
- We need to identify the assumptions in our project: the real customer needs, the cost of the product, the duration of the service, etc. – and test them early.
- Doing that leads to effective and innovative teams!
- *It's also a lot of fun!*

9 "Pass the Ball"

Purpose: Improve team communication regarding defined issues.

Materials needed: Any type of ball, e.g., tennis ball.

Instructions:
- Organize the team(s) into a circle(s) - 6 to 10 people
- Throw ball to another team member, in random order
- The receiver (catcher) must call out his or her suggestion, according to the theme
- The theme should be a real issue or concern for the team/organization, e.g.,

  - reasons why customers complain
  - causes of stress at work
  - things that motivate us/me/staff
  - benefits of a given product or service
  - management challenges that we face (for managers)
  - ideas to save cost
  - ways to improve quality
  - ways to delight customers outside of their normal expectations
  - time management tips and ideas

10 "The Egg Drop"

Purpose: Improve team communication and innovative problem solving around a given task. (and have fun)

Materials needed: Raw egg, 30 straws, Masking tape (2 meters), String (2.5 meters), Scissors.

Instructions: Build an "egg package" that can sustain an eight foot drop to the floor - without breaking the egg. Each team must present their 'packing' idea to the whole group before the drop.

Note: it can get messy if the egg breaks - so use a plastic sheet as the target.

11 "Build the Tallest Tower"

<u>Purpose</u>: Improve team communication and innovative problem solving.

<u>Materials needed</u>: 20 sheets of blank paper.

<u>Goal</u>: Build the Tallest Tower:
- Use the paper to build the tallest tower
- You can cut, fold, tear, crush the paper
- You cannot use paper clips, tape, scissors or anything else
- The tower must be stable - it must not fall down at the end of the allotted time!

Making Transparent Decisions

4 Fundamental Decision Making Methods

Teams perform better when they know in advance how decisions will be made. One technique you can use is to introduce the four basic decision making methods, and then discuss as team, as follows:

Discuss & Agree:

- Facilitate a discussion about which method will work best for the work you will be doing. If the choice is not obvious, you may need to list the pros and cons for each type.
- Listen to everyone's opinion.
- Make an agreement.
- Note: When new team members join, tell them what type of decision making is being used and why.

High

Consultative	**Consensus**
• Key decision maker accepts input and advice of the team, then decides. • Allows for team members to share their ideas and opinions.	• Everyone can "work with" the decision • Full discussion of all the issues. • Takes a long time to reach conclusion. • Good for special processes and project teams.
Executive	**Voting**
• Decisions are designated to a single person or committee. • Good for making quick decisions.	• Majority or 2/3 "yes" vote can make decision. • Some people are happy with results, others are not. • Good for formal committees and organizations.

Time

Involvement → High

Making Transparent Decisions

Criteria Matrix/ Dot Voting for Group Decisions

A quick, visual, analytical method to make group-based decisions when there are several options/ solutions to choose from.

Evaluation Criteria
- For a given issue/ problem/ challenge, discuss as a group and then list up the key Evaluation Criteria, such as: Quality, Schedule, Cost, etc.
- Team members get a fixed number of "votes," say 3-5, which they can then show by dots on a whiteboard - or asterisks using a shared on-line tool (see below)
- In the example below, "Schedule" got the most votes, and so has the highest weighting.

Option Assessment against Evaluation Criteria:
- Then, repeat the voting method, this time using the second table, which lists the Evaluation Criteria against the Options.
- Score each Option = Number of votes x Weighting

Discuss "Evaluation Criteria" and prioritize through dot-voting.

Evaluation Criteria	
Quality	***
Schedule	*****
Cost	****
Risk	*
Features	**

Then use dot-voting again to assess each option against the evaluation criteria.

Weight	Evaluation Criteria	Option 1	Option 2	Option 3
5	Schedule	***	*****	**
4	Cost	**	***	*****
3	Quality	***	*	*
2	Features	**	***	**
1	Risk	**	****	*
	Total Points	38	50	38

In this case, Option 2 scored the highest - so that implies it is the best choice!

Risk Analysis

What is it?
- A method for evaluating the impact of a problem/ issue.

Why Use it?
- To prioritize issues that need to be resolved.

Method
- Assess the probability/likelihood and impact of each issue.
- Write in the issue in the appropriate box in the chart.
- Prioritize high-impact and high-probability issues accordingly.

Risk Rating = Likelihood x Impact/Severity

Impact/ Severity						
Catastrophic/ Disastrous	5	Monitor	Action	Urgent Action	Stop	Stop
Significant	4	Monitor	Action	Action	Stop	Stop
Moderate	3	No Action	Monitor	Action	Action	Urgent Action
Low	2	No Action	Monitor	Monitor	Action	Action
Negligible/ Almost Zero	1	No Action	No Action	No Action	Monitor	Monitor
		1	2	3	4	5
		Very Unlikely/ Rare	Unlikely	Occasional/ Moderate	Probable/ Likely	Frequent/ Almost Certain

Likelihood

The Risk Analysis Matrix

Risk Rating = Likelihood x Impact/Severity

Impact/Severity		Likelihood				
		1	2	3	4	5
		Very Unlikely/ Rare	Unlikely	Occasional/ Moderate	Probable/Likely	Frequent/ Almost Certain
Catastrophic/ Disastrous	5					
Significant	4					
Moderate	3					
Low	2					
Negligible/ Almost Zero	1					

Developing Innovative Business Ideas

Business school graduates and/ or experienced managers will already have some good tools available to them for building the strategy.

However, if your background is different, or your organization does not have a set of tools on the company intranet, then here's a few ideas to get you started.

You *can* use them by yourself, but they are designed for a group/ team workshop, using the collective power of everyone's innovative inputs and insights to develop new business concepts and actionable ideas.

1) Business Trend Analysis

This method will help:
- To introduce your team to new technologies and trends that can trigger innovative ideas.
- To explore how specific trends and technologies can impact the business challenges.

What to do:
- First, pick a business challenge to work on.
- For the business challenge, evaluate trends that are taking place now.
- What impact will they have?
- What opportunities will they bring?
- How could you use them?
- What products or services could you create?

https://www.trendhunter.com/

Also see "Let the Ideas Fly" on page 166

Business Trend Analysis

What new products or services could your organization create for each challenge?

	Trend/Technology	Trend/Technology	Trend/Technology
For our goal/ challenge:			
For our goal/ challenge:			
For our goal/ challenge:			

Inspired by the "Board of Innovation"

2) Brainstorm Categories

Brainstorming Categories
This provides a more structured approach, but gives space for creative individual input and team discussion.

What to do:
- First, pick a business challenge to work on.
- Everyone individually writes their ideas on post-it notes, then attaches then to the chart.
- The team gathers around the chart and discusses the ideas.
- The team rates each idea for feasibility/ ease of implementation or impact to the "Challenge Statement."

Also see "Let the Ideas Fly" on page 166

Brainstorm Categories

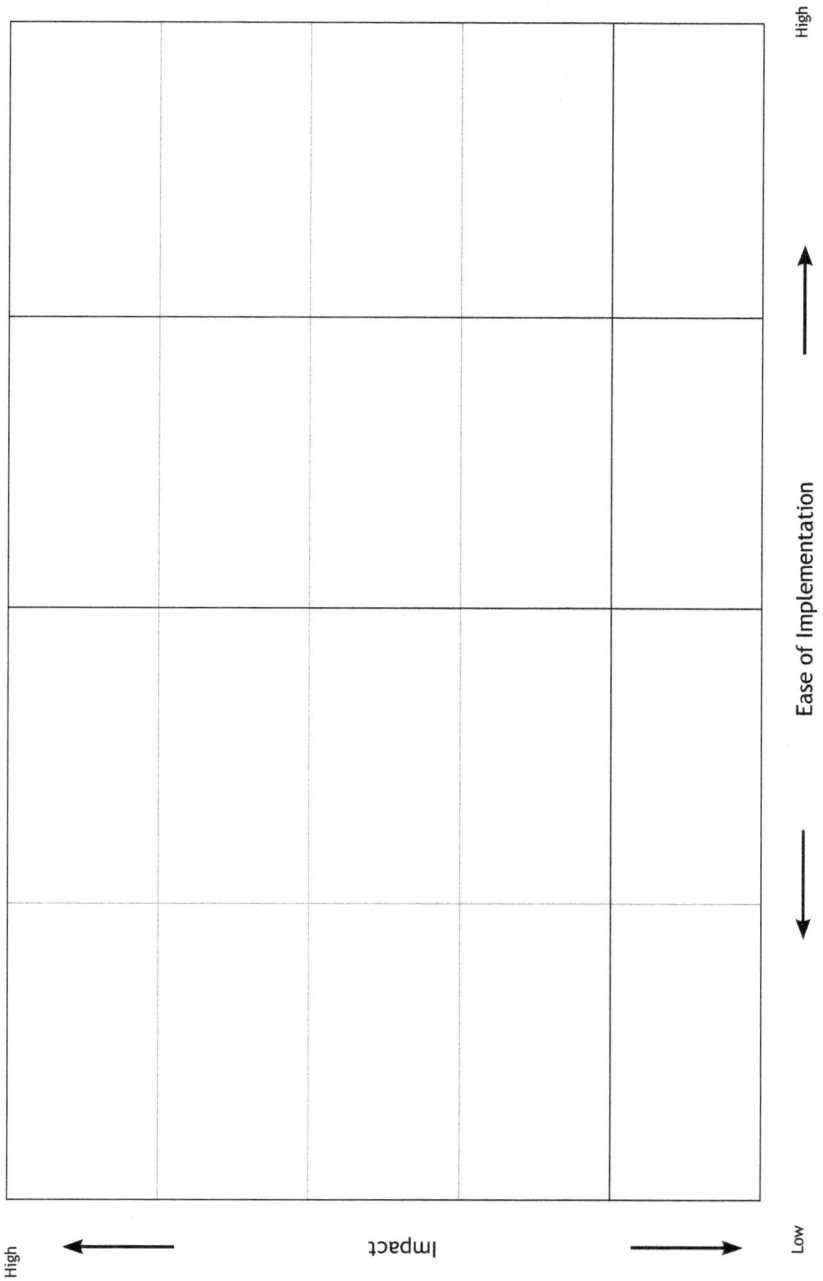

The Highly-Engaged & High-Performing Organization

Next Actions/ Follow-up
- Create step-by-step plans for how the business concept will be put into motion.
- Assign responsibility/ ownership for each task.
- Develop a follow-up plan to make sure each step is accomplished.

Due Date							
Owner							
KPI/ Success Measure							
Actions to Take							
Item/ Initiative							

Developing the Strategy

For more structured approach, try this method.

What to do:
- You'll need whiteboards and/ or flip charts.
- Gather your team.
- You'll need one large room for all-hands discussion, and smaller breakout rooms for the group assignments.
- No need to follow the process exactly - pick and choose what you feel will work best for you.

The Highly-Engaged & High-Performing Organization

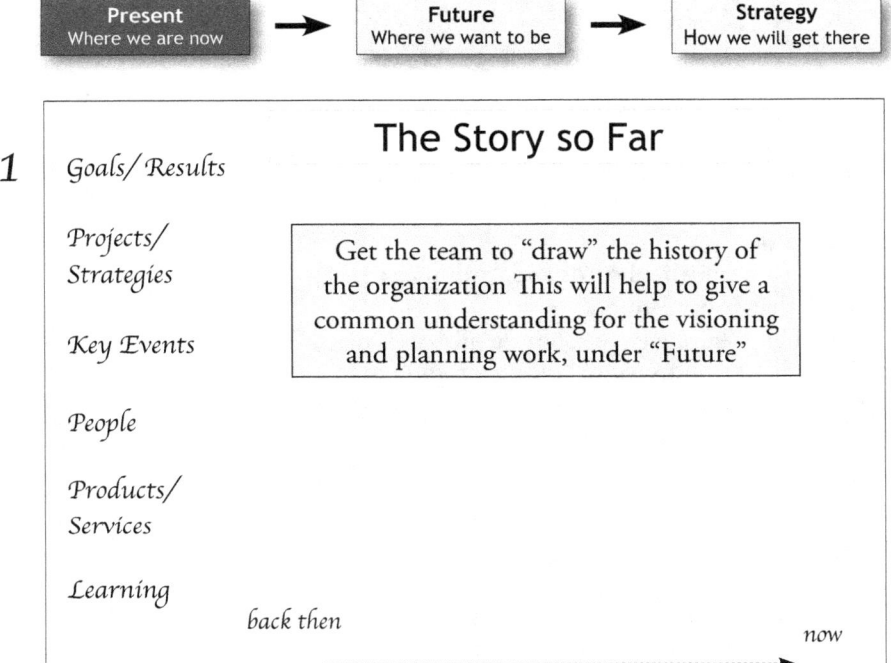

Present - Where Are are Now

3

Strengths	Weaknesses
Capabilities, competitive advantages	Gaps in capabilities
USPs (unique selling points)	Lack of competitive strength
Resources, assets, people	Reputation, presence, vulnerabilities
Experience, knowledge, data	Time-scales, deadlines
Financial reserves, likely returns	Cash flow, supply chain
Marketing - reach, distribution, awareness	Distractions from core activities
Innovation aspects, location/ geography	Morale, leadership
Value, quality, qualifications, certifications	Qualifications, certifications
Processes, systems, IT, communications	Processes, systems, IT, communications
Opportunities	**Threats**
Market developments,	Political effects
Competitors' vulnerabilities	Legislative effects
Industry or lifestyle trends	Environmental effects
Technology development, innovation	IT developments
Global influences, new markets, niche markets	Market demands, competitor intentions
Geography, export, import	Vital contracts, partners
Business and product development	Sustaining internal capabilities
Information & research	Obstacles, loss of key staff
Partnerships, agencies, distribution	Financial backing, Economy
Seasons, weather, fashion influences	Seasons, weather effects

Conduct a SWOT analysis

4

Ask - Are we where we need to be?

High Business Potential

Should we really be doing these? Or should we do more? | **Taking us to the future!**

- Web Hosting
- E-Commerce Application Development
- Business Consulting Services
- Mobile Solutions
- Interactive Marketing Platforms
- We're missing something here!!

- Portal Redirection
- Server Maintenance and Support
- Knowledge Management Solutions
- Web Page Interface Design

Get out of this? | **Cash Generator**

Low ← Ability to Compete → High

The Highly-Engaged & High-Performing Organization

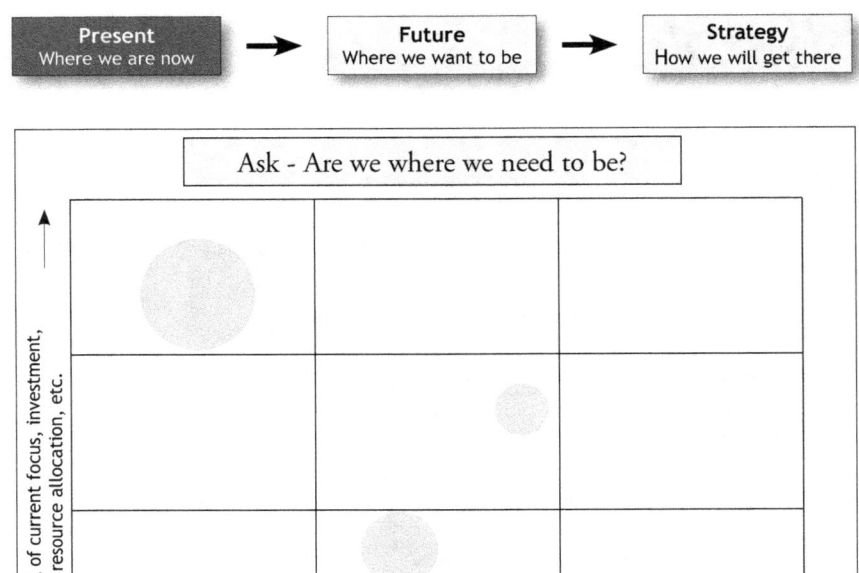

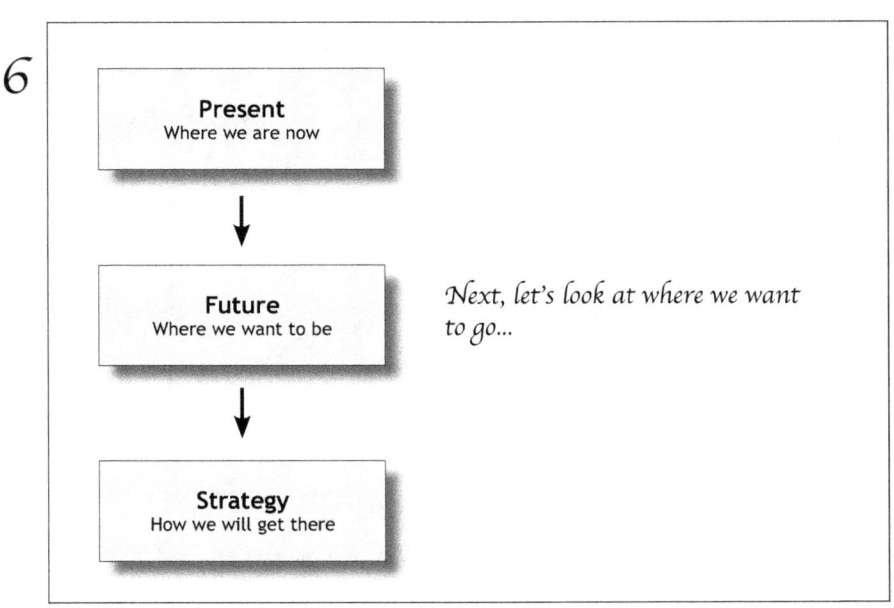

Future - Where We Want to Be

| Present — Where we are now | → | **Future — Where we want to be** | → | Strategy — How we will get there |

7 Looking Ahead

"What would you like to say about Our Organization three years from now?"

For example

"We Shocked the Industry with our Innovation, Leadership and Quality...

.... And we are proud of what we have done"

> This can be a 'brainstorming' session, perhaps in small teams then report back to the main group.

8 Our Purpose

1) List products/ services
- What themes do we see?
- What's unique? What differentiates us from others?

2) List customers/ customer types
- Who are our customers?
- What do they really want/need from us?

3) Describe our business from the viewpoint of customers
- To them, what is the purpose of our organization/ our team?

4) What is the end result we offer?
- What result do we offer, not just products and services

In ~25 words, create the purpose of your organization/ team

For example:
"We help leaders create highly-engaged and high-performing organizations that achieve extraordinary results"

> If you need to revisit the Vision/ Mission, try running this session from page 63.

The Highly-Engaged & High-Performing Organization

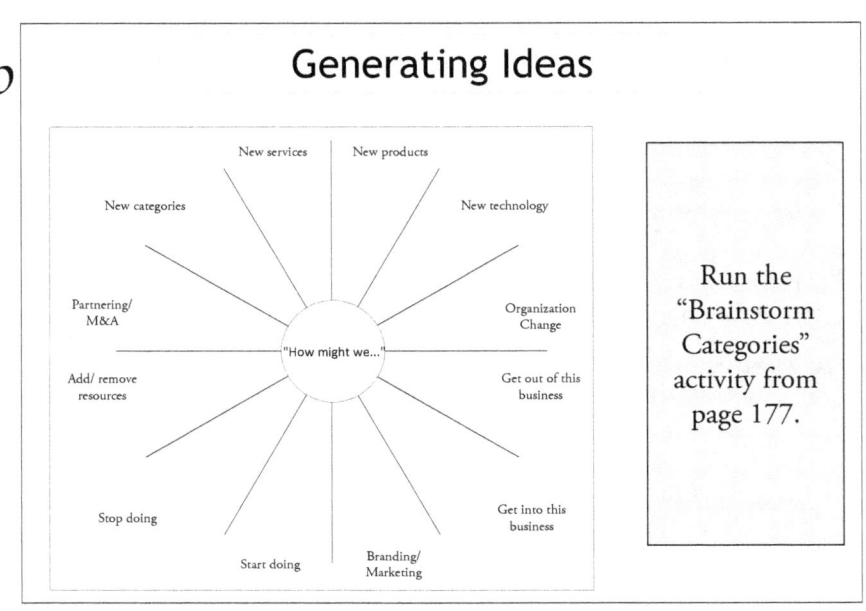

Future - Where We Want to Be

11
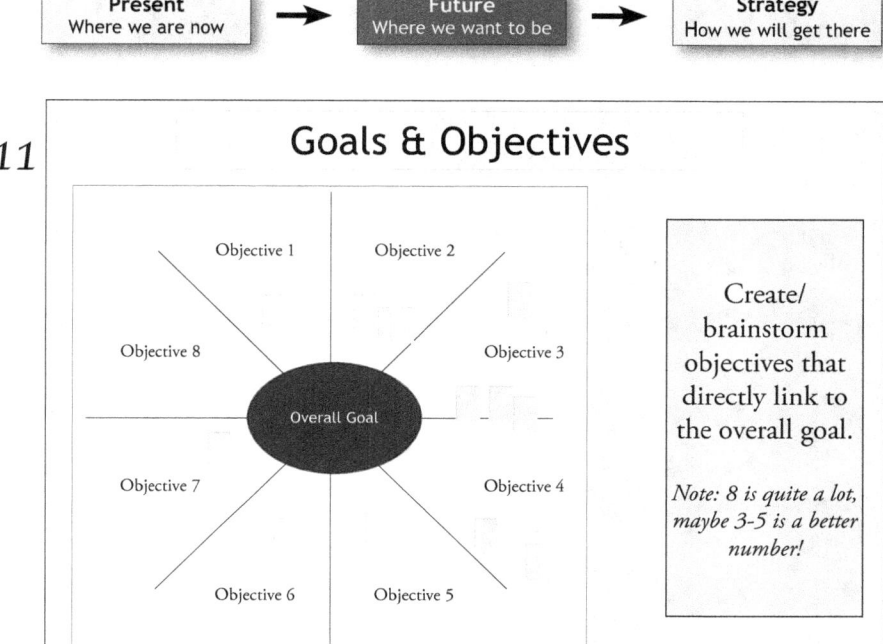

12
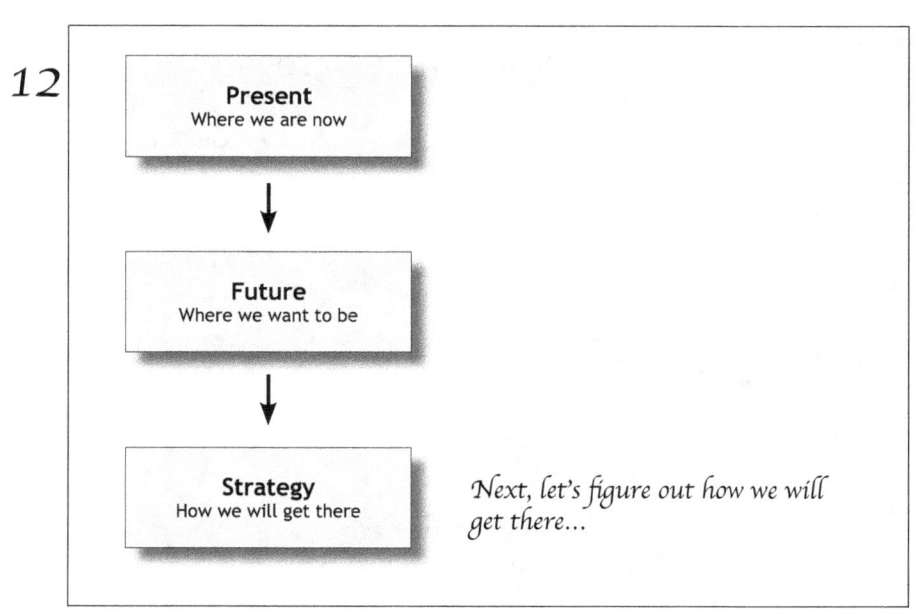

The Highly-Engaged & High-Performing Organization

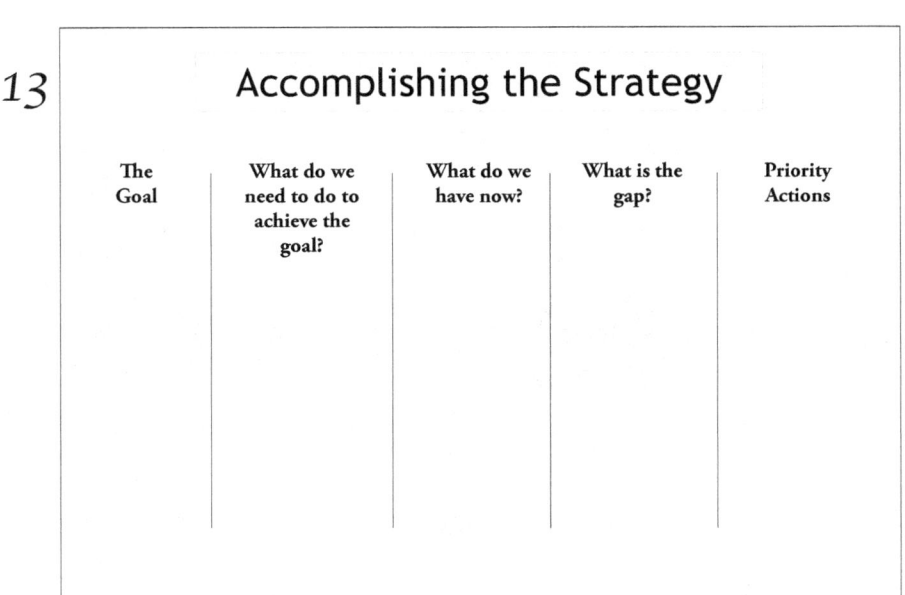

Strategy - How We Will Get There

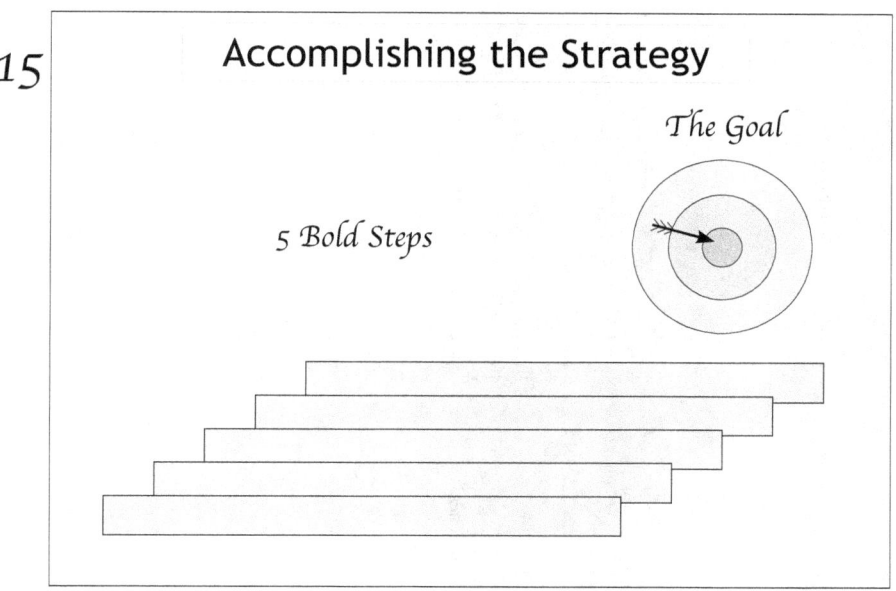

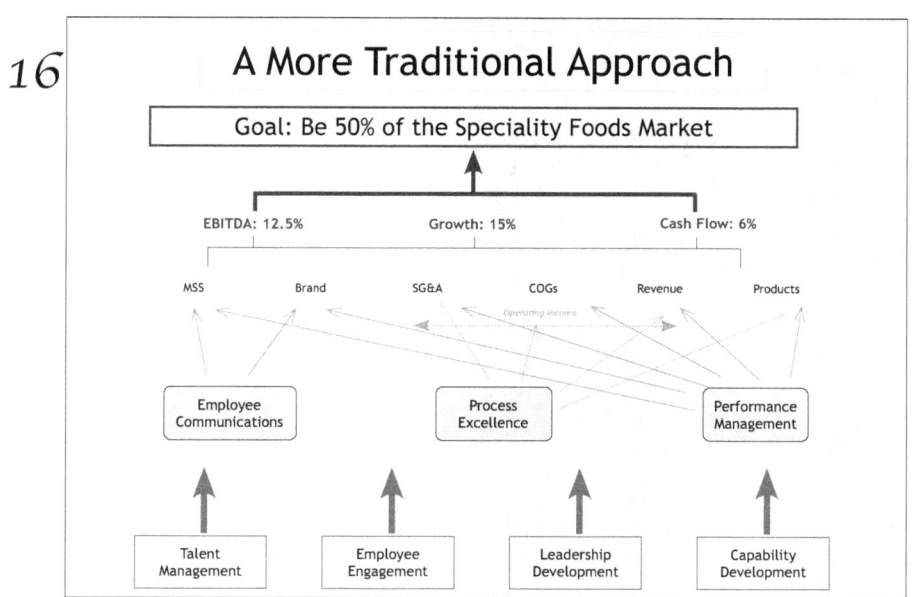

Presentation Structure: Presenting a Product Category/ Service/ New Business Area

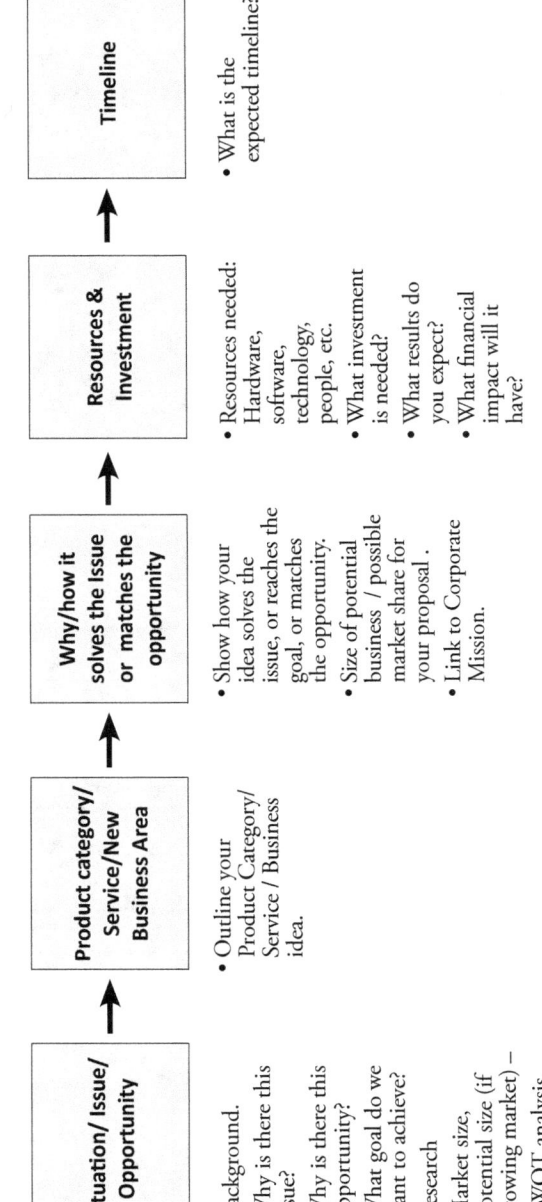

Strategy - How We Will Get There

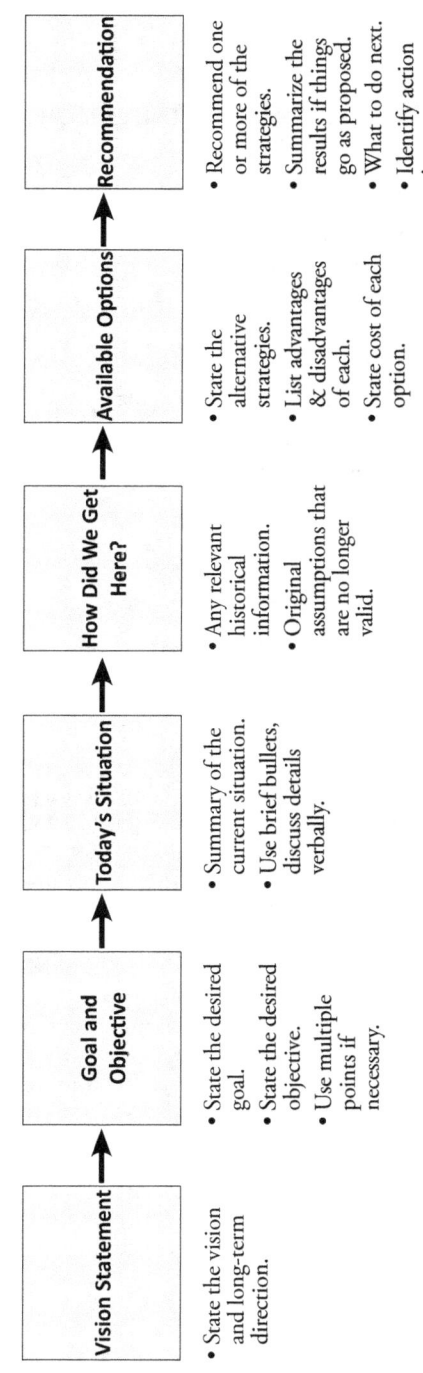

The Highly-Engaged & High-Performing Organization

> **Delivering Objectives & Performance Reviews**

The examples on the following pages were originally developed as a reference for non-native English speakers when designing & delivering objectives, together with a structure & 'vocabulary' for handling formal performance reviews.

We've included them here as a reference for native and non-native speakers alike, as the examples might prove helpful for anyone in a managerial/leadership role, wherever they are in the world..

A Process for Deploying SMART Objectives

**Team Meeting
Align team Objectives
to Corporate Objectives**

1. Explain that the purpose of this meeting is to establish the Team's Objectives for the coming year.
2. Start by reviewing the Corporate mission and objectives.
3. Show the linkage through the Division, Dept Mission & Objectives.
4. Then move on to the creating Team's Objectives.
5. Note: The team manager should come to the meeting with provisional/draft objectives. However, these might change as a result of this team meeting.

Delivering Objectives

2 — Individual Preparation
Objectives, KPIs,
Individual Development Plan

1. Individuals choose the objectives that will deliver the most value to their customers and that will impact team objectives to the furthest extent.
2. Note that not all individual objectives impact the team objectives.
3. KPIs/Measurements: Individuals should choose measures of success, which consider both the final result as well as the process of getting there.

3 — 1:1 Manager/Employee
Finalize Individual Objectives
Finalize Individual Development Plan

1. Clarify how the individual's Job Role align to/supports the Dept., BU and Company Mission & Objectives. You can make use of Job description here, too.
2. Employee presents his/her objectives (or manager presents objectives to the employee, depending on which method you use).
3. Manager/ employee discussion & agreement.
4. Confirm performance expectations according to those objectives - i.e, how you will measure your staff.
5. Finalize IDP.

1 Conducting the Team Meeting

State Meeting Purpose

"The objective of this meeting is to understand our team's mission and objectives and how they relate to the corporate mission and objectives. We'll define our customers, the products/services that we offer, and what our team can do to achieve our objectives.

Then we'll see if we can improve on the team objectives. Then, after the meeting, we'll work on our individual objectives, which we'll discuss in 1:1 meetings next week."

Link Corporate Mission & Objectives to Team Mission and Objectives

- Re-affirm the corporate mission, strategy and team mission.
- Discuss each team objective as it relates to the overall mission, strategy and customers.
- Ensure everyone understands how the provisional/draft objectives are important for the team.

Discuss Customers

- Which customers do we spend the majority of our time on?
- Which customers account for the highest revenue for the team?
- If the team mainly has internal customers: Which people/BUs derive the most value from our efforts?
- Does the team spend the appropriate amount of time on our most time-consuming customers?
- Does the team deliver value to our most valuable customers?

Delivering Objectives

Discuss Products/ Services

↓

- Which products/services do you spend the most time and effort on?
- If the team mainly has external customers: What products/services account for the highest revenue for the team?
- If the team mainly has internal customers: Which products/services deliver the most value to our customers?

Improving & Supporting the Team Objectives

↓

- Does everyone understand the objectives and feel they are important?
- How can these objectives be improved?
- Individual brainstorming to Identify actions to take to support the objectives.
- Discuss how the individual actions support the team objectives.

 When complete, move to Step 2: Individual Preparation
(not covered in this section)

Useful Framework for Discussing Customers & Products/ Services

Customers / Revenue from Products

Time/Effort ↑ High

External Customer - Revenue/ Value <u>to</u> our team
Internal Customer - Value <u>from</u> our team   → High

193

3 Delivering Objectives in a 1:1 Meeting

Clarify how the individual's Job Role aligns to/supports the Dept., BU and Company Mission & Objectives

"As you know, our overall company mission is to 'Be a world-class company that inspires the planet through innovation and infotainment technologies.' And, our BU Mission continues to be to 'Produce and market the best in-vehicle infotainment equipment in the world.'

In support of these missions, our BU is focusing on four key areas: Revenue growth of 30%; Being the market leader by achieving 25% market share; Improving operational income by achieving $20 million operational income for our BU; and launching 10 innovative new products that inspire our customers.

In your role as a Product Development & Marketing Engineer, your main responsibility is to develop and launch two new products for this year and also create the roadmap for the coming three years. Also, you'll need to improve quality of some of our phase two products. Your role closely links to our BU goal of launching integrated new products and gaining market share, which will make a strong contribution to operating income and hopefully result in delighted customers. Your role is very important and is also changing, and so I've created an updated job description for the coming year."

Employee presents his/her objectives
(or manager presents objectives to the employee, depending on which method you use)

"Ok, next let's look at your objectives for the coming year. Three of your objectives support the department goal of launching 10 new products, which supports the BU goal of 'New products that inspire and perform,' which itself comes under the Company goal of 'New product introductions that delight our customers.'

You also have a more personal objective of improving prioritization and time management, which comes under the company goal of building 'a Highly engaged and innovative organization that achieves extraordinary results.'

Delivering Objectives

Employee presents his/ her objectives *contd.*	So, let's look at the first objective, which is to develop and launch 2 "A" products that delight customers, and which will also be on track to achieve launch sales projections, by the end of the fiscal year. This is the most important goal and has a weighting of 40%. How do you see this objective?"
Manager/ employee discussion around those objectives ↓	Discussion continues around the objectives. For example: • "Do you feel this goal is achievable?" • "What resources do you need to achieve this goal?" • "Is this something you feel is a worthwhile activity for you?" • "Well, I can understand that you feel this goal is very difficult and challenging, however I would like to ask you to do your very best to achieve it, as it's very important contribution towards the team goal of 10 new product introductions this year." • "Ok, I see, I wasn't aware that the technology required for this objective is not yet available in the market. Let's see what we can do to modify the expectations for this objective." • "Let's see if this objective passes the SMART test. Specific – it's easy to tell exactly what is being produced: yes. Measurable – there are concrete success indicators: yes, we have those. Achievable – it can reasonably be accomplished: we have some challenges here but I believe you can do this. Relevant – it fits with our business objectives: definitely yes. Time-bound – the completion date and conditions are clear: yes, although we may need to add some more time for the technology study to be completed."
Confirm performance expectations according to those objectives	"Good , I'm glad we have been able to agree on those key objectives for the coming year. Next, let's confirm the performance expectations. For each objective there is a key measurement, and also a weighting. Let's look again at the first objective, which is to 'Develop and launch 2 "A" products that delight customers and also be on track to achieve launch sales projections,' by end of fiscal year, with a weighting of 40%.

Confirm performance expectations according to those objectives
contd.

In terms of performance, if all the criteria are achieved then that will be "Meets Expectations." However, if one product is launched more than one month earlier than planned, then I'll consider that as "Exceeds Expectations." And if both products are launched more than one month early, then I'll see that as "Outstanding."

Of course, there are other objectives with different weightings, so we'll have to take those into account in order to get view your overall performance. So, please do not forget about your time management goal - even though it has a weighting of 10%, it can still make a big difference to the final assessment. Shall we go through each objective one-by-one and confirm performance expectations?"

Finalize IDP

"Let's look at some short-term development opportunities. I'd like to suggest that we put you into a writing skills workshop. There is a very good one available through the company university. I think this will help you to not only write better product proposals, but also will help you with writing emails that are precise, to the point and get better results.

I'd also like to suggest that you attend both an assertive communications seminar, and also a presentation skills workshop. These will help you to develop positive and powerful communication skills, which will then help you improve interactions with your internal and external stakeholders. How does that sound?"

Finish

"Great. I think we have covered everything. So, let's confirm where are. We've finalized your objectives for the coming year, but we have extended the deadline for the sound quality objective due to the need to develop new technologies and processes.

We've discussed and agreed performance expectations for all the objectives. And we set your individual development plan to focus on writing skills, but also we've added an advanced Code R programming course to help you get up to speed on the latest developments, which you'll need for

Delivering The Performance Review

Finish
contd.

the noise canceling software.

That's it. If, when you get back to your desk, you find that we have overlooked something, then please let me know. I look forward to working with you, and I'm sure we can make a great contribution to 'Producing and marketing the best in-vehicle infotainment equipment in the world.'"

Delivering the Performance Review

Opening Statement: Appreciation and Purpose

"Thank you for your time today. As you know, we are meeting to discuss your performance during the past year, and the contribution you've made to achieving our team objectives, as well as the overall company objectives.

For the process, I'd like to ask you to start by summarizing how you see that things went, where you achieved your objectives, or surpassed them, and where you see yourself as having fallen short of the goals you had, if any. Then I'll respond with my views and observations, and from there we'll agree on an assessment.

I do see this very much as a two-way conversation, and so there will be plenty of time for you to ask questions or raise any concerns that you have. However, if for some reason we are unable to agree on a performance level, you of course have the option to ask Human Resources for an independent review. Is that OK, or are there any other items you would like to include?"

> Employee Gives Self-Assessment

The Highly-Engaged & High-Performing Organization

Manager Responds

"Thank you, that's a good summary of how things went, and I agree with what you said about the improvements you made in getting contracts completed on time. I think you have made significant developments in that area, so I'd like to recognize you for the work you did, particularly regarding how you started using the 7 Habits time-management method. Very good.

That said, I think there are still some areas regarding quality of contracts that we need to discuss. As you know, there are two goals for contracts. The first is to be completed on time, but the second is to meet the requirements of the client without the need for further revisions. And, although your on-time-completion rate moved from 60% to 90%, the quality rate didn't improve in the same way. In fact, 65% of the contracts submitted required significant revisions, whereas the goal is that no more than 10% should require changes. And the weighing of that goal is 75%, compared to the on-time weighting of 25%.

How do you see that? Why do you think there were so many revisions needed?

Well, although I accept that there were several misunderstandings regarding the needs of the client, I do think it is important for you to make sure these needs are fully understood - and agreed - with the client before starting to write the contract. And, I think that you didn't fully do that.

So, I think it's reasonable to say that your performance for this goal is 'Needs Improvement.'"

Career Discussion

"Now let's move on to career goals. Last year we discussed a move overseas, to be part of the London team, which would hopefully lead to a future role in the international section after you return to headquarters. Are you still looking for the same career path, or have things changed since then?"

Delivering The Performance Review

Development Discussion

"Let's look at some short-term development opportunities. I'd like to suggest that we put you into a writing skills workshop. There is a very good one available through the company university. I think this will help you to not only write better customer contracts, but also will help you with writing emails that are precise, to the point and get better results.

I'd also like to suggest that you attend both an assertive communications seminar, and also a presentation skills workshop. These will help you to develop positive and powerful communication skills, which will then help you improve interactions with your internal clients. How does that sound?"

Wrap up

"We had a very good and productive discussion, and I'm glad we are in agreement on your achievements for the past year, plus the areas for improvement and development going forward. I'll write up the full appraisal with my signature, and then submit that to you for your signature. If after reading the appraisal you have any other questions or concerns, then please do ask me.

And as you know, next week we'll meet for objectives planning for the coming year. So, before then I'd like to ask you to prepare your ideas for your personal objectives based, which will discuss in more detail next week."

Note: Originally developed as a reference for non-native English speakers

Leading Change Initiatives

Most organizations need to make changes in how business is conducted in order to meet a new and more challenging market environment, whether internally or externally driven. However, whether these are 'big' organizational changes or 'smaller' changes to operating procedures or workflows, change initiatives often finish somewhere between failure and success:

- Many companies hit their cost savings targets, but do not always succeed in hitting their employee performance or employee engagement goals.
- Projects are delivered on time and within budget, but there is still resistance in the organization from the people it affects most: those who are in the front-line of the business.
- Changes that are not handled well can result in reduced buy-in for future change initiatives – making things tougher the next time around.
- Or, in the worst case: Projects are not delivered, new initiatives fail, things don't change, things get even worse.

Points to Consider
- Are you getting the business results you want from change?
- Have changes impacted employee engagement, organizational morale?
- Is the organization executing well, but employees either do not show buy-in, or even do not understand?
- Do you see resistance to change in your organization?
- Does performance dip after a redesign?
- Do you have good data to tell you how employees feel about change, or where the real issues are?
- Do you sense that your organization is suffering from "Change Fatigue?"
- Is the organization learning from its mistakes?

Shortening the "Change Curve"

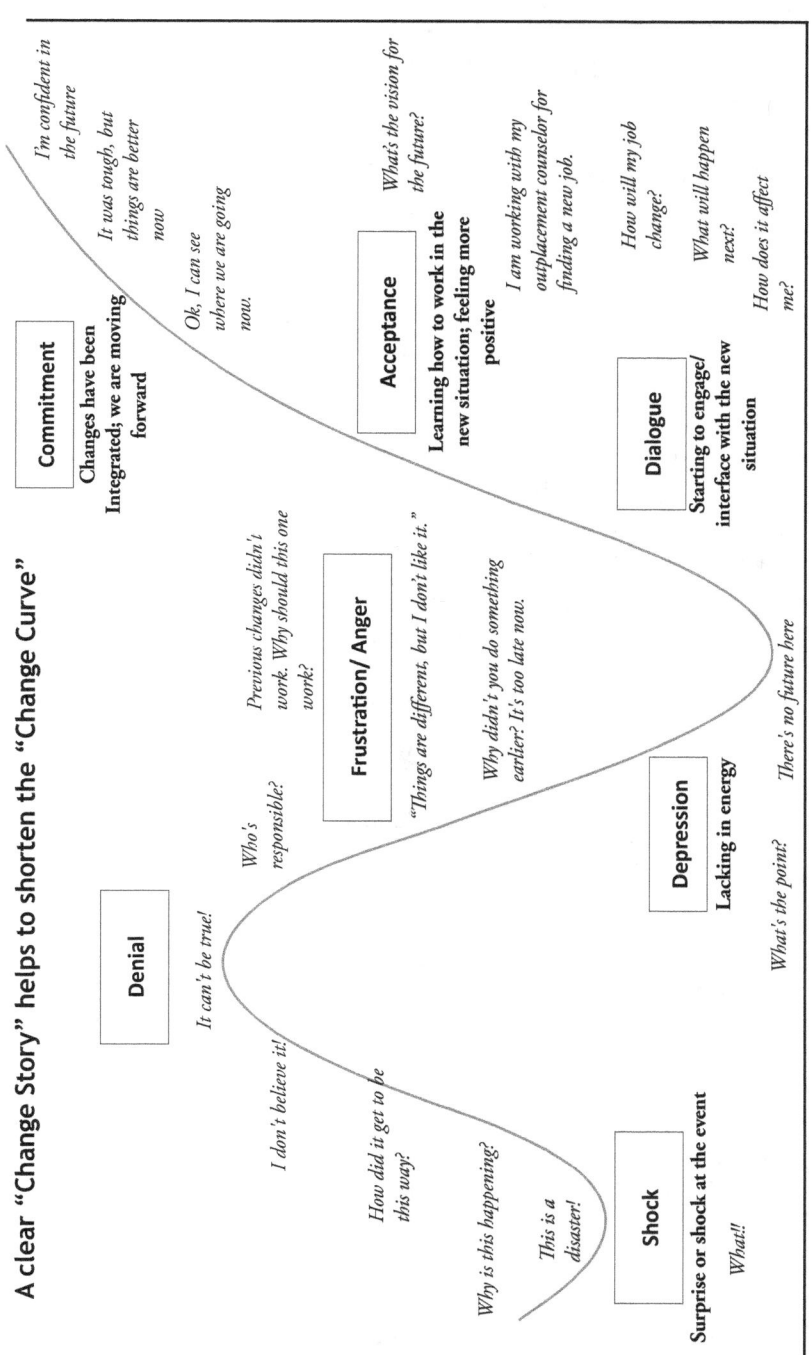

201

The Highly-Engaged & High-Performing Organization

7 Steps to Creating the Change Story

1) Clarify Why Change is Needed
- Why do we need to change?
- What is the vision for the change?
- Why is it the most effective solution?

2) Establish Needs Different Attitudes, Mindsets & Behaviors
- What new attitudes and mindset(s) will be necessary?
- What new behaviours will be needed?

3) Evaluate Impact How People & Business will be impacted
- How will people be impacted?
- How will people be affected?
- How will their world/environment change?
- How will it affect accountability, decision making, responsibility, etc.?
- What are the financial impacts – personal, company?
- What are the likely issues?
- What do we need to prepare for?

4) Conduct RACI Analysis
- Responsible, Accountable, Consulted, Informed.

5) Identify Change Agents
- Key people who can promote this change to other people within the organization.

6) Set Milestones & Measures
- Dates
- Events
- Timings

7) Create the Change Story
- Case/Reason for Change
- The Challenge Ahead
- Individual Impact

7 Steps to Creating the Change Story

1) Clarify Why Change is Needed

↓

1) Why do we need to change?
- What are the driving forces, the threats?
- What are the opportunities?
- What happens if we do nothing?
- What is the vision for the change?
- What will be the outcome?
- What is the focus of the change (e.g. productivity, quality...)
- What will success look like?
- What measures/KPIs will we use?
- Why is it the most effective solution?

2) Establish Needs Different Attitudes, Mindsets & Behaviors

↓

2) Key Mindsets
- What new attitudes and mindset shifts will be necessary?
- Key Behaviours:
- What will people do and say differently?

3) Evaluate Impact How People & Business will be impacted

↓

3) What Will the Impact be?
- What are the driving forces, the threats?
- What are the opportunities?
- How will people be affected?
- How will their world/environment change?
- How will it affect accountability, decision making, responsibility, etc.?
- What are the financial impacts – personally, company?
- What issues are there likely to be?
- What do we need to prepare for?

4) Conduct RACI Analysis

Responsible	• People who perform an activity / decision.
Accountable	• The person who is ultimately accountable for an activity / decision. • Includes yes / no and power of veto. • Only one "A" can be assigned to an activity or decision. • Can also be "Responsible" for the activity.
Consulted	• People who must be consulted before a decision or action.
Informed	• People who must be informed after a decision or action.

Item/Event	Responsible	Accountable	Consulted	Informed

7 Steps to Creating the Change Story

5) Identify Change Agents

Change Agent: Any person who:
- Understands the need for change.
- Proactively takes part in the change process.
- Promotes change to other people within the organization.
- Influences other people to go through the change process.

Name	Why this person would be a good Change Agent

6) Set Milestones & Measures

Milestones & Measures
- Items
- Actions
- Date
- KPI
- Owner

Item/Event	Actions	Date	KPI	Owner

7) Create the Change Story

Case for Change

- Why do we have to change? e.g.,
  - The industry – economics, success factors, change drivers.
  - Our capabilities vs. the competition.
- What is the focus of the change (e.g., productivity, quality…)
- What is the vision of the future after this change?
- How will our organization look and feel after we have changed?
- What are the anticipated costs and benefits?

Challenge & Opportunity Ahead

- What challenges will we face during this change?
- What strengths can we build on during the transformation?
- The new opportunity ahead, and why/how we will get there.

Individual Impact

- What will it mean for the people affected?
- What new skills/behaviours will be needed
- What do people need to stop/start/continue doing?

7 Steps to Creating the Change Story

Forms of Communication

		Shock/ Denial	Frustration/ Anger	Depression	Dialogue	Acceptance
Expect		• "No one warned us this was coming."	• "This is really a stupid idea…."	• "What's the point? It will never finish."	• "Is it OK to try doing it like this?"	• "It makes sense, its beginning to work."
Communicate		• Why the change is needed. • When people will know more.	• Listen and understand. • Repeat the vision.	• Evidence on progress. • Honest and realistic. • How jobs will change. • Milestones ahead.	• Examples of where change is working. • Problems / solutions. • Repeat the vision.	• Remind of the past. • The wider impact of the team's effort – how others are learning from us.
How		• Bring people together. • Take-away note/hand-out explaining the Change / Follow up.	• Group discussions. • One to one. • Proof points on why change is needed.	• Weekly 10 min update. • Easy short-term tasks. • Outside input and individual feedback.	• Celebrate successes. • One to one support. • Regular problem solving meetings.	• Celebrate a major milestone. • Arrange workshops to pick-up what was learned.

The Highly-Engaged & High-Performing Organization

Communication Plan Template

Audience	Item	Messages	Media/ method	Who	When/ Frequency	Where

Employee Engagement Full Question Set

The Highly-Engaged Organization

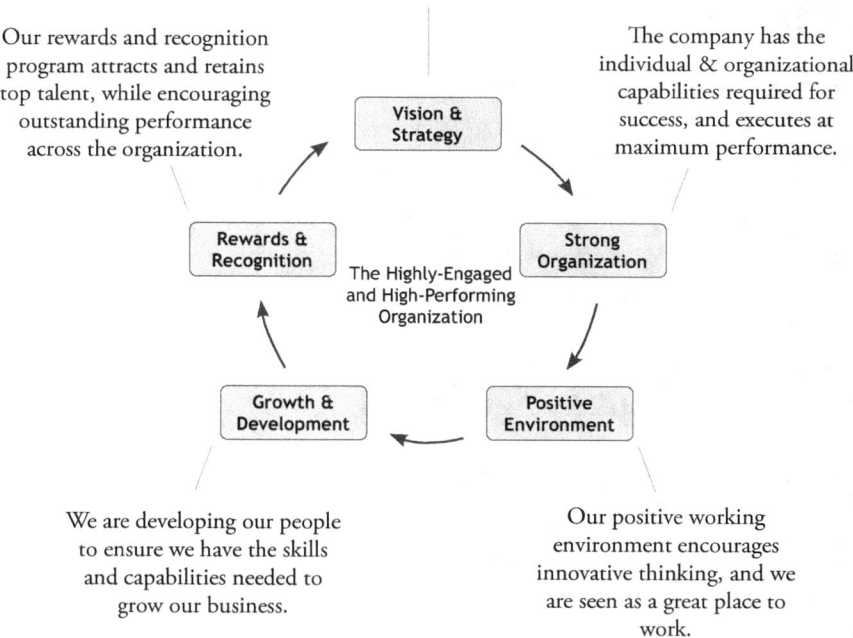

The whole organization is aligned to the vision, and working together to implement and achieve the business strategy and objectives.

Our rewards and recognition program attracts and retains top talent, while encouraging outstanding performance across the organization.

The company has the individual & organizational capabilities required for success, and executes at maximum performance.

We are developing our people to ensure we have the skills and capabilities needed to grow our business.

Our positive working environment encourages innovative thinking, and we are seen as a great place to work.

"Engaged" employees are aligned to the organization's mission & vision, and personally want the organization to succeed

The Highly-Engaged & High-Performing Organization

Employee Engagement Full Question Set
For reference - you might decide on a completely different approach!

Vision & Strategy
1. I understand the Vision of my company.
2. I can empathize with the Vision of my company.
3. I understand the strategies by which my Business Group will achieve its goals.
4. I feel connected to organizational strategies.
5. I understand what is expected of me.
6. I think that I am given the authority necessary for getting my job done.
7. I have confidence in my Business Group's senior management to lead us to achieve our goals and objectives.
Strong Organization
8. I feel the organization where I work is strong.
9. I feel there is a strong sense of urgency.
10. Our Business Group's leaders place appropriate focus on strengthening our organization.
11. My company is making the changes necessary to compete effectively.
12. My Work Group eliminates non-critical tasks and processes.
13. The decision-making process in my Business Group is consistent and trustworthy.
14. I am proud to work for my company.
Positive Environment
15. I like the kind of work that I do.
16. My job makes good use of my skills and abilities.
17. I am encouraged to take risks.
18. I feel encouraged to come up with new and better ways of doing things.
19. In my Work Group, innovation and creative thinking are actively encouraged.
20. My Work Group has a clear understanding of our customers' needs.
21. I hope to continue working at my company into the future.
22. Looking at my situation as a whole, I am satisfied with working at my company.
23. The office environment at my company helps me to work productively.
24. I have the flexibility to balance the needs of my work and personal life.
25. In my Work Group, diversity among members is respected.
26. In my company, people can trust one another.

Employee Engagement Full Question Set

27. In my Business Group, inappropriate behaviours are clearly set out as being unacceptable.
28. In my Work Group, different viewpoints and values are recognized.
29. In my Work Group, bottom-up approaches are respected.
30. I am able to speak candidly with the leader of my Work Group about problems and matters I am concerned about.
31. I would want to introduce a family member/ friend to my company as an excellent place to work.
Growth & Development
32. I think my company possesses the appropriate mechanisms to support the development of individual skills.
33. I have received the training I need to do a quality job.
34. I feel my skills are developing.
35. I receive ongoing feedback that helps me improve my performance.
36. I am satisfied with the feedback I receive.
Rewards & Recognition
37. My manager evaluates me fairly and in accordance with my ability to perform.
38. I think that if I am able to fulfill the role expected of me, my successes will be recognized.
39. The leader of my Business Group is always prepared to assume management responsibility for the results of his/her subordinates' work.
40. I feel my ideas are listened to/heard.

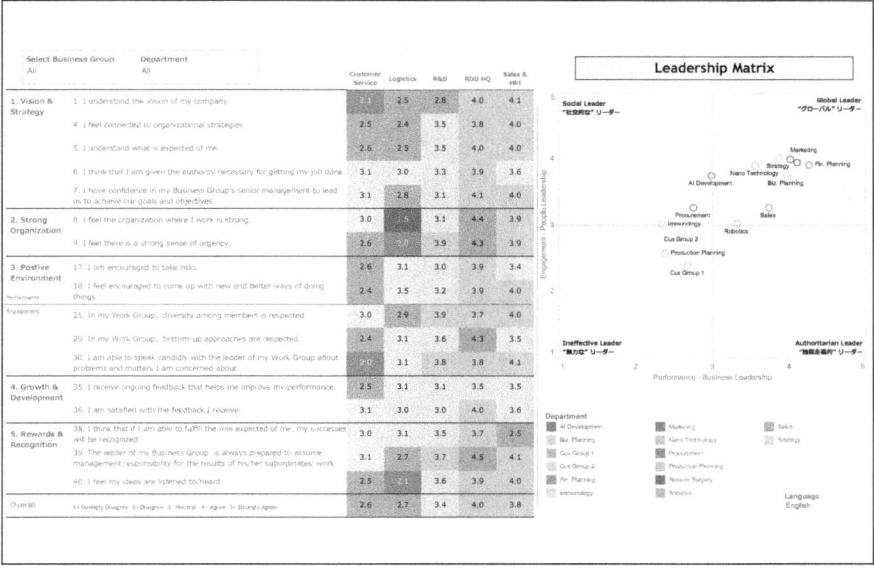

The Highly-Engaged & High-Performing Organization

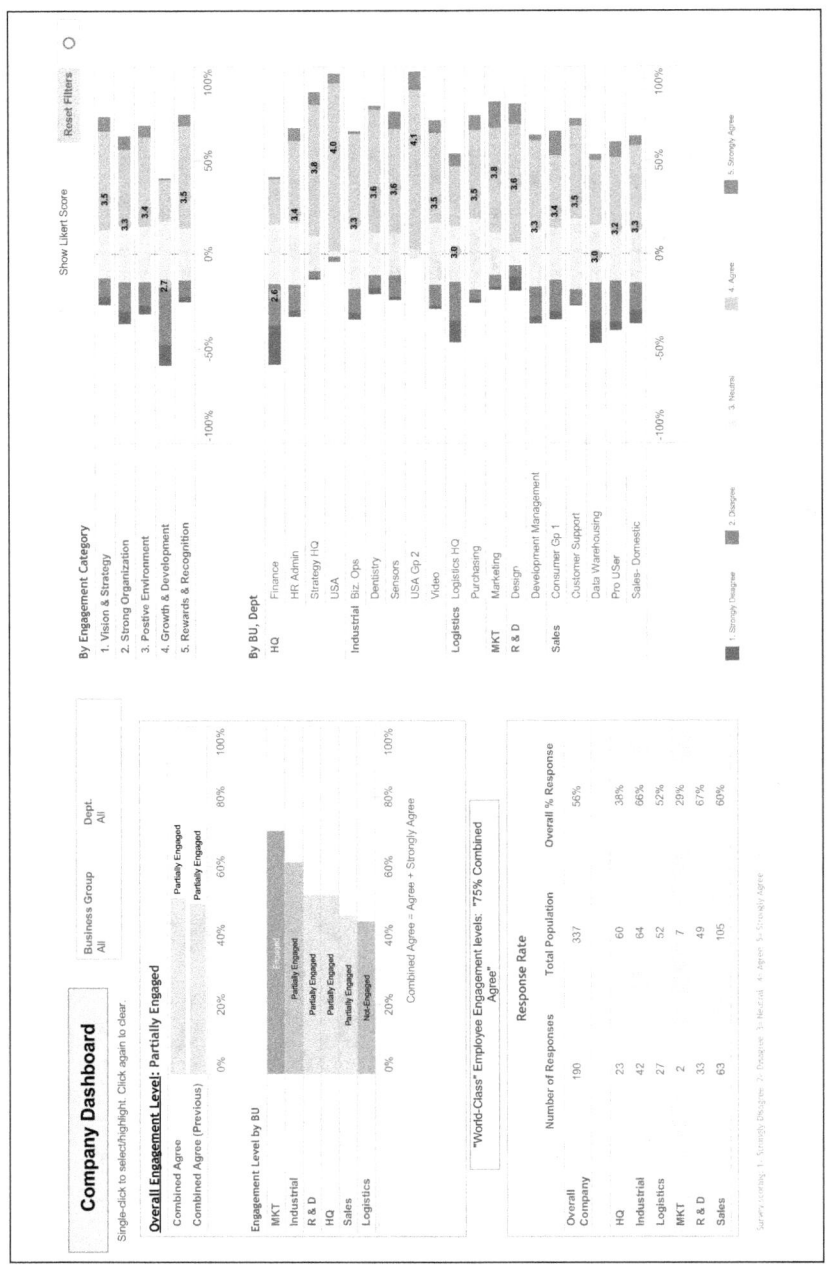

Working With HR on Leadership Interventions

Working with HR to develop an HR solution/ strategy to help the organization succeed

The Highly-Engaged & High-Performing Organization

What HR "Leadership Interventions" Might Look Like

In this section we'll look at organizational and leadership solutions from the HR point of view.

So, why do we think this will be useful?
- We define an HRBP like this:
  - "A Strategic HR Business partner is an HR professional who interfaces with the business, providing human capital solutions to enable the organization to implement its strategy and achieve business and organizational goals. The goal is to create a Highly-Engaged and High-Performing Organization that Achieves Extraordinary Results"
- So, you can see that, ideally, the HRBP is working with you to achieve the same goals.

And...
- The working relationship with your HR Business Partner can be critical to the success of your organization - so we feel it will be helpful to see things from the HR point of view.

Two Examples
- Example Organizational Analysis Report   page 216
- Example HR Intervention/ Case Study   page 225

Working With HR

Please note that the following pages are written for HRBPs* - so at times you might feel we are talking to HR rather than to you as a leader of your team or organization

We hope this doesn't cause too much confusion!, but it will give you some insights into the kind of leadership interventions you might need - or want - to implement in your own organization

* Taken from *The Practical HRBP*, available on Amazon

Working With HR - Case Studies

> **Example Organizational Analysis Report**
> *Created by one of our consultants for a client*
> *(full report withheld - sorry!)*

Here's the question-set used for the 1:1 meetings with the leadership team, as well as other key managers:

Overall
1. Please tell me about your business, what you do, your customers (Internal, external) etc.
2. What challenges are you facing at the moment?
3. What are the positive/negative aspects of working for this new "international" organization?
4. Do you feel the company employees have a good understanding of the new partnership with xxxx?
5. Overall, what's working well, not working so well?

Strategy
6. How would you summarize the organization's strategy?
7. What are your team/BU priorities for the next 3 years?
8. Imagine the CEO, is talking about the success we've achieved (in 3 years from now). What would you like him to say?
9. Right now, how do we compare to the "Desired" State?

Organization
10. How would you describe the organizational culture?
11. What are the organizational Strengths and weaknesses?
12. How effective is cross-department communications?
13. How effective is the decision-making process?
14. What opportunities do you see for improvement?
15. What is the meeting/ information sharing process? How is info shared, is there a regular team meeting, senior level, departmental level?

People
16. How would you assess the quality of people in the organization?
17. Do you feel your organization has the right skills and capabilities to take us to the future?
18. Are there gaps in recruiting, job training, and development that need to be addressed?

Leadership*
19. What do the organization's leaders need to do more of?
20. What do they need to stop doing or do less of?

Measurements
21. How are goals set for you and your group?
22. How are you measured?
23. What additional or different measures would you suggest?
24. Performance appraisal system: How do you see it?

Moving Forward
25. What additional tools and resources do you need, if any? (e.g. technology, systems, information, people)

Finally
26. What are the three priority issues that, if addressed/solved, would have the greatest impact on the organization overall
27. What recommendations do you have with regard to organizational structure, culture, etc?

The Executive Summary from the final report

COMPANY = Name of this organization
Parent/HQ Company Family = Name of new owners
Previous Management Company = Name of previous owners

Building a Highly-Engaged and Innovative Organization that Achieves Extraordinary Results

Situation
COMPANY has recently become part of the "Parent/HQ Company Family," having previously been under the management of "Previous Management Company", which will bring changes to COMPANY's:
- Business strategy and product range
- People, culture and organization
- Way of thinking, operating
- Way of communicating: internally, externally and internationally
- Brand image

An organizational assessment was conducted at COMPANY, with the objective of gaining a high-level view from senior management and their direct reports on issues, concerns, positive aspects, and recommendations for the future.

Working With HR - Case Studies

Decision required:
Which of the below recommendations to implement/ prioritize:

Background
Although COMPANY has many gifted and talented people in the workforce, in recent years there has been a reduced emphasis on people and organizational development, mainly due to cost reduction requirements under the previous ownership. With the change of ownership and direction, this presents an opportunity to do things differently and build a "Highly Engaged and Innovative Organization that Achieves Extraordinary Results."

Assessment

Vision & Strategy - Not clear
Although there are several areas that need addressing, the most consistent message from the interviews is the need to create a clear "Direction" for COMPANY, comprising Vision, Mission and Strategy - and to communicate this so that Employees understand the organizational Vision & Strategy, and are clear on how their work relates to it. Much of this story is already underway within the current marketing department.

Strong Organization - Is Structure properly aligned to Strategy?
The current structure may not be optimal, especially for supporting and implementing the emerging strategy. As part of this, the decision-making process needs clarification, as does the level of responsibility of the various managers (or the level of responsibility that they themselves take). In addition, some mid-level managers are reported to be "decision averse," meaning they prefer not to make decisions or take responsibility for the decision.

Strong Organization - Process and procedures not documented. Resource allocation likely inefficient
Many processes and procedures are not documented and are instead located in the mind/ experience of the person in the role. Also, it is not clear if resources have been best allocated. The combination of these two factors raises the issues:
    a) What is the output and corresponding "value" of every role?
    b) Are we working at optimal efficiency and effectiveness?
    c) If a person joins or takes a new role, there is no given process to follow
    d) Different departments do things differently - there may be an opportunity to share best practices

Positive Environment - Engagement levels dropping?
COMPANY has not yet conducted an Employee Engagement survey to measure employee engagement, but it seems possible that engagement levels may have dropped, at least in some parts of the business. Innovation and innovative thinking

are reported to also have dropped – but without objective data this is hard to quantify.

Growth & Development - Lack of opportunities, Lack of Diversity
Many people have been in the same department or same job for many years, which has resulted in some lack of vitality in the organization. In recent years there has also been reduced focus on people development, with almost no training, nor career discussion/ development.

The number of employees aged below 35 is low. This can potentially lead to a stagnating workforce. There are very few female managers, indicating a lack of diversity.

Rewards & Recognition - Performance Management lacks objective performance / pay differentiation
The current performance management system lacks objective performance / pay differentiation and does not incorporate the best practices used by other organizations. For example, it is not easy to identify high performers, neither is there a bonus scheme related to individual performance. There is, however, a base salary adjustment based on performance, but this is rather limiting and does not fully reward high-performers, although it does punish low-performing managers.

The system can also unnecessarily increase someone's salary year-on-year if there is one year of high performance followed by several years of acceptable performance (i.e., the base increase stays in place, at corresponding additional cost). A bonus scheme would introduce more flexibility, especially at manager level.

Main Recommendations

1) Clarify Vision/Mission
Hold a one-day workshop with the senior management team – possibly including some of their key direct reports. Outputs from this session would be:

- Clarification of COMPANY Direction, with aligned understanding of the management team – for a consistent "Voice."
- Agreement on change management/communications plan to get all employees aligned to the new Direction
- Review of organizational structure, capabilities, processes, rewards, and people development.
- Optional: Re-visiting of the COMPANY brand and how it relates to Innovation/User Experience

2) Align Structure to Strategy
- Structure should follow strategy, i.e., define the strategy first, then figure

out the structure and set accountability & decision-making authority, then communicate clearly. Note: Sales has already defined a new structure. Industrial is also taking steps. These should be continually reviewed and optimized as necessary
- Introduce a Leadership program to establish what is expected of managers at all levels in the organization.
- Conduct study for re-locating sales/marketing office.

3) Implement a Culture and Method of Process Excellence (PEX)
- Set up a PEX-Desk, comprised of 2-3 dedicated members, and train them in PEX methodology.
- This team would then identify and address the major issues and opportunities with the relevant departments. The initial focus areas would likely be 1) Cost reduction and 2) Sales process improvement, which would have the biggest impact on operating income.
- The team would be in place for as long as necessary, but this could be a two+ year project.

This will have major benefits in all areas: improving processes, reducing costs, increasing customer satisfaction, reducing waste, and so on.

4) Improve Performance Management
- Improve Performance Management system to ensure all employees have clear individual & departmental goals, aligned to COMPANY strategy, ready for next year's objectives
- Revise salary system to reflect true pay for performance. Due to complexity of revisions and Union negotiations required, the revised pay for performance system is likely to be implemented in 20XX.

5) Improve People Development and Employee Engagement
- Run an EES - Employee Engagement Survey - and use the results to initiate actions to address issues
- Create internal/external Communications function, under CMO
- Set up Talent Development function to focus on people development
- Review COMPANY VALUES – create an updated, more relevant version

Communications
All decisions and initiatives to be effectively communicated through a combination of
- Email
- Open Forums
- Intranet
- Manager/team meetings
- 1:1 meetings with key individuals

Example Organizational Analysis Report

Cost Estimation:

		Cost/Day	Days x Classes	Total Cost (yen)
Process Excellence	PEX Consultant	120,000	22	2,640,000
Business Acumen	Project management	600,000	2 X 3	3,600,000
	Business Communication Presentation/ Negotiation/ Assertiveness	450,000	2 x 5	4,500,000
	Finance for non-finance managers	600,000	2 x 2	2,400,000
	Marketing boot camp	500,000	2 x3	3,000,000
	Business Acumen: case Study	600,000	1 X 4	2,400,000
Leadership	Fundamental Management Skills	600,000	2 x 6	7,200,000
	Global Leadership Skills for Senior Leaders	750,000	2 x 2	3,000,000
EES survey	Annual Survey cost			950,000
Management Offsite: Mission and Direction	Tokyo Location	700,000	2 x 1	1,400,000
				31,090,000

Full report follows below
(sorry, details withheld)

Working With HR - Case Studies

Leadership Interviews
Inputs & comments from the Leadership Questions

<table>
<tr><th colspan="2">Category</th><th>Input/ Comment</th></tr>
<tr><td rowspan="1">Self-Leadership</td><td>Leadership Philosophy, Values</td><td>
• Leadership needs to be based on company fundamental philosophy, values.
• Managers need to be more greedy, more ambitious.
• Many skills are needed to be a leader, but fundamentally the person needs ambition for him/herself as a start.
</td></tr>
<tr><td rowspan="5">Business-Leadership</td><td>Communications</td><td>
• Need better communication from top leadership all the way down to individual contributor: Day to day, Quarterly, Annually, etc. Could be verbal, email, newsletter.
• Directors have responsibility for effective communications in their BU, to ensure employees a) know where COMPANY is going and b) stay informed.
• All directors/Managers need to improve.
• Need to be good listener and good storyteller, too.
• Communication is two way <-->. Can learn a lot from employees with respect.
• Business leaders need to be good communicators.
• Leaders should be a great supporter of the bottom-up system, presenting ideas of the team to the top management.
</td></tr>
<tr><td>Positive Environment</td><td>
• The leader should be a problem solver - and should scan the environment looking for issues and then apply help, advice or resources to solve the problem.
• Promote a Positive Environment for employees to work efficiently and effectively.
</td></tr>
<tr><td>Problem Solving</td><td>
• Managers need to ask the "5 Whys" as a business analysis and/or problem-solving technique.
</td></tr>
<tr><td>Strong Organization</td><td>
• The Leader's job is to create a "Professional Organization" that understands the needs of the market, is market oriented and talks to customers, has direct interaction with customers and can gain trust with them.
• Issue: many employees only know COMPANY, only know their own boss for many years and are not aware of other departments, other products. Need more rotations, especially of younger people.
• Silo Thinking - need to break down these walls/barriers.
• Less flexibility = Less growth.... need more flexibility.
• Create more X-functional teams for driving innovation.
</td></tr>
<tr><td>Technical Competency</td><td>
• Business skill is needed, such as knowledge of costs. P/L. etc. Better data/information is needed. We have so many systems/tools... need simpler, clearer management data.
</td></tr>
</table>

Leadership Interviews - Inputs

	Category	Input/ Comment
Business-Leadership	Vision & Strategy, Goals and KPIs	• Become a Global business unit - (think like one) - with strong products and focus on core competency. • Must have Vision and Clear goals and objectives - create feeling of Purpose, Worthwhile, Belonging. • Direction, Path must be clear and understandable, with clear targets. • Vision gap --> Where we are now and Where we want to be: Leaders must fill this gap. • Goals need to be broken down to individuals more clearly, and clearly connected to the strategy. However, support functions don't always have clear, measurable goals. • Currently, many managers focus on what is in front of them rather than looking ahead to the future. This needs to be addressed. • Many employees feel that their only accountability is their "assigned job" - and that leadership is the manager's job. Need to create a concept of "leadership at all levels." • Global thinking, Global view --> not just "my department, my job". In this case, 'Global' also means having a Group company-wide view. • Excellence: achieve excellence in all things, continue to change/ Improve. • Link: Individual goal --> Department goal --> BU goal --> COMPANY goal --> Vision.
People-Leadership	Building Trust	• Leaders should be Fair: don't have a "favourite" in your team. If you take one person to lunch, you need to take everyone to lunch. • Employees are quiet, possibly "satisfied" with things as they currently are. Perhaps given up on being promoted. • We need some "Loud/Active" people to stir things up. Impact: if people are quiet, then the company loses the chance to change. Maybe people have seen so much re-structuring/redundancies that they have become reluctant to speak up.
	Empowerment	• Top-down instruction was strong in recent years, especially under OWNER, so that people have become reactive instead of proactive - why submit something if it will be rejected?
	Flow: Skills & Capabilities	• Does HR have career details of staff, so that Managers can see this and understand the current skill level of their staff? So directors can see all organization and so make overall, organizational decisions. • The leader must know his/her people and their skill/capability.
	Growth & Development	• We have few successors for senior leadership roles. Let's find key talent and invite to senior management meetings for discussion opportunities - use a more interactive approach.

Working With HR - Case Studies

Use this page for notes

Robo-Doc Case Study

A quick reminder
Please note that the following pages are written for HRBPs - so at times you might feel we are talking to HR rather than to you as a leader of your team or organization

We hope this doesn't cause too much confusion!, but it will give you some insights into the kind of leadership interventions you might need - or want - to implement in your own organization

Working With HR - Case Studies

> "Putting it all Together"

Developing The HR Response
Let's look at a complete example, based on a case study that we use in one of our HRBP workshops, which includes 'instructions' for the participation HRBPs.

We won't go into *all* the details, but there'll be enough information in here to show you the approach we used, which was the Organizational Analysis process combined with several aspects of the 7R method. As we said before, they might seem to be two separate methods, but essentially they are the same thing.

We'll give you the data used, along with the key templates filled in, but won't go into how we got there because a) it would take too long and b) we think you can figure it out anyway. Note that the 'answers' are typically what participants came up with in the workshops.

The Robo-Doc Division
"The Future of Health Care, Right Now"

Background
Six months ago, ABC Healthcare (that's you) acquired The Yokohama Robotic Devices Company - YRDC - which became the main part of the "Robo-Doc" Division based in Japan.

Robo-Doc's purpose is to develop robot-based medical treatments, based on two key technologies:
- "Robotic Surgeon" - remote surgery devices that can be operated at a distance by a doctor or locally by AI
- "Nano-bots" - tiny robots that will be injected into the human bloodstream to seek out & destroy unwanted elements in the human body as a supplement to the normal immune system. These Nano-bots will also deliver medication, or even perform surgical procedures from inside the body.

The Robo-Doc Division has 199 staff, of which 118 came from the Yokohama Robotic Devices Company. The other 81 people came from ABC Healthcare Systems and the existing, but small, ABC Healthcare Robo-Doc division - which itself was formed 2 years previously. Together, these 199 people are specialized in immunology, medical research, robotics, computer programming, nano technology, bio-mechanical engineering, etc.

The Robo-Doc Case Study

Everything was rushed
At first, things were very hectic. The acquisition was done quickly, in order to stop a competitor from buying YRDC and getting hold of both its breakthrough nano-bot technology and its market-leading robotic surgery equipment. The Robo-Doc division expanded quickly as part of this acquisition. People were transferred from other parts of ABC Healthcare quickly, without a thorough assessment of the capabilities required for the growing organization.

HR did its best to be fully involved, but things were happening so fast. There was only enough time to process the administrative side of the acquisition - there wasn't enough time to complete a proper organizational analysis.

Message from the Head of Robo-Doc
You are the newly appointed HRBP for the Nano-Doc Division - the previous HRBP returned to the European HQ.

Bob Rogers, the head of the Robo-Doc division, has requested a meeting to evaluate the needs of the organization. Bob's email message to you:

> Congratulations on your new appointment - I'm looking forward to working with you!
>
> For our meeting next week I'd like to discuss the issues that I see in the new organization. Six months have passed and the situation is less hectic than it was at the start, but things are not satisfactory from my point of view.
>
> By that I mean:
> - I sense that several former YRDC employees are not working well with their new ABC Healthcare colleagues, and vice versa.
> - R&D is going slower than I expected.
> - Different teams are working on different projects, but seem to be going in different directions.
> - People are working late, and working hard, but productivity does not seem to be high - although it's hard to be precise about that.
> - We just had the Employee Engagement Survey results - not good!
> - I don't yet have a good understanding of key issues in the organization such as diversity, capability gaps, overtime hot-spots, key people and so on.
>
> And, on top of all that, I need to know what I don't know. In other words, what organizational issues am I overlooking or not informed about? Please help me understand if there are things that I am missing.
>
> B. Rgds,
> Bob

The Task
Prepare for the meeting with Bob by conducting an organizational analysis with the information provided.

Working With HR - Case Studies

Presentation from Bob Rogers, Head of Robo-Doc

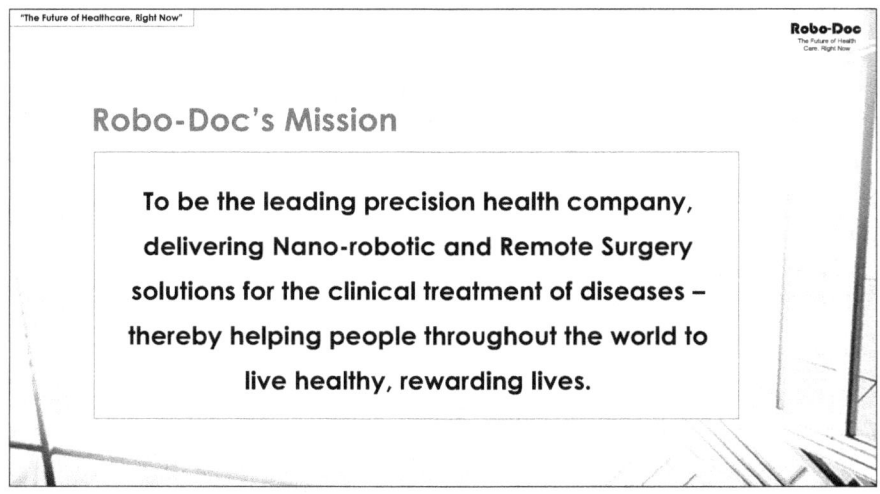

Presentation from Bob Rogers, Head of Robo-Doc

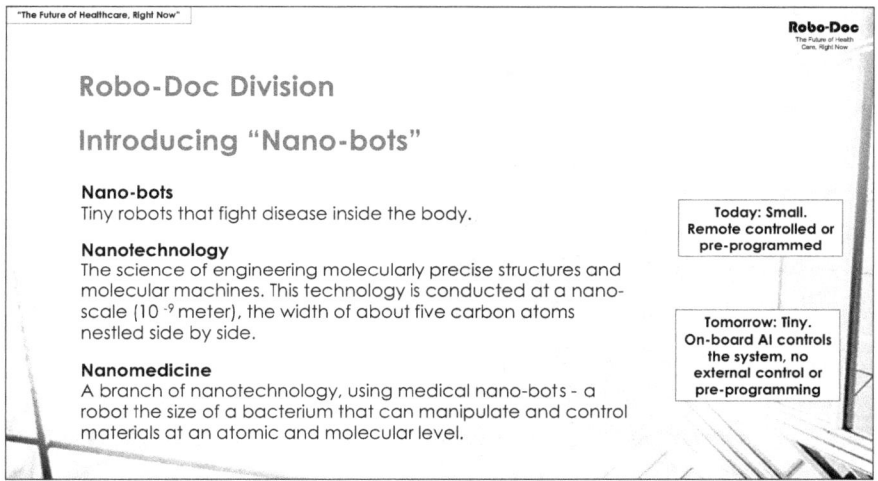

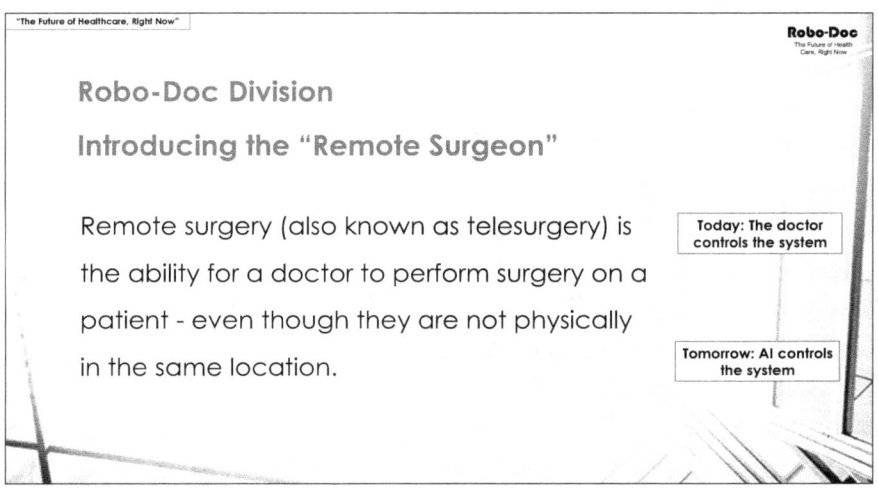

Working With HR - Case Studies

Presentation from Bob Rogers, Head of Robo-Doc

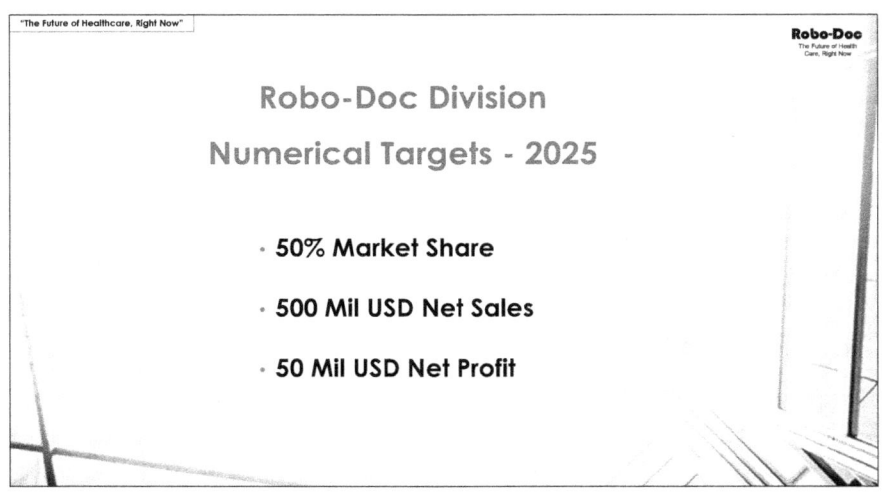

Presentation from Bob Rogers, Head of Robo-Doc

"The Future of Healthcare, Right Now" Robo-Doc
The Future of Health Care, Right Now

Where we are now

- Acquisition of Yokohama Robotics Devices Company (YRDC) completed 6 months ago
- Approximately 200 employees based in Yokohama (120 YRDC / 80 ABC)
- Company Mission and Strategy re-aligned
- R&D resources fully deployed

"The Future of Healthcare, Right Now" Robo-Doc
The Future of Health Care, Right Now

Where we are now

- Current Revenue projection: $50 Million - 2019
- Loss making – mainly due to high R&D costs, but this is expected during the development phase
- Expected breakthrough in AI/Nano-technology not yet delivered: lack of key experts? inadequate systems? outdated processes?

Working With HR - Case Studies

Presentation from Bob Rogers, Head of Robo-Doc

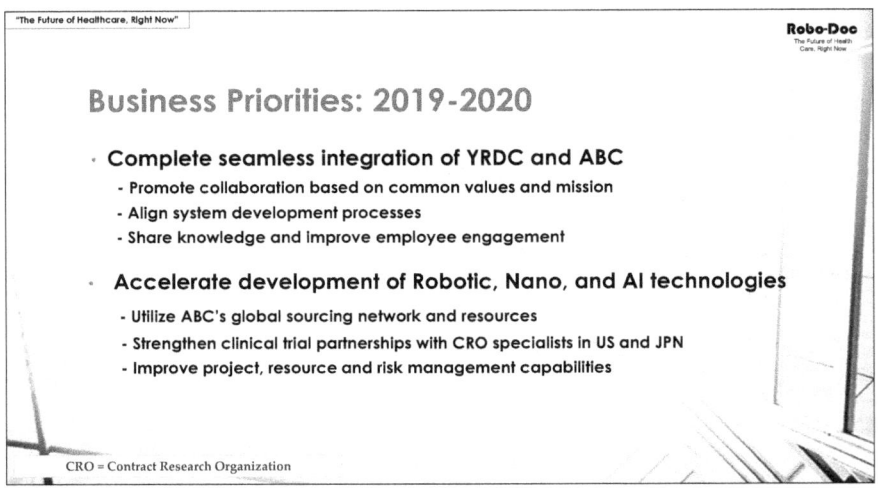

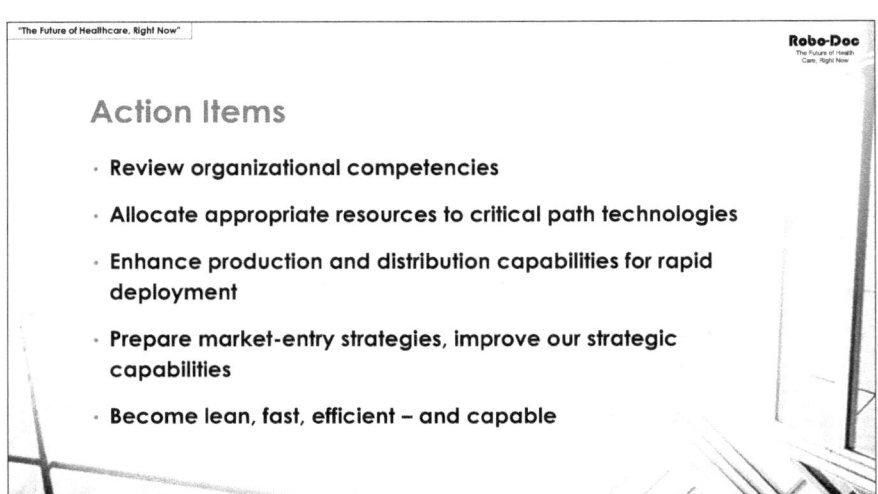

Next Steps

Presentation from Bob Rogers, Head of Robo-Doc

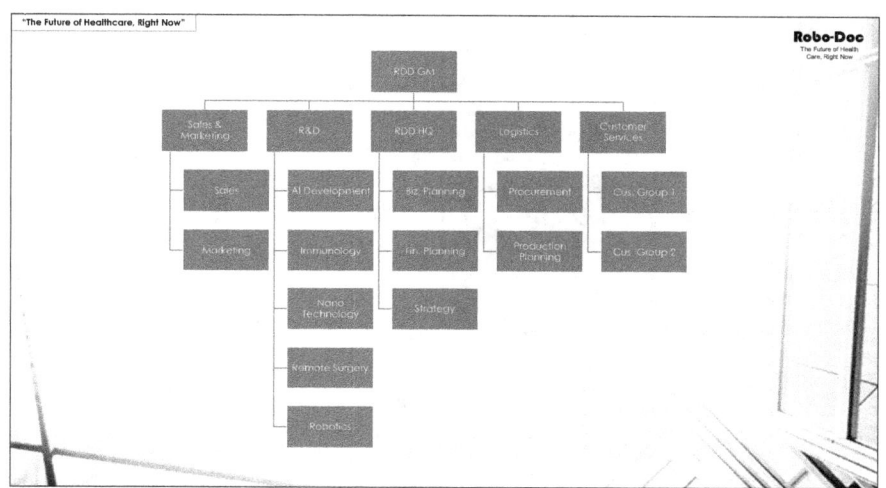

Next Steps

So far we have:
- The email from Bob
- The presentation

Next we'll:
- Summarize our understanding of Bob's issues and concerns (see next page).
- Gather & analyze HR data (from the HRIS).
- Use that analysis to deepen our understanding of what the issues are and why they are occurring.
- Create a framework of ideas/ insights/ possible solutions, ready for our meeting with Bob.
- Note: we'll probably have gaps in our data/ understanding, which we'll need to table as part of our discussion with Bob.

Working With HR - Case Studies

Summary of Bob's Issues, Concerns, etc.

Business Strategy	Culture & Organization
Vision: • Be the leading precision health company • Leadership in chosen markets, Innovation, Excellence in operations • By 2025 - 50% M-Share, $500 Mil sales (currently %50mil), $50 Mil profit • New mission/ strategy in place, aligned But: • Loss making now - High R&D cost • Expected AI/Nano tech breakthroughs not yet delivered Priorities: • Complete seamless integration • Accelerate development of Robotic, Nano, AI	• AI/Nano tech - inadequate systems, outdated processes? • YRDC M&A - 118 new employees, plus 81 from ABC group • Integration rushed, things were hectic • YRDC and ABC folk not working well together • R&D is slow • Some projects not aligned • People working hard, but productivity not so high • Engagement survey - some issues • Lack of clarity on overtime hot-spots • Goal: be lean, fast, efficient, capable • Allocate resources to critical path technologies • Review needed for organizational competencies
Talent & Capability Needs • AI/Nano tech issues - lack of key experts? • However, org is skilled in immunology, medical research, robotics, Nano tech, bio-mech eng, etc. • No full capability analysis done • Lack of clarity on diversity, capability, key people • Need to improve strategic capabilities • Need to improve production & distribution capabilities	**What's Needed from HR** • Help solve Bob's perceived issues • Bring insights and analysis on both what he does and does not know. • Be a true Business Partner

HR Data Analysis

HR Data - Overview

Bob mentioned several issues/ concerns where HR data analysis could provide insights.
- Employee Engagement scores are 'not good'
- Overtime hot-spots
- Productivity is not good
- Organizational competencies need reviewing
- Who are the key people?
- Lack of clarity on diversity
- No capability analysis done
- And .. what should he know that he does not already know

We'll start with taking a look at the overall organization, then move on to engagement results, and from there into overtime, key talent, etc.

The previous HRBP (who got transferred back to Europe), already did some work in relation to Robo-Doc, so you are not starting from scratch. That said, due to her urgent relocation back to Paris, there wasn't time for a proper handover (mmmm... things seem to often be a bit rushed in this organization!)

Note:
- *Instead of doing a deep analysis, there are brief comments/ annotations to the various graphics.*
- *Some of the text might be a bit small - but hopefully you'll be able to get enough of the story*
- *Some clarity might be lost moving from colour (the original graphics) to monochrome.*

Working With HR - Case Studies

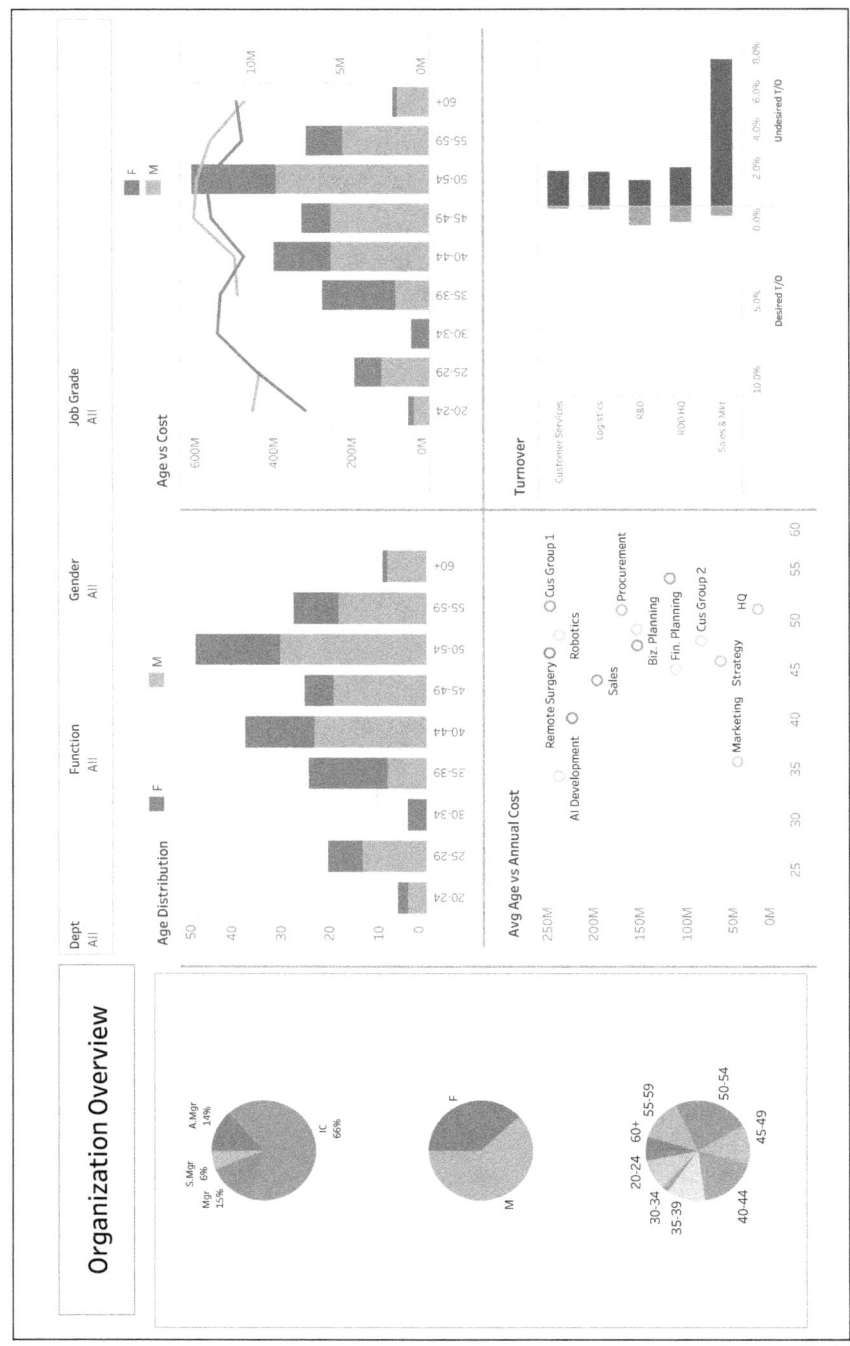

236

Organization Overview

Opposite page:
- High undesired staff turnover in Sales & Mkt - why?
- Large population age 50+ - impact on org, diversity, flexibility, promotions, headcount costs?
- Low population 30-34 - impact on talent pipeline?
- M/F only - how does the org track/ measure/ encourage diversity?
- Gap in M/F costs at higher age groups - are there differences in salary levels for same job/JG?

Below:
- Avg overtime higher than last year - due to M&A, but are there other factors?
- High number of JG 5/6 (mgr role starts at JG7) - could be due to M&A, but is there an issue with promotions? Long-term mgrs blocking career paths?
- No data on spans & levels - will need to conduct an assessment
- High headcount in R&D - scope for role/position assessment?

Overtime

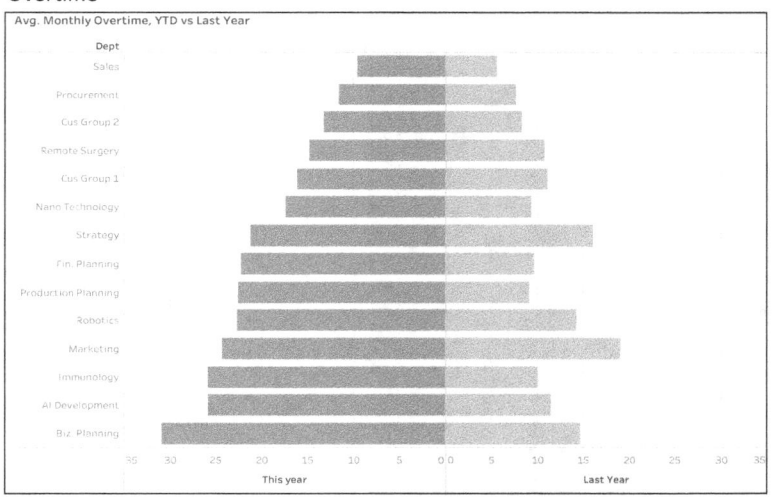

Job Grade Distribution

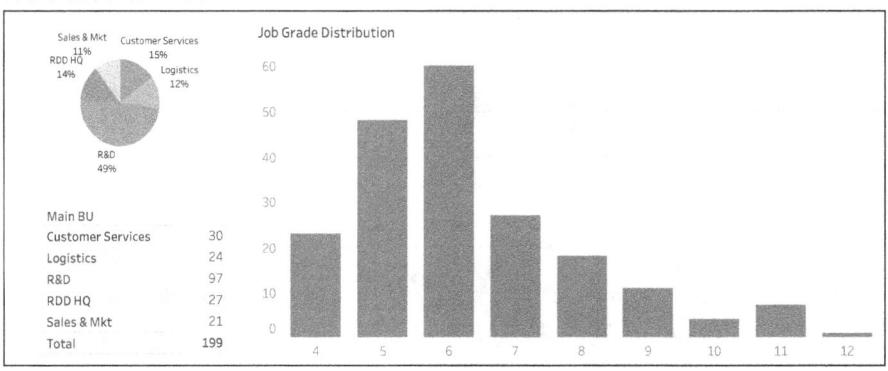

Engagement

Working With HR - Case Studies

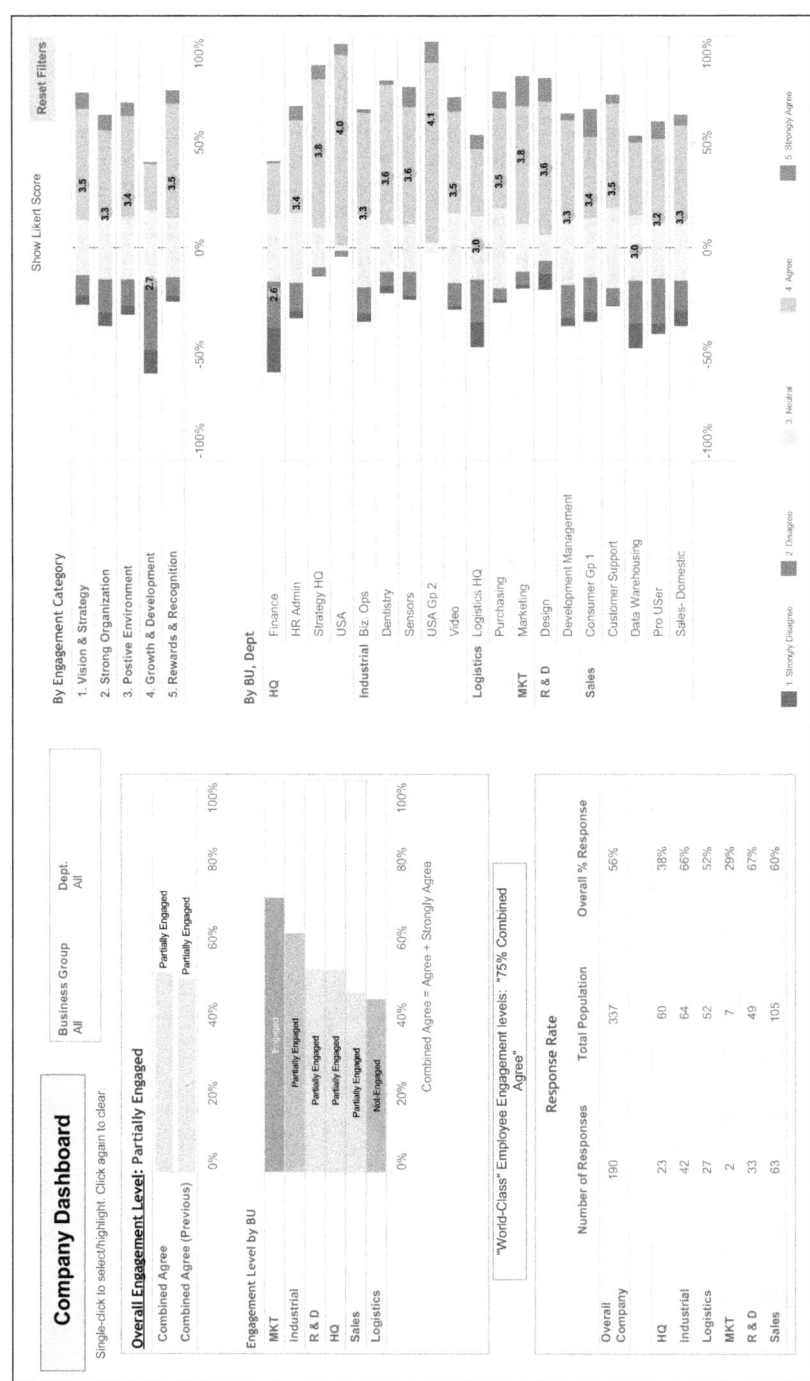

Engagement Survey

Opposite page:
- Overall: only 'Partially-engaged'
- Only Marketing 'engaged' - but only 2 people responded.
- Other groups partially engaged, with Logistics un-engaged.
- Engagement Category Growth & Development - high ratio of "disagree"
- BU/ Dept: Issues in Finance, Logistics HQ, Sales group.

Below:
- Wide range of engagement levels, some depts OK, others not
- Customer Groups 1&2 look pretty bad, with big -ve changes since previous survey.
- Same for Immunology, Production Planning
- Some R&D groups engaged, others un-engaged.
- Work to be done here to understand reasons behind low engagement

Engagement by dept.

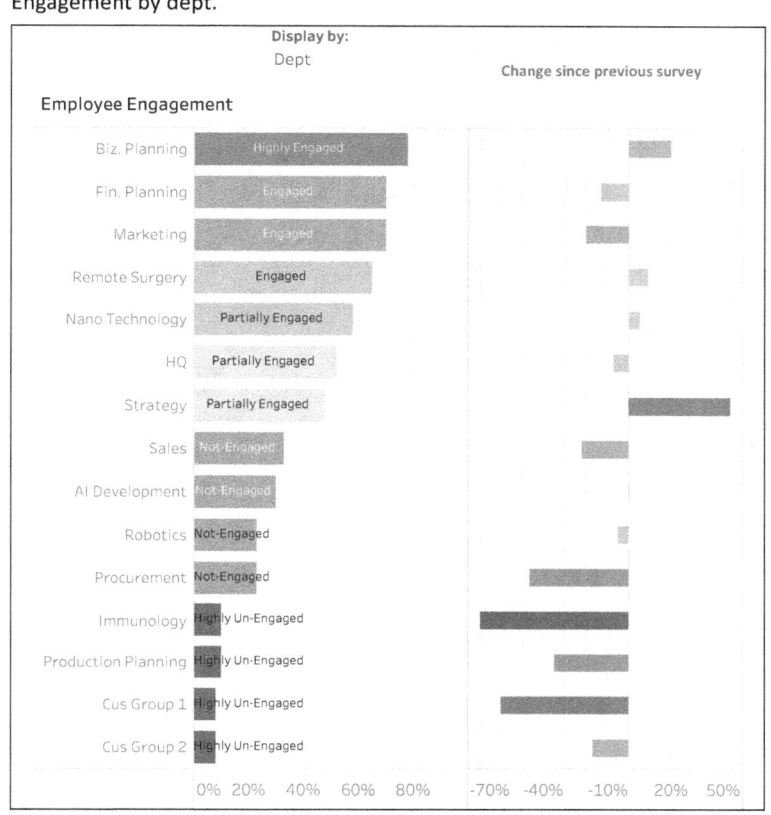

Working With HR - Case Studies

Engagement - Leadership focus

Select Business Group: All
Department: All

		Customer Service	Logistics	R&D	RDD HQ	Sales & Mkt
1. Vision & Strategy	1. I understand the Vision of my company.	2.1	2.5	2.8	4.0	4.1
	4. I feel connected to organizational strategies.	2.5	2.4	3.5	3.8	4.0
	5. I understand what is expected of me.	2.6	2.5	3.5	4.0	4.0
	6. I think that I am given the authority necessary for getting my job done.	3.1	3.0	3.3	3.9	3.6
	7. I have confidence in my Business Group's senior management to lead us to achieve our goals and objectives.	3.1	2.8	3.1	4.1	4.0
2. Strong Organization	8. I feel this organization where I work is strong.	3.0	1.5	3.1	4.4	3.9
	9. I feel there is a strong sense of urgency.	2.6	2.0	3.9	4.3	3.9
3. Positive Environment	17. I am encouraged to take risks.	2.6	3.1	3.0	3.9	3.4
	18. I feel encouraged to come up with new and better ways of doing things.	2.4	3.5	3.2	3.9	4.0
Engagement	25. In my Work Group, diversity among members is respected.	3.0	2.9	3.9	3.7	4.0
	29. In my Work Group, bottom-up approaches are respected.	2.4	3.1	3.6	4.3	3.5
	30. I am able to speak candidly with the leader of my Work Group about problems and matters I am concerned about.	2.0	3.1	3.8	3.8	4.1
4. Growth & Development	35. I receive ongoing feedback that helps me improve my performance.	2.5	3.1	3.1	3.5	3.5
	36. I am satisfied with the feedback I receive.	3.1	3.0	3.0	4.0	3.6
5. Rewards & Recognition	38. I think that if I am able to fulfill the role expected of me, my successes will be recognized.	3.0	3.1	3.5	3.7	2.5
	39. The leader of my Business Group is always prepared to assume management responsibility for the results of his/her subordinates' work.	3.1	2.7	3.7	4.5	4.1
	40. I feel my ideas are listened to/heard.	2.5	2.1	3.6	3.9	4.0
Overall		2.6	2.7	3.4	4.0	3.8

1= Strongly Disagree 2= Disagree 3= Neutral 4= Agree 5= Strongly Agree

Leadership Matrix

Axes: Engagement - People Leadership (vertical, 2–5) vs Performance - Business Leadership (horizontal, 1–5)

- Social Leader "社交的な" リーダー (upper left)
- Global Leader "グローバル" リーダー (upper right)
- Ineffective Leader "無力な" リーダー (lower left)
- Authoritarian Leader "独裁主義的" リーダー (lower right)

Plotted departments: Marketing, Strategy, Fin. Planning, Biz. Planning, Nano Technology, Sales, AI Development, Robotics, Immunology, Procurement, Cus Group 2, Production Planning, Cus Group 1, Remote Surgery

Department legend: AI Development, Biz Planning, Cus Group 1, Cus Group 2, Fin. Planning, Immunology, Marketing, Nano Technology, Procurement, Production Planning, Remote Surgery, Robotics, Sales, Strategy

Language: English

Leadership Effectiveness

Opposite page:
- Leadership Focus from engagement survey - shows issues/ concerns in Customer Service, Logistics
- Leadership effectiveness in those groups could be driver behind low engagement
- Conversely, leadership in Sales & Mkt quite strong - so why the high staff turnover in sales?
- Range of leadership results across depts (in the 4-box matrix)
- Overall, not where Leadership should be (avg 4.0 = "Agree")

Below:
- 360 results show wide spread of leadership capability
- Goal - get everyone to top right quadrant.
- Need for actions/ decisions for leaders in extremes of Social, Authoritarian leadership
- De-select ineffective leaders?
- What's the status/ effectiveness of the leadership development program?

Latest 360 survey results

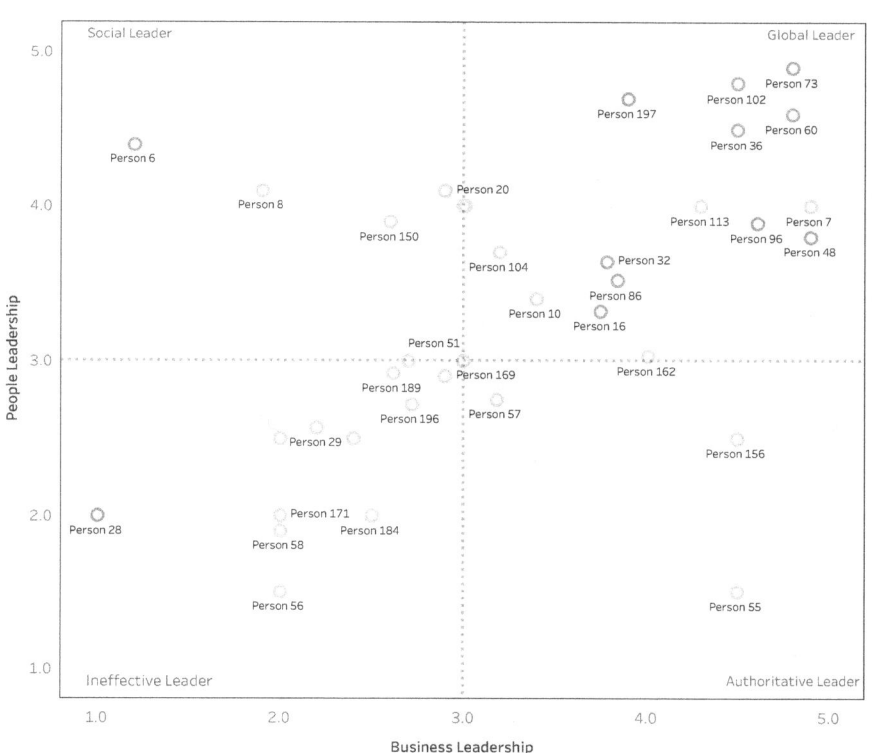

Working With HR - Case Studies

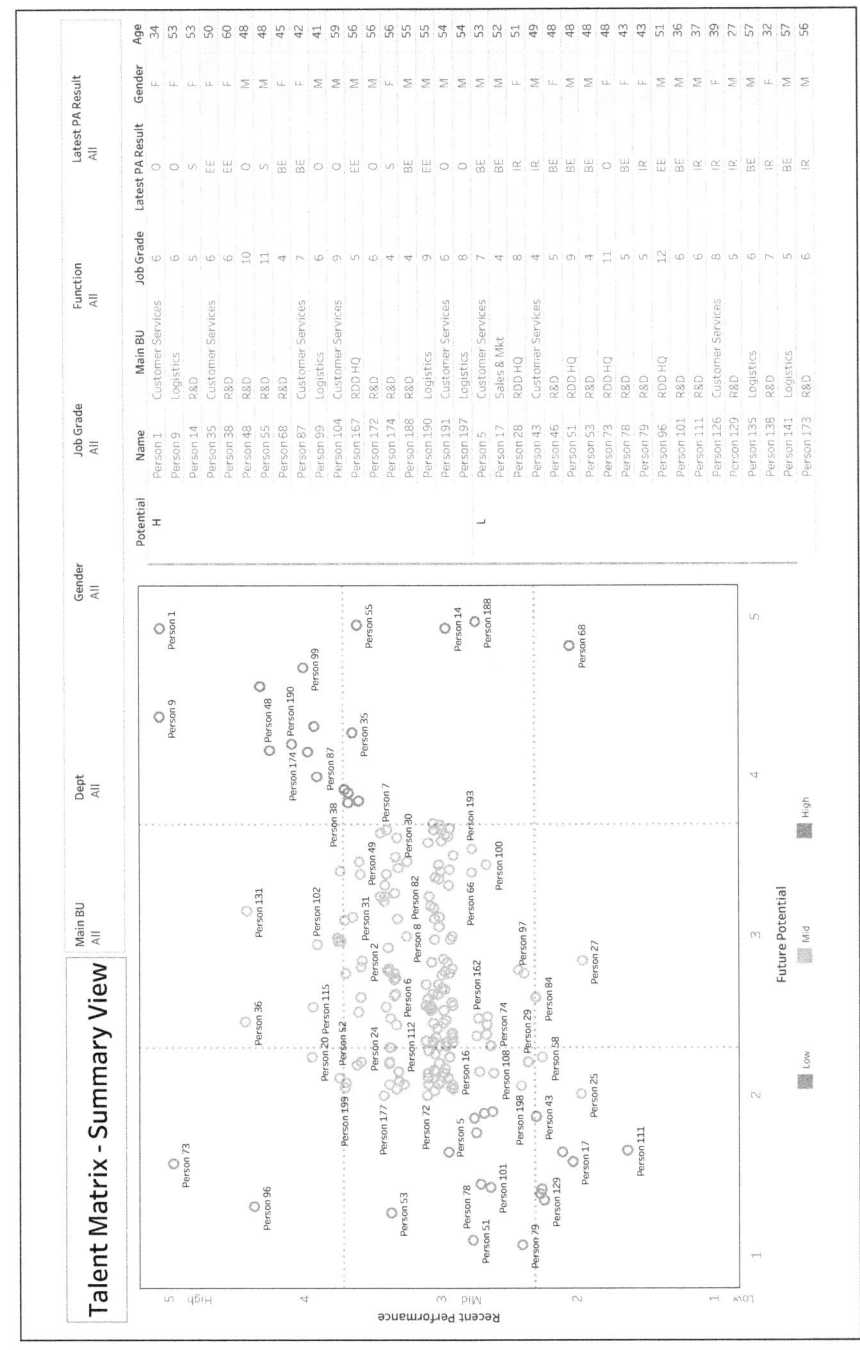

Key People, Key Positions

Opposite page:
- Data view itself is rather messy, complicated - need to re-design?
- Need for actions/ decisions for those with Low Future Potential, Low Performance
- Have we done a C&B analysis for pay to market for high-performers? Any retention issues there?
- Do managers of Hi-Potentials have development plans in place for them?

Below:
- Another messy data-view!
- Top left box, Key Position (high-impact), but Low Performer in role - actions needed?
- Bottom right, Low Impact Position, but High-Performer in role - actions needed?
- In any case, need review of all people in all roles.

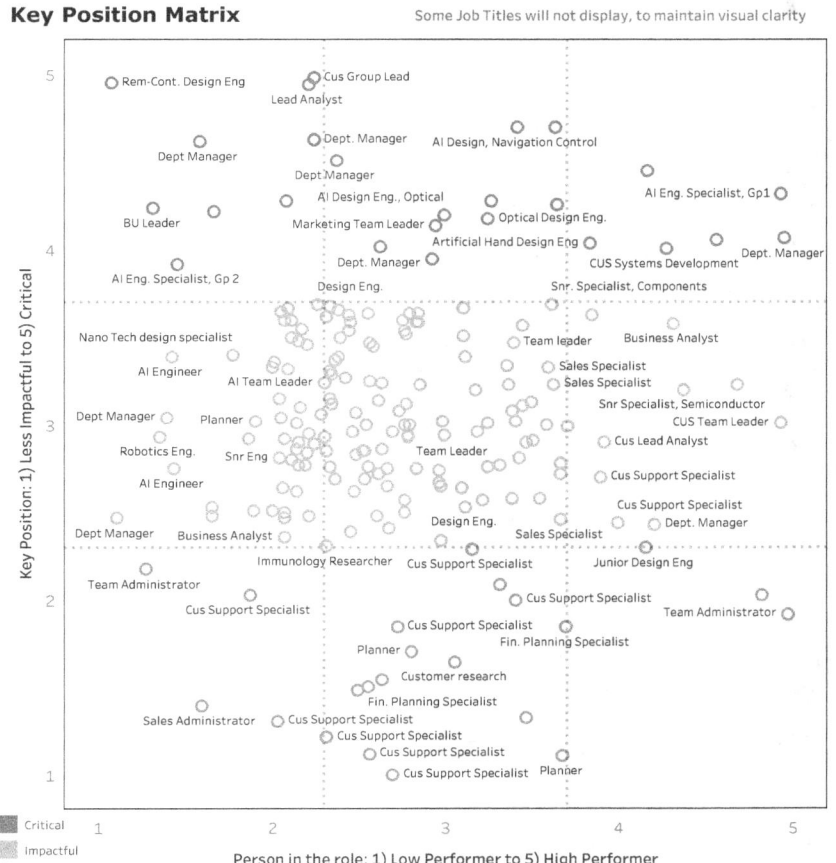

Working With HR - Case Studies

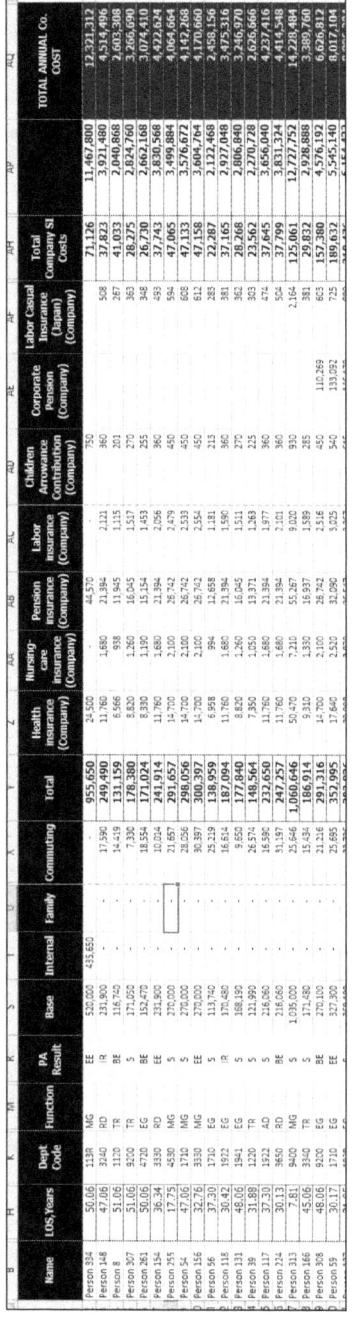

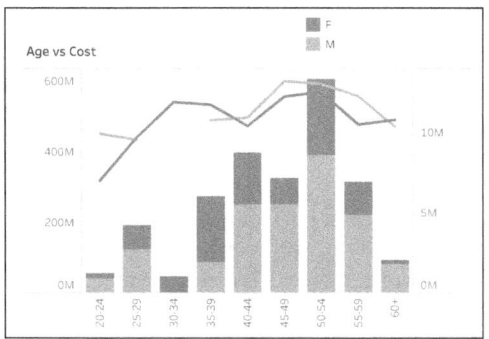

This page:
- Full headcount and related costs behind above chart
- Does Bob want a fuller/ deeper analysis?

Opposite page:
- Capability assessment done by previous HRBP with Robo-doc head leadership team
- What actions taken so far? (if any)
- How involved is L&D, Recruiting?
- What are the success measures for developing these capabilities?
- Do the Robo-doc leadership team still see it this way?
- Does Bob see it this way?
- New assessment needed?

Headcount Cost, Capabilities

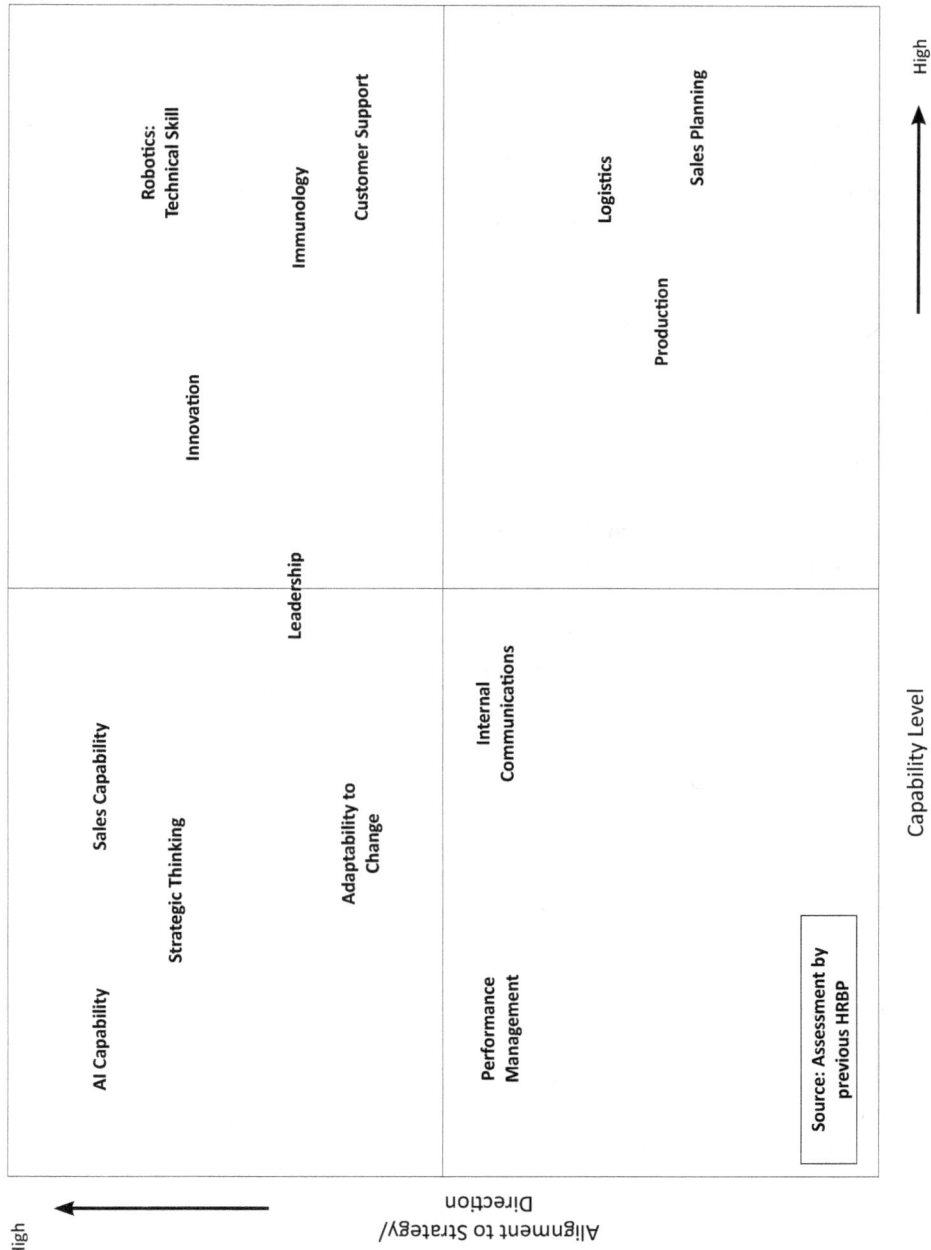

Data Gathering & Analysis

Summarize and Analyze the HR Data
Ok, so you've got a whole bunch of HR data along with the original email from Bob. There is probably more data you could dig up from the HRIS, but we'll leave it there for this example.

The next step is to summarize and analyze the information you have, and relate it to Bob's message and presentation.

Previously, under "Summarizing Gathered Information" (page 90) we suggested several different ways of doing this, and said it's up to you to choose which one to use. We also made a note that in our HRBP workshops we saw that participants used whichever method/ approach the table-team preferred (we leave the choice up to them). Some choose free brainstorming, whereas others prefer a more structured approach.

Below we'll look at a combined method (which is how the author does it), which uses brainstorming followed by the more structured method. For me, this works best, as it allows free thinking followed by "step back and try to figure it all out, and add structure." This works well with HR teams, too: everyone pitches in with their ideas and assessments, then the team discusses each idea more deeply, before heading to solutions.

You might feel you have enough already - i.e, with the summary (opposite page) and the HR data review, you're ready to bypass brainstorming/analysis and go straight to the "solution development & impact analysis" phase. In which case, feel free to go ahead! There's no "you must do it this way" to this kind of thing.

Note: Bob's email and presentation are a good starting point, almost as if you have had your first 1:1 meeting with him already - and along with the HR data analysis you'll have a good platform for the actual first meeting next week with Bob.

Analysis & Solution Development

Summary of Bob's Issues, Concerns, etc.

Business Strategy	Culture & Organization
Vision: • Be the leading precision health company • Leadership in chosen markets, Innovation, Excellence in operations • By 2025 - 50% M-Share, $500 Mil sales (currently %50mil), $50 Mil profit • New mission/ strategy in place, aligned But: • Loss making now - High R&D cost • Expected AI/Nano tech breakthroughs not yet delivered Priorities: • Complete seamless integration • Accelerate development of Robotic, Nano, AI	• AI/Nano tech - inadequate systems, outdated processes? • YRDC M&A - 118 new employees, plus 81 from ABC group • Integration rushed, things were hectic • YRDC and ABC folk not working well together • R&D is slow • Some projects not aligned • People working hard, but productivity not so high • Engagement survey - some issues • Lack of clarity on overtime hot-spots • Goal: be lean, fast, efficient, capable • Allocate resources to critical path technologies • Review needed for organizational competencies
Talent & Capability Needs	**What's Needed from HR**
• AI/Nano tech issues - lack of key experts? • However, org is skilled in immunology, medical research, robotics, Nano tech, bio-mech eng, etc. • No full capability analysis done • Lack of clarity on diversity, capability, key people • Need to improve strategic capabilities • Need to improve production & distribution capabilities	• Help solve Bob's perceived issues • Bring insights and analysis on both what he does and does not know. • Be a true Business Partner

Working With HR - Case Studies

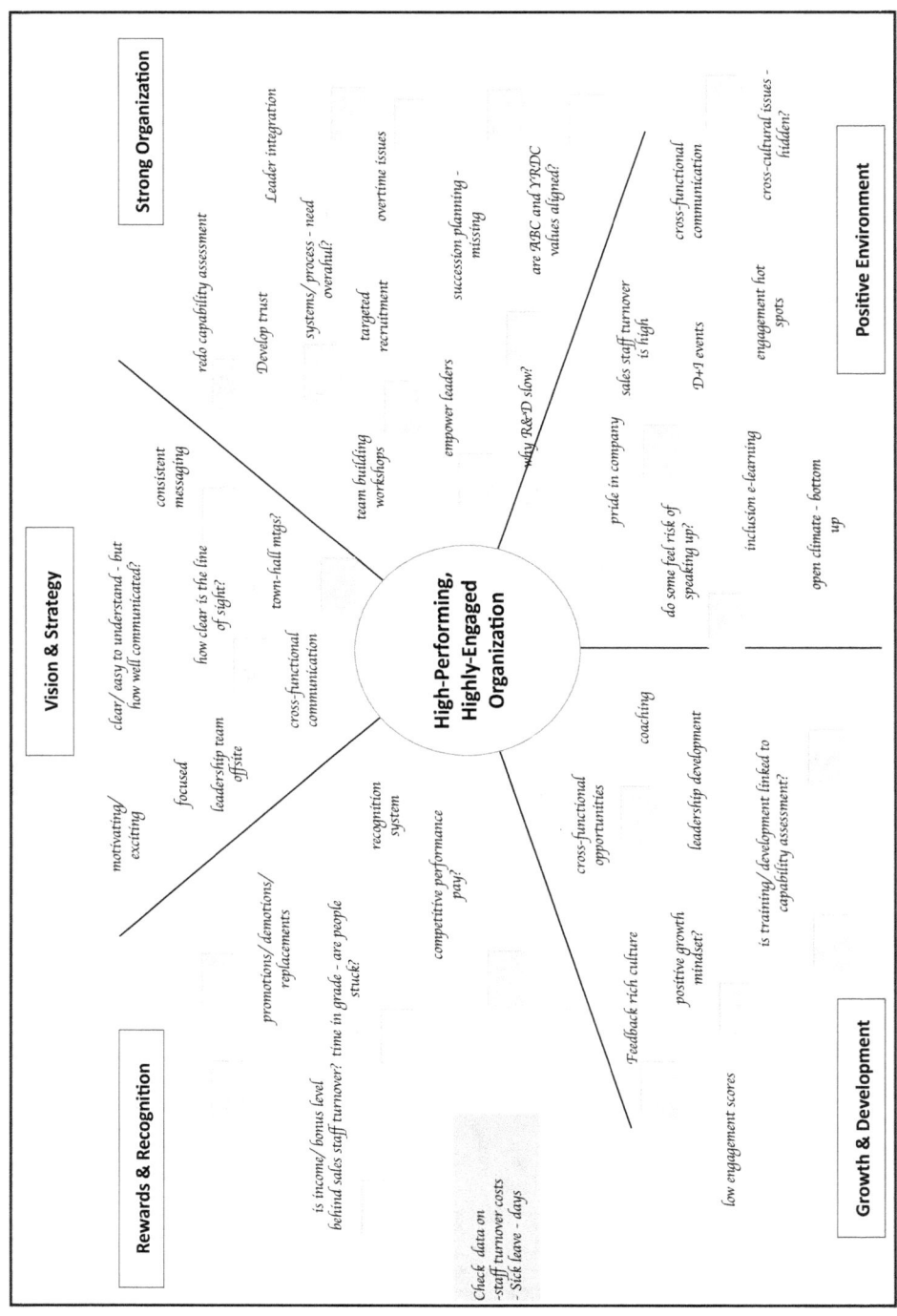

Brainstorming Issues & Solutions, Adding Structure

Opposite page: HR team discussion - more issues/ solutions on post-its *(excluded for visual clarity)*. Below - a more structured summary.

	Issues/ Status	HR Response
Vision and Strategy	• motivating/ exciting • focused/ clear/ easy to understand - but how well communicated? • Not all groups feel the connection • consistent messaging? • how clear is the line of sight? • cross-functional communication	• Leadership team offsite - re-affirm vision, esp. for depts. with low connections • Town-hall mtg for a) engagement review & honesty b) re-connect and re-align all to vision • Communication plan in place
Strong Organization	• redo capability assessment • Leader integration? • Develop trust • targeted recruitment • overtime issues • succession planning - missing • are ABC and YRDC values aligned? • empower leaders • systems/ process - need overahul? • R&D too slow - why	• Team building workshops - linked to vision/ engagement issues, plus improving ABC/YRDC relationships • Re-visit values - conduct workshops, possibly part of team building. • Re-run capability assessment. Invite L&D, Talent management/Recruiting, so they are aware and ready • Create process excellence team? • Full talent review: key people/ key roles • Deep dive on R&D - what's causing slow results
Positive Environment	• pride in company • sales staff turnover is high • cross-functional communication • cross-cultural issues - hidden? • engagement hot spots • D+I events • inclusion e-learning • open climate - bottom up • do some feel risk of speaking up?	• Figure out sales staff turnover - contact leavers, see if they'll disclose • Diversity/ Inclusion - make leadership team priority • Engagement feedback to teams and action planning
Growth & Development	• low engagement scores • is training/ development linked to capability assessment? • leadership development/ coaching • cross-functional opportunities • positive growth mindset? • Feedback rich culture	• Get L&D more involved in capability needs discussions • Full review of leadership development program - develop coaching skills • Get managers better trained on creating development plans
Rewards & Recognition	• promotions/ demotions/ replacements • time in grade - are people stuck? • is income/ bonus level behind sales staff turnover? • competitive performance pay? • recognition system	• Full talent review • Deeper analysis on time in grade, etc. • Sit with C&B for performance pay review • Re-visit recognition and awards

Working With HR - Case Studies

Below: You could also run the brainstorm/ analysis sessions (by yourself or as an HR team) with some added structure around fairly typical HR responses linked to the given business priorities. I prefer the method on the previous page, as the layout is easier to use on a whiteboard.

Either way, when you get to discussing/ presenting with your customer (i.e., Bob in this case), you'll need to connect the HR response to the needs of the business.

		Complete seamless integration/ Accelerate development of Robotic, Nano, AI
A more structured approach - but it's harder to do on a whiteboard compared to the method on the previous pages 	Talent Management	
	Organization/ Culture Change	
	Innovation Strategy	
	Organizational Mission & Vision	
	Leadership Coaching & Development	
	Capability Development	
	Employee Engagement	
	Workforce Planning	
	Diversity Strategy	
	Performance Management, Rewards, C&B	
	Other	

text excluded for visual clarity

Below - Impact analysis. *(from one of our HRBP workshops. There is no need to agree with this assessment - you might have some quite different views!).*

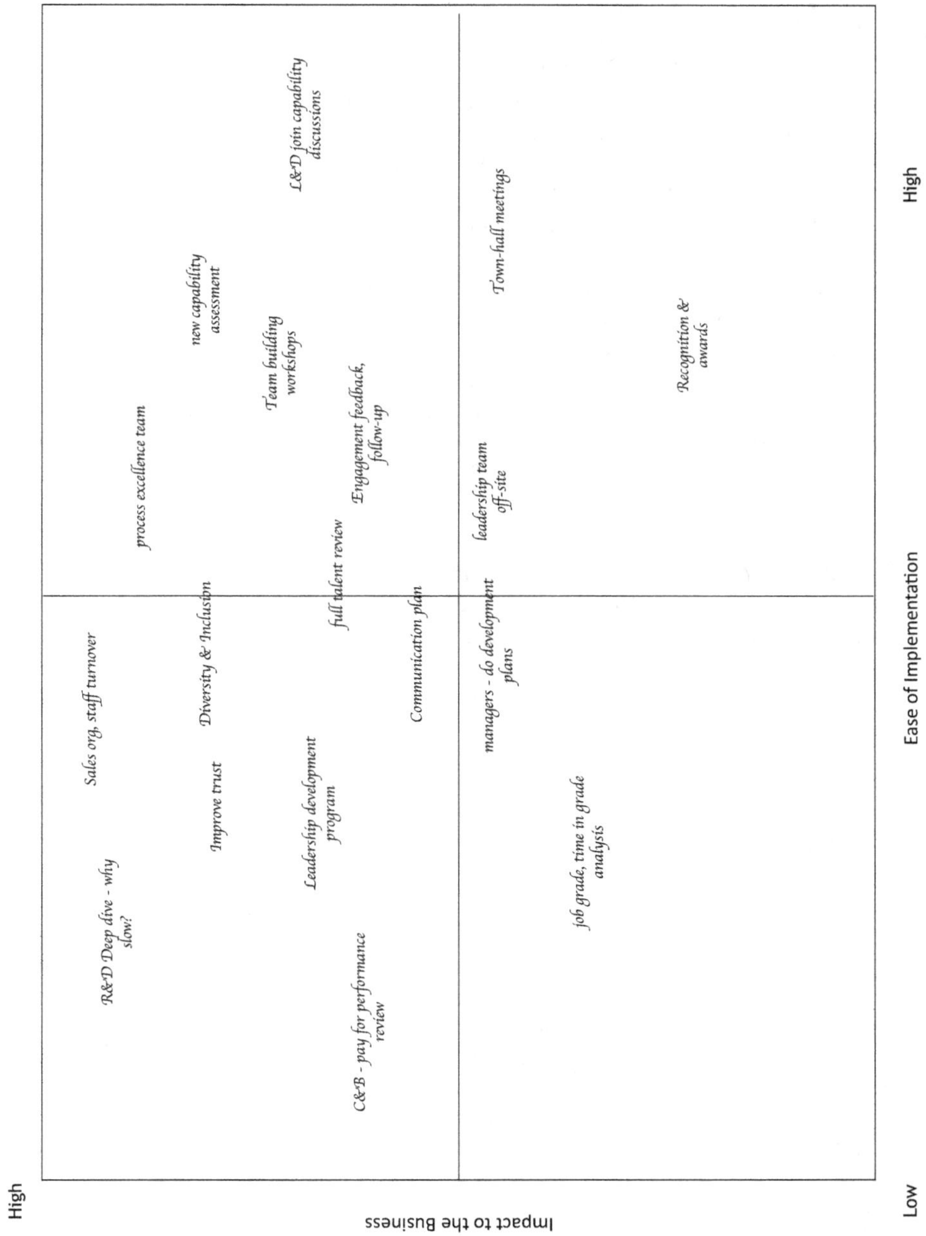
L&D join capability discussions
Town-hall meetings
new capability assessment
Team building workshops
Recognition & awards
Engagement feedback, follow-up
process excellence team
leadership team off-site
full talent review
Diversity & Inclusion
Communication plan
managers - do development plans
Sales org, staff turnover
Improve trust
Leadership development program
job grade, time in grade analysis
R&D Deep dive - why slow?
C&B - pay for performance review
High
Ease of Implementation
Low
High
Impact to the Business

Working With HR - Case Studies

Next Steps

So, we've gathered a lot of data, done some initial analysis, and have some ideas of what the HR response could be. As we prepare for the meeting with Bob, there are several points to keep in mind:
- We can't do everything, so don't fall into the trap of presenting a shopping-list of issues/ solutions to fix everything in the next 6 months. (*I did that a few years ago. The country GM looked at me and said, "This is a 3 year program!"*)
- Bob will be looking for HR solutions that address his needs/ concerns.
- HR are here to help make the business successful - so we'll need to a) show how we'll do that, and b) use business-relevant KPIs.
- Be mentally prepared for tough discussions, idea rejection, emerging strategies, things you hadn't thought of but wish you had, etc. This can happen no matter how great and well thought-out your presentation is - although in this case Bob doesn't look like he'll do that kind of thing.

Let's jump straight to the presentation itself. This is how I would do it, although you might do it very differently! Also, we'll just look at the PowerPoint slides, rather than a transcript of the discussion itself.

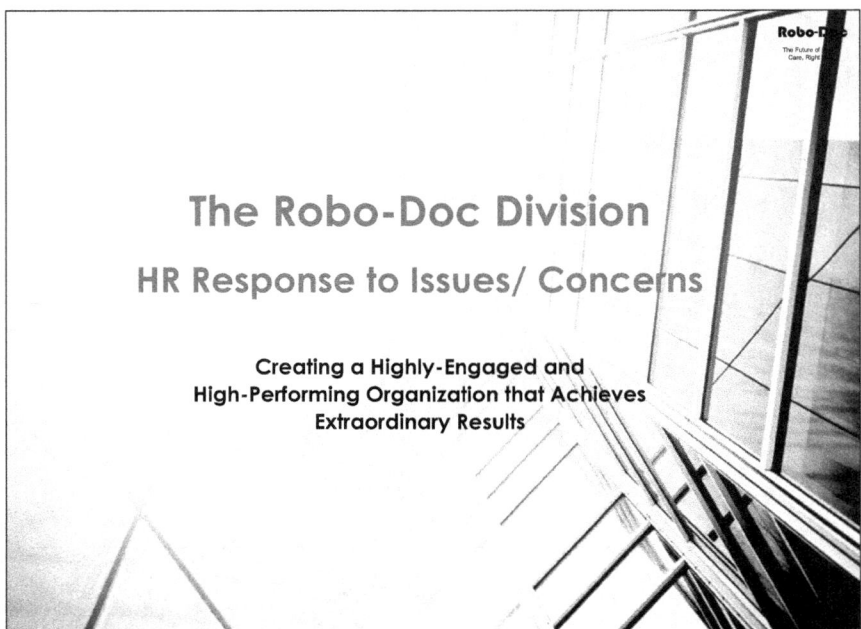

Presenting the HR Response

Robo-Doc
The Future of Health Care, Right Now

Today

- Issues, Concerns, Challenges
- HR Data Review & Analysis
- Recommendations, Next Steps

Robo-Doc
The Future of Health Care, Right Now

Business Strategy

Vision:
- Be the leading precision health company
- Leadership in chosen markets, Innovation, Excellence in operations
- By 2025 - 50% M-Share, $500 Mil sales (currently %50mil), $50 Mil profit
- New mission/ strategy in place, aligned

But:
- Loss making now - High R&D cost
- Expected AI/Nano tech breakthroughs not yet delivered

Priorities:
- Complete seamless integration
- Accelerate development of Robotic, Nano, AI

Working With HR - Case Studies

Cultural & Organizational Challenges

Several challenges/roadblocks...

- YRDC M&A - folk not working well together
  - Integration rushed, things were hectic
- AI/Nano tech - inadequate systems, outdated processes?
- R&D is slow
- Some projects not aligned

... require analysis/assessment

- People working hard, but productivity not so high
- Engagement survey - some issues
- Lack of clarity on overtime hot-spots
- Goal: be lean, fast, efficient, capable
- Need to allocate resources to critical path technologies
- Review organizational competencies

Talent & Capability Needs

Do we have the right people in the right roles?...

- AI/Nano tech issues - lack of key experts?
- However, org is skilled in immunology, medical research, robotics, Nano tech, bio-mech eng, etc.

... with the right skills/capabilities?

- Need to improve strategic capabilities
- Need to improve production & distribution capabilities
- No full capability analysis done
- Lack of clarity on diversity, capability, key people

Presenting the HR Response

What's needed from HR

- Bring insights and analysis to help solve these issues/challenges
- Be a true Business Partner

⟹ Support Robo-Doc in Achieving its Business & Organizational Goals

Analysis & Recommendations

- Issues, Concerns, Challenges
- **HR Data Review & Analysis**
- Recommendations, Next Steps

Working With HR - Case Studies

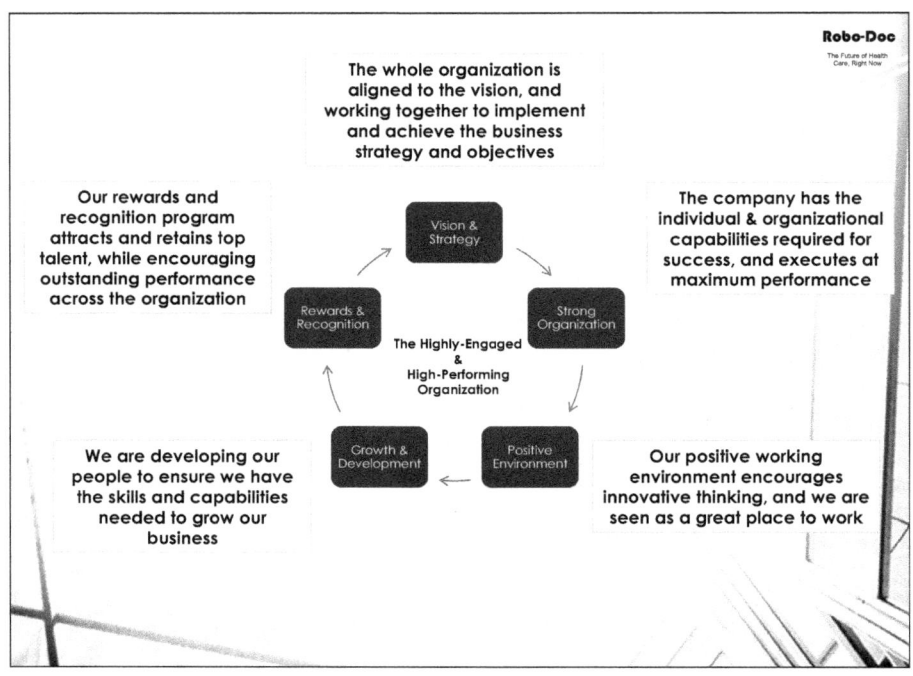

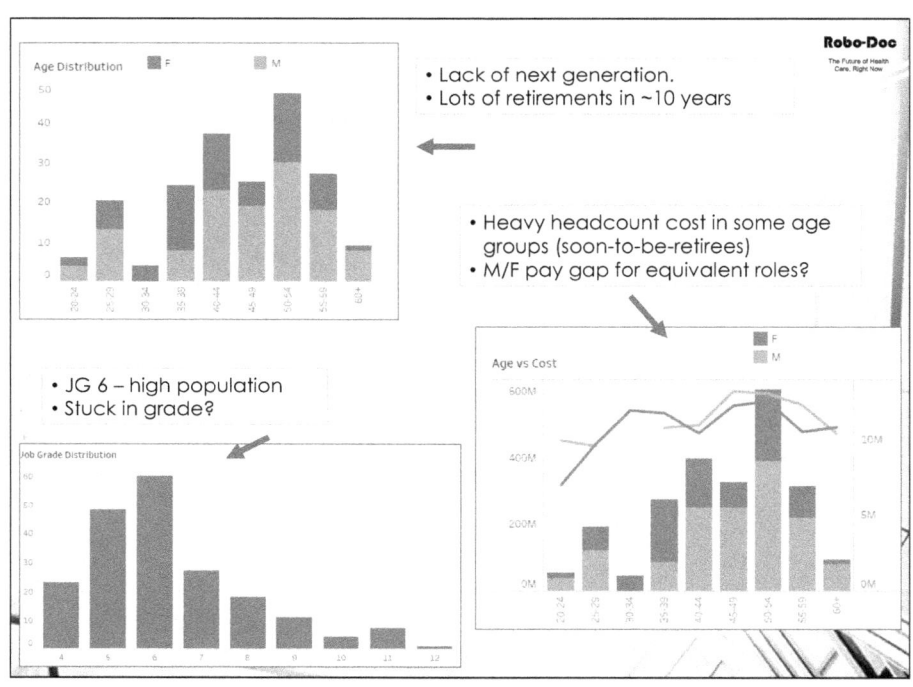

Presenting the HR Response

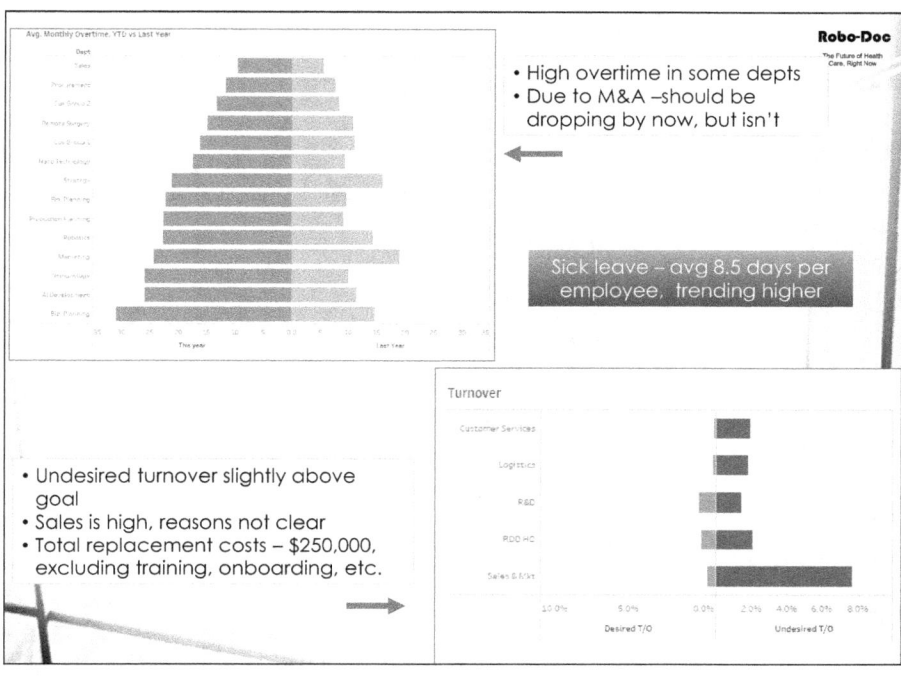

- High overtime in some depts
- Due to M&A – should be dropping by now, but isn't

Sick leave – avg 8.5 days per employee, trending higher

- Undesired turnover slightly above goal
- Sales is high, reasons not clear
- Total replacement costs – $250,000, excluding training, onboarding, etc.

Engagement Survey
- Organization only 'Partially Engaged' – 50% vs 75% goal
- MKT looks good – but only 2 responses
- Logistics group behind
- Several depts doing quite badly

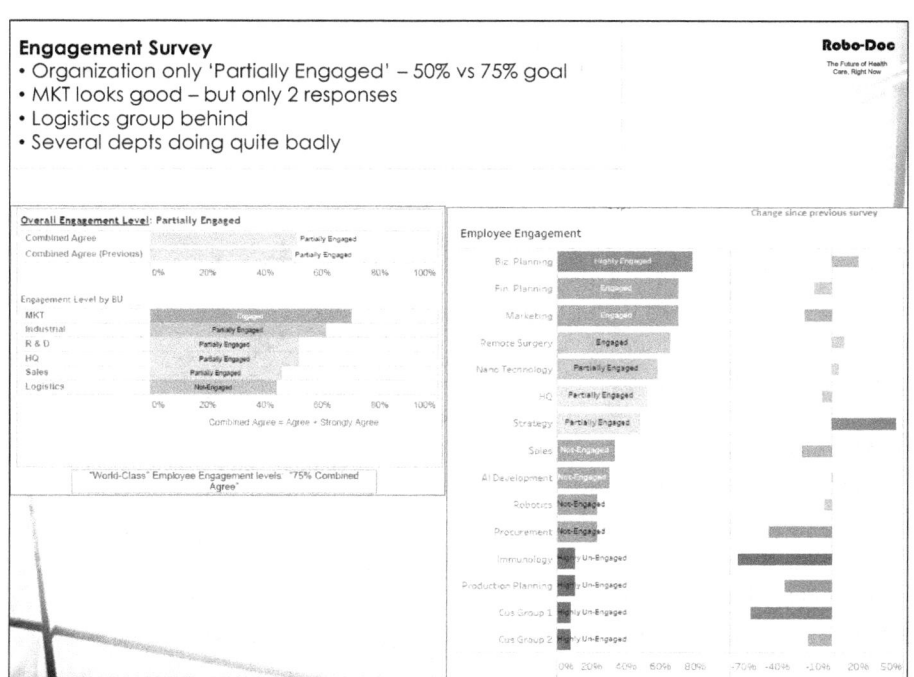

Working With HR - Case Studies

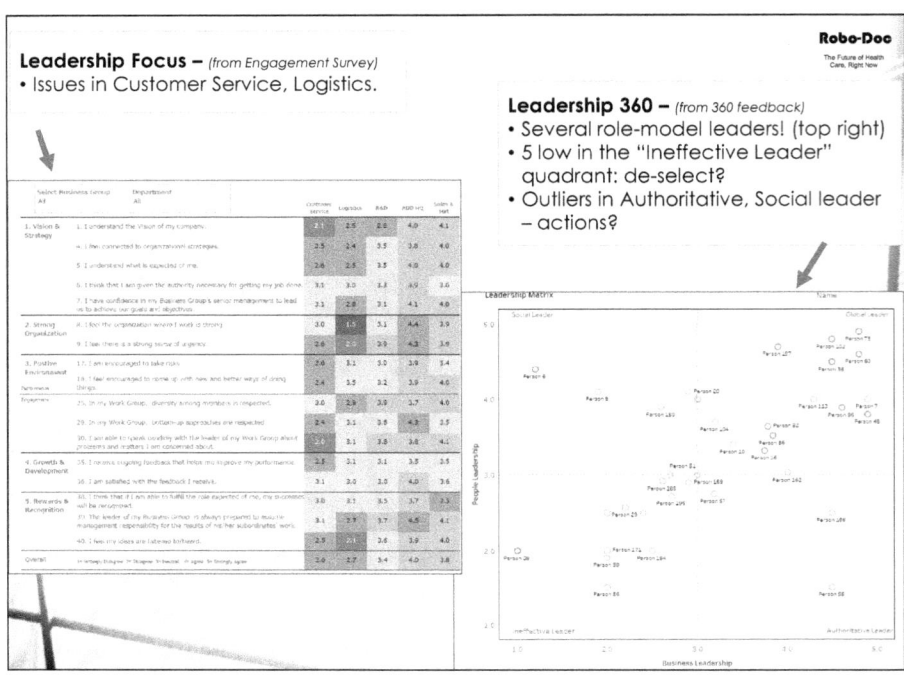

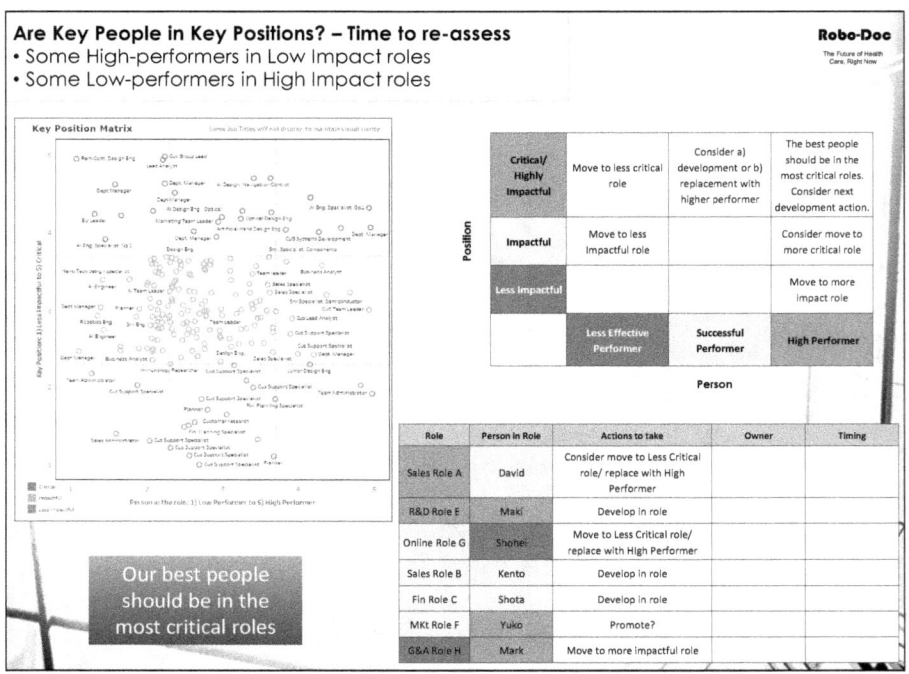

Presenting the HR Response

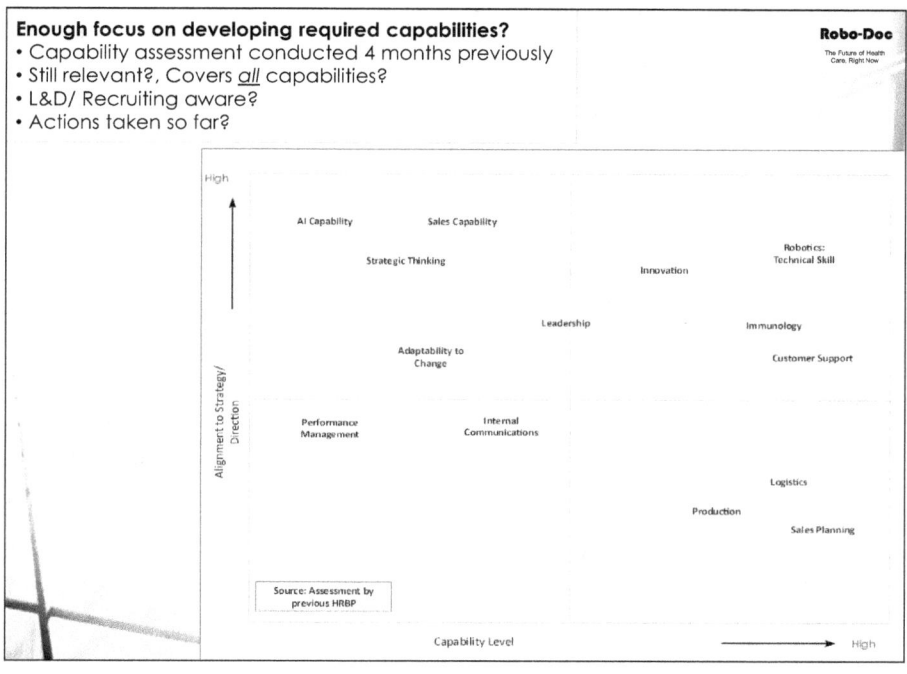

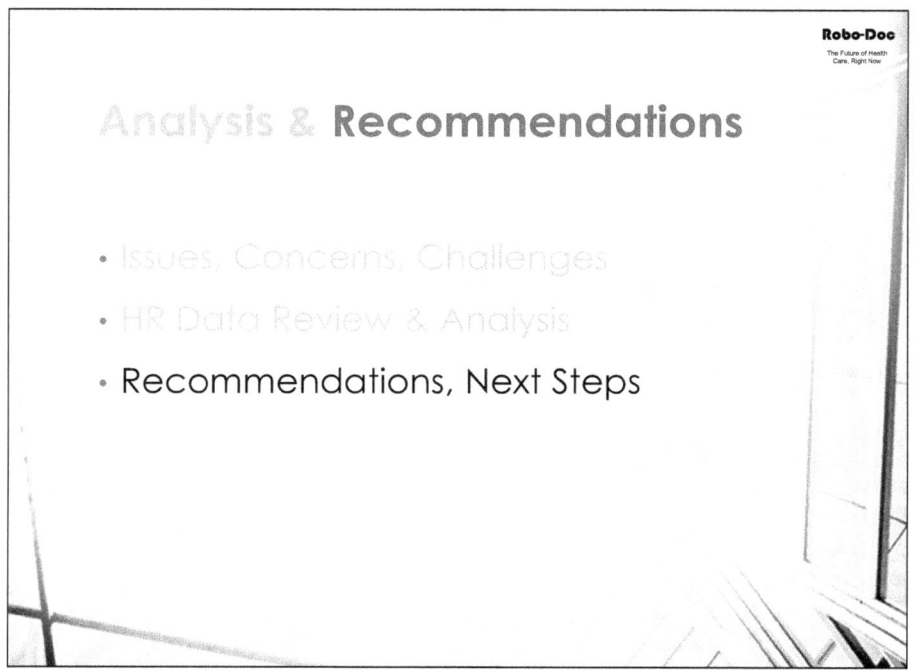

Working With HR - Case Studies

	Issues/ Challenges	Recommendations
The Leading Precision Health Company 2025 – 50% MSS, $500M Rev, $50M Prof.	• Vision not well understood (some depts.) • Leadership – several issues need attention • Excessive headcount costs • High undesired staff turnover in Sales – link to compensation?	• Leadership team offsite - re-affirm vision, esp. for depts with low engagement scores • Town-hall mtg for a) engagement review & honesty b) re-connect and re-align all to vision • Diversity/ Inclusion – make leadership team priority • Figure out sales staff turnover - contact leavers • Review of all Leaders – de-select, train, change roles, etc.
Complete seamless integration	• Organization 'Partially Engaged' • ABC/ YRDC folk not working well together? • Right person in key positions? • Talent pipeline – gaps in next generation, Long 'time in grade' • Diversity & Inclusion – work needed • Overtime – heavier than previous year • Capabilities – enough focus on current/ future needs? • Sick leave trending high	• Team building workshops - linked to vision/ engagement issues, plus improving ABC/YRDC relationships • Re-visit values - conduct workshops, possibly part of team building. • Re-run capability assessment. Invite L&D, Talent management/Recruiting, so they are aware and ready • Full talent review: key people/ key roles • Deeper analysis on time in grade. • Re-visit recognition and awards – fit for purpose? • Develop leaders' coaching skills/ creating development plans
Accelerate development of Robotic, Nano, AI	• Slow R&D – needs investigation • Productivity – slipping? • Multiple parallel projects – org. moving in one direction?	• Deep dive on R&D - what's causing slow results • Create process excellence team?

	Current Metrics	Metrics in 12 Months
The Leading Precision Health Company 2025 – 50% MSS, $500M Rev, $50M Prof.	• $50 Million revenue • Loss making • Vision (Engagement Survey) ➢ I understand the Vision - 60% ➢ I can empathize with the Vision – 55%	• On track, on schedule to 2025 revenue goals • Vision (Engagement) ➢ I understand the Vision - 80 % ➢ I can empathize with the Vision - 80%
Complete seamless integration	• Organization 'Partially Engaged' – 50% Agree • Sales undesired turnover – 7.5%, Other BU undesired turnover ~ 2.0 % • Replacement costs $250,000 (3.5% turnover) • Sick leave 8.5 days • Leadership – 5 managers in low "Ineffective Leader" quadrant	• Organization 'Engaged' – 70% Agree • All undesired turnover < 2.0% • Replacement costs <$120,000 • Sick leave < 3.5 days (not a strict goal) • Leadership – 0 managers in low "Ineffective Leader" quadrant
Accelerate development of Robotic, Nano, AI	• Expected breakthrough in AI/Nano-technology not yet delivered • Productivity (no measure)	• Expected breakthroughs realized, as per schedule • Productivity - method/ measure in place

Presenting the HR Response

Now we're in the discussion phase. Maybe Bob will agree, maybe he won't. Maybe he'll push back, perhaps he'll accept everything.

I sense, though, that Bob has his own ideas and will add a few things from his side. But, that's good - you are after all, the Business Partner for the Robo-Doc division, and so the end result should ideally be a joint decision.

Again, you might choose to do the whole thing differently from this example - no problem! And we did miss a few things, such as SWOT and PEST.

But, overall, the presentation tries to link to Bob's business priorities and concerns, so we will (hopefully) be off to a good start.

The End

Thank You

Thank you for taking your time to read *The Practical Leader*. We hope it proved useful for you. If you would like to know more about our Leadership or HRBP workshops, please let us know. You can contact us through LinkedIn:

If you are in HR check out the *The Practical HRBP,* on Amazon.

Kevin Reynolds:
https://www.linkedin.com/in/kevin-reynolds-026b391/

Brent Conkle:
https://www.linkedin.com/in/brentconkle/

Kevin Reynolds has nearly 30 years' experience in Human Resource Management and People Development for Japanese, American and European organizations in Japan, most recently as Human Resources Director for Maersk Line and Intel Japan, where he was responsible for Leadership Development and Employee Engagement programs, and for TEAC Corporation.

Kevin also writes novels about Japan, which you can see here: https://www.kevinareynolds.com/

Since 2002, Brent has been an executive & leadership coach in Japan. He is a master coach for the International Christian Universities' Global Leadership Studies program. He is the co-creator of Leadership Development Solutions, a comprehensive HRM tool kit, that develops highly engaged organizations through consulting, training & coaching.

www.ingramcontent.com/pod-product-compliance
Lightning Source LLC
Chambersburg PA
CBHW052345220526
45465CB00003BA/960